Pro Android Apps
Performance
Optimization

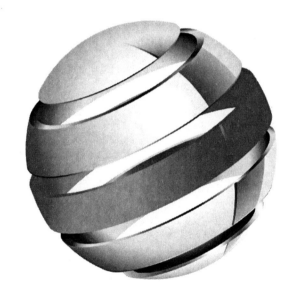

Hervé Guihot

Apress®

Pro Android Apps Performance Optimization

ISBN-13 (pbk): 978-1-4302-3999-4

ISBN-13 (electronic): 978-1-4302-4000-6

President and Publisher: Paul Manning
Lead Editor: James Markham
Technical Reviewer: Charles Cruz, Shane Kirk, Eric Neff
Editorial Board: Steve Anglin, Mark Beckner, Ewan Buckingham, Gary Cornell, Morgan Ertel, Jonathan Gennick, Jonathan Hassell, Robert Hutchinson, Michelle Lowman, James Markham, Matthew Moodie, Jeff Olson, Jeffrey Pepper, Douglas Pundick, Ben Renow-Clarke, Dominic Shakeshaft, Gwenan Spearing, Matt Wade, Tom Welsh
Coordinating Editor: Corbin Collins
Copy Editor: Jill Steinberg
Compositor: MacPS, LLC
Indexer: SPi Global
Artist: SPi Global
Cover Designer: Anna Ishchenko

Distributed to the book trade worldwide by Springer Science+Business Media, LLC., 233 Spring Street, 6th Floor, New York, NY 10013. Phone 1-800-SPRINGER, fax (201) 348-4505, e-mail orders-ny@springer-sbm.com, or visit www.springeronline.com.

For information on translations, please e-mail rights@apress.com, or visit www.apress.com.

Apress and friends of ED books may be purchased in bulk for academic, corporate, or promotional use. eBook versions and licenses are also available for most titles. For more information, reference our Special Bulk Sales–eBook Licensing web page at www.apress.com/bulk-sales.

Any source code or other supplementary materials referenced by the author in this text is available to readers at www.apress.com. For detailed information about how to locate your book's source code, go to http://www.apress.com/source-code/.

Contents at a Glance

Contents

About the Author

Hervé Guihot started learning about computers more than 20 years ago with an Amstrad CPC464. Although the CPC464 is most likely the reason why he still appreciates green-screened devices (ask him about his phone), Hervé started working with Android as it became a popular platform for application development. It was also was the only platform that combined two of his main passions: software and pastries. After many years working in the world of interactive and digital television, he is focused on bringing Android to more devices to encourage more developers to leverage the power of Android and more people to have access to the technology. Hervé is currently a software engineering manager in MediaTek (www.mediatek.com), a leading fabless semiconductor company for wireless communications and digital multimedia solutions. He holds an engineering degree from the Institut de Formation Supérieure en Informatique et Télécommunication in Rennes, Brittany, and you can sometimes find him waiting in line for an éclair on 18th and Guerrero.

About the Technical Reviewers

Charles Cruz is a mobile application developer for the Android, iOS, and Windows Phone platforms. He graduated from Stanford University with B.S. and M.S. degrees in Engineering. He lives in Southern California and, when not doing technical things, plays lead guitar in an original metal band (www.taintedsociety.com) and a classic rock tribute band. Charles can be reached at cruzcj@soundandcodecreations.com and @CodingNPicking on Twitter.

Shane Kirk earned his B.S. in Computer Science from the University of Kentucky in 2000. He's currently a software engineer for DeLorme, a mapping and GPS technology company based in Yarmouth, Maine, where he spends his days writing C++ and Java code for mobile and desktop applications. When Shane isn't coding, you'll usually find him making lots of noise with his guitar or lost in the pages of a good book.

Eric Neff is an experienced technical architect with more than 14 years of overall experience in as a technical architect and senior software developer. He is an expert in full life-cycle application development, middle-ware, and n-tier application development, with specific expertise in Microsoft .NET application development. He specializes in object-oriented analysis and design in systems development with a focus on the scheduling of service personal or manufactured items and was instrumental in the design and implementation of data relation schemas for the lexicography industry. Eric was recently promoted to Director of Mobile Innovations at Kiefer Consulting, Inc, putting into practice several years of hobbyist development in the mobile space on iPhone, Android, and Windows Mobile. Eric is active in the local development community through his participation in the Sacramento Google Technology Group and as a board member of the Sacramento Dot Net User Group. He has given presentations on mobile web technologies, mobile development, and ASP.NET techniques.

Acknowledgments

I thank the team at Apress who made this book possible: Steve Anglin, Corbin Collins, Jim Markham, and Jill Steinberg. Working with all of them was a real pleasure and I can with confidence recommend them to any author.

I also want to thank the tech reviewers: Charles Cruz, Shane Kirk, and Eric Neff. They provided invaluable feedback, often catching mistakes I would not have seen even after dozens of readings.

To all my friends whom I did not get to see as often as I would have liked while I was working on this book, I give my thanks too: Marcely, Mathieu, Marilen, Maurice, Katie, Maggie, Jean-René, Ruby, Greg, Aline, Amy, and Gilles, I promise I will make up for the lost time. Last but not least, I owe a lot to three people: Eddy Derick, Fabrice Bernard, and Jean-Louis Gassée. Sometimes all it takes is an injured toe and a broken suitcase.

Introduction

Android quickly became almost ubiquitous. With the world transitioning from feature phones to smartphones, and then discovering that tablets are, after all, devices we can hardly live without, application developers today have a choice between mostly two platforms: Android and iOS. Android lowered, some may even say broke, the barrier of entry for application developers, because all you need to write Android applications is a computer (and of course some programming knowledge). Tools are free, and almost anyone can now write applications reaching millions of customers. With Android now spreading to a variety of devices, from tablets to televisions, it is important to make sure your applications can not only run well on all these devices but also run better than competing applications. After all, the barrier of entry was lowered for all application developers and you will in many cases find yourself competing for a slice of the ever-growing Android applications market. Whether you write applications to make a living, achieve stardom, or simply make the world a better place, performance will be one of the their key elements.

This book assumes you already have some familiarity with Android application development but want to go one step further and explore what can make your applications run faster. Although the Android tools and online documentation make it easy to create applications, performance optimization is sometimes more of an art than a science and is not documented as thoroughly. I wrote *Pro Android Apps Performance Optimization* to help you find easy ways to achieve good performance on virtually all Android devices, whether you are trying to optimize an existing application or are writing an application from scratch. Android allows developers to use Java, C/C++, and even assembly languages, and you can implement performance optimizations in many different ways, from taking advantage of the CPU features to simply using a different language more tailored to a specific problem.

Chapter 1 focuses on optimizing your Java code. Your first applications will most likely exclusively use the Java language, and we will see that algorithms themselves are more important than their implementation. You will also learn how to take advantage of simple techniques such as caching and minimizing memory allocations to greatly optimize your applications. In addition, you will learn how to keep your applications responsive, a very important performance indicator, and how to use databases efficiently.

Chapter 2 takes you one step further (or lower, depending on who you talk to) and introduces the Android NDK. Even though the Java code can be compiled to native code since Android 2.2, using C code to implement certain routines can yield better results. The NDK can also allow you to easily port existing code to Android without having to rewrite everything in Java.

Chapter 3 takes you to the abyss of assembly language. Albeit rarely used by most application developers, assembly language allows you to take advantage of every platform's specific instruction set and can be a great way to optimize your applications, though at the cost of increased complexity and maintenance. Though assembly code is typically limited to certain parts of an application, its benefits should not be ignored as tremendous results can be achieved thanks to carefully targeted optimizations.

Chapter 4 shows you how using less memory can improve performance. In addition to learning simple ways to use less memory in your code, you will learn how memory allocations and memory accesses have a direct impact on performance because of how CPUs are designed.

Chapter 5 teaches you how to use multi-threading in your Android applications in order to keep applications responsive and improve performance as more and more Android devices can run multiple threads simultaneously.

Chapter 6 shows you the basics of measuring your applications' performance. In addition to learning how to use the APIs to measure time, you will also learn how to use some of the Android tools to have a better view of where time is spent in your applications.

Chapter 7 teaches you how to make sure your applications use power rationally. As many Android devices are battery-powered, conserving energy is extremely important because an application that empties the battery quickly will be uninstalled quickly. This chapter shows you how to minimize power consumption without sacrificing the very things that make Android applications special.

Chapter 8 introduces some basic techniques to optimize your applications' layouts and optimize OpenGL rendering.

Chapter 9 is about RenderScript, a relatively new Android component introduced in Honeycomb. RenderScript is all about performance and has already evolved quite a bit since its first release. In this chapter you learn how to use RenderScript in your applications and also learn about the many APIs RenderScript defines.

I hope you enjoy this book and find many helpful tips in it. As you will find out, many techniques are not Android specific, and you will be able to re-use a lot of them on other platforms, for example iOS. Personally, I have a sweet tooth for assembly language and I hope the proliferation of the Android platform and support for assembly language in the Android NDK will entice many developers, if only to learn a new skill. However, I do want to emphasize that good design and good algorithms will often already take care of all performance optimizations you need. Good luck, and I am looking forward to your Android applications!

Chapter 1

Optimizing Java Code

Many Android application developers have a good practical knowledge of the Java language from previous experience. Since its debut in 1995, Java has become a very popular programming language. While some surveys show that Java lost its luster trying to compete with other languages like Objective-C or C#, some of these same surveys rank Java as the number 1 language popularity-wise. Naturally, with mobile devices outselling personal computers and the success of the Android platform (700,000 activations per day in December 2011) Java is becoming more relevant in today's market than ever before.

Developing applications for mobile devices can be quite different from developing applications for personal computers. Today's portable devices can be quite powerful, but in terms of performance, they lag behind personal computers. For example, some benchmarks show a quad-core Intel Core i7 processor running about 20 times faster than the dual-core Nvidia Tegra 2 that is found in the Samsung Galaxy Tab 10.1.

> **NOTE:** Benchmark results are to be taken with a grain of salt since they often measure only part of a system and do not necessarily represent a typical use-case.

This chapter shows you how to make sure your Java applications perform well on Android devices, whether they run the latest Android release or not. First, we take a look at how Android executes your code. Then, we review several techniques to optimize the implementation of a famous mathematical series, including how to take advantage of the latest APIs Android offers. Finally, we review a few techniques to improve your application's responsiveness and to use databases more efficiently.

Before you jump in, you should realize code optimization is not the first priority in your application development. Delivering a good user experience and focusing on code maintainability should be among your top priorities. In fact, code optimization should be one of your last priorities, and may not even be part of the process altogether. However, good practices can help you reach an acceptable level of performance without having you go back to your code, asking yourself "what did I do wrong?" and having to spend additional resources to fix it.

How Android Executes Your Code

While Android developers use Java, the Android platform does not include a Java Virtual Machine (VM) for executing code. Instead, applications are compiled into Dalvik bytecode, and Android uses its Dalvik VM to execute it. The Java code is still compiled into Java bytecode, but this Java bytecode is then compiled into Dalvik bytecode by the dex compiler, dx (an SDK tool). Ultimately, your application will contain only the Dalvik bytecode, not the Java bytecode.

For example, an implementation of a method that computes the nth term of the Fibonacci series is shown in Listing 1–1 together with the class definition. The Fibonacci series is defined as follows:

$F_0 = 0$
$F_1 = 1$
$F_n = F_{n-2} + F_{n-1}$ for n greater than 1

Listing 1–1. *Naïve Recursive Implementation of Fibonacci Series*

```
public class Fibonacci {
    public static long computeRecursively (int n)
    {
        if (n > 1) return computeRecursively(n-2) + computeRecursively(n-1);
        return n;
    }
}
```

> **NOTE:** A trivial optimization was done by returning n when n equals 0 or 1 instead of adding another "if" statement to check whether n equals 0 or 1.

An Android application is referred to as an APK since applications are compiled into a file with the apk extension (for example, APress.apk), which is simply an archive file. One of the files in the archive is classes.dex, which contains the application's bytecode. The Android toolchain provides a tool, dexdump, which can convert the binary form of the code (contained in the APK's classes.dex file) into human-readable format.

> **TIP:** Because an apk file is simply a ZIP archive, you can use common archive tools such as WinZip or 7-Zip to inspect the content of an apk file..

Listing 1–2 shows the matching Dalvik bytecode.

Listing 1–2. *Human-Readable Dalvik Bytecode of Fibonacci.computeRecursively*

```
002548:                    |[002548] com.apress.proandroid.Fibonacci.computeRecursively:(I)J
002558: 1212              |0000: const/4 v2, #int 1 // #1
00255a: 3724 1100         |0001: if-le v4, v2, 0012 // +0011
00255e: 1220              |0003: const/4 v0, #int 2 // #2
002560: 9100 0400         |0004: sub-int v0, v4, v0
```

```
002564: 7110 3d00 0000  |0006: invoke-static {v0},
    Lcom/apress/proandroid/Fibonacci;.computeRecursively:(I)J
00256a: 0b00             |0009: move-result-wide v0
00256c: 9102 0402        |000a: sub-int v2, v4, v2
002570: 7110 3d00 0200  |000c: invoke-static {v2},
    Lcom/apress/proandroid/Fibonacci;.computeRecursively:(I)J
002576: 0b02             |000f: move-result-wide v2
002578: bb20             |0010: add-long/2addr v0, v2
00257a: 1000             |0011: return-wide v0
00257c: 8140             |0012: int-to-long v0, v4
00257e: 28fe             |0013: goto 0011 // -0002
```

The first number on each line specifies the absolute position of the code within the file. Except on the very first line (which shows the method name), it is then followed by one or more 16-bit bytecode units, followed by the position of the code within the method itself (relative position, or label), the opcode mnemonic and finally the opcode's parameter(s). For example, the two bytecode units 3724 1100 at address 0x00255a translate to "if-le v4, v2, 0012 // +0011", which basically means "if content of virtual register v4 is less than or equal to content of virtual register v2 then go to label 0x0012 by skipping 17 bytecode units" (17_{10} equals 11_{16}). The term "virtual register" refers to the fact that these are not actual hardware registers but instead the registers used by the Dalvik virtual machine.

Typically, you would not need to look at your application's bytecode. This is especially true with Android 2.2 (codename Froyo) and later versions since a Just-In-Time (JIT) compiler was introduced in Android 2.2. The Dalvik JIT compiler compiles the Dalvik bytecode into native code, which can execute significantly faster. A JIT compiler (sometimes referred to simply as a JIT) improves performance dramatically because:

- Native code is directly executed by the CPU without having to be interpreted by a virtual machine.
- Native code can be optimized for a specific architecture.

Benchmarks done by Google showed code executes 2 to 5 times faster with Android 2.2 than Android 2.1. While the results may vary depending on what your code does, you can expect a significant increase in speed when using Android 2.2 and later versions.

The absence of a JIT compiler in Android 2.1 and earlier versions may affect your optimization strategy significantly. If you intend to target devices running Android 1.5 (codename Cupcake), 1.6 (codename Donut), or 2.1 (codename Éclair), most likely you will need to review more carefully what you want or need to provide in your application. Moreover, devices running these earlier Android versions are older devices, which are less powerful than newer ones. While the market share of Android 2.1 and earlier devices is shrinking, they still represent about 12% as of December 2011). Possible strategies are:

- Don't optimize at all. Your application could be quite slow on these older devices.

- Require minimum API level 8 in your application, which can then be installed only on Android 2.2 or later versions.

- Optimize for older devices to offer a good user experience even when no JIT compiler is present. This could mean disabling features that are too CPU-heavy.

> **TIP:** Use android:vmSafeMode in your application's manifest to enable or disable the JIT compiler. It is enabled by default (if it is available on the platform). This attribute was introduced in Android 2.2.

Now it is time to run the code on an actual platform and see how it performs. If you are familiar with recursion and the Fibonacci series, you might guess that it is going to be slow. And you would be right. On a Samsung Galaxy Tab 10.1, computing the thirtieth Fibonacci number takes about 370 milliseconds. With the JIT compiler disabled, it takes about 440 milliseconds. If you decide to include that function in a Calculator application, users will become frustrated because the results cannot be computed "immediately." From a user's point of view, results appear instantaneous if they can be computed in 100 milliseconds or less. Such a response time guarantees a very good user experience, so this is what we are going to target.

Optimizing Fibonacci

The first optimization we are going to perform eliminates a method call, as shown in Listing 1–3. As this implementation is recursive, removing a single call in the method dramatically reduces the total number of calls. For example, computeRecursively(30) generated 2,692,537 calls while computeRecursivelyWithLoop(30) generated "only" 1,346,269. However, the performance of this method is still not acceptable considering the response-time criteria defined above, 100 milliseconds or less, as computeRecursivelyWithLoop(30) takes about 270 milliseconds to complete.

Listing 1–3. *Optimized Recursive Implementation of Fibonacci Series*

```
public class Fibonacci {
    public static long computeRecursivelyWithLoop (int n)
    {
        if (n > 1) {
            long result = 1;
            do {
                result += computeRecursivelyWithLoop(n-2);
                n--;
            } while (n > 1);
            return result;
        }
        return n;
    }
}
```

> **NOTE:** This is not a true tail-recursion optimization.

From Recursive To Iterative

For the second optimization, we switch from a recursive implementation to an iterative one. Recursive algorithms often have a bad reputation with developers, especially on embedded systems without much memory, because they tend to consume a lot of stack space and, as we just saw, can generate too many method calls. Even when performance is acceptable, a recursive algorithm can cause a stack overflow and crash an application. An iterative implementation is therefore often preferred whenever possible. Listing 1–4 shows what is considered a textbook iterative implementation of the Fibonacci series.

Listing 1–4. *Iterative Implementation of Fibonacci Series*

```java
public class Fibonacci {
    public static long computeIteratively (int n)
    {
        if (n > 1) {
            long a = 0, b = 1;
            do {
                long tmp = b;
                b += a;
                a = tmp;
            } while (--n > 1);
            return b;
        }
        return n;
    }
}
```

Because the nth term of the Fibonacci series is simply the sum of the two previous terms, a simple loop can do the job. Compared to the recursive algorithms, the complexity of this iterative algorithm is also greatly reduced because it is linear. Consequently, its performance is also much better, and computeIteratively(30) takes less than 1 millisecond to complete. Because of its linear nature, you can use such an algorithm to compute terms beyond the 30th. For example, computeIteratively(50000) takes only 2 milliseconds to return a result and, by extrapolation, you could guess computeIteratively(500000) would take between 20 and 30 milliseconds to complete.

While such performance is more than acceptable, it is possible to to achieve even faster results with a slightly modified version of the same algorithm, as showed in Listing 1–5. This new version computes two terms per iteration, and the total number of iterations is halved. Because the number of iterations in the original iterative algorithm could be odd, the initial values for a and b are modified accordingly: the series starts with a=0 and b=1 when n is odd, and it starts with a=1 and b=1 (Fib(2)=1) when n is even.

Listing 1–5. *Modified Iterative Implementation of Fibonacci Series*

```
public class Fibonacci {
    public static long computeIterativelyFaster (int n)
    {
        if (n > 1) {
            long a, b = 1;
            n--;
            a = n & 1;
            n /= 2;
            while (n-- > 0) {
                a += b;
                b += a;
            }
            return b;
        }
        return n;
    }
}
```

Results show this modified iterative version is about twice as fast as the original one.

While these iterative implementations are fast, they do have one major problem: they don't return correct results. The issue lies with the return value being stored in a long value, which is 64-bit. The largest Fibonacci number that can fit in a signed 64-bit value is 7,540,113,804,746,346,429 or, in other words, the 92nd Fibonacci number. While the methods will still return without crashing the application for values of n greater than 92, the results will be incorrect because of an overflow: the 93rd Fibonacci number would be negative! The recursive implementations actually have the same limitation, but one would have to be quite patient to eventually find out.

> **NOTE:** Java specifies the size of all primitive types (except boolean): long is 64-bit, int is 32-bit, and short is 16-bit. All integer types are signed.

BigInteger

Java offers just the right class to fix this overflow problem: `java.math.BigInteger`. A BigInteger object can hold a signed integer of arbitrary size and the class defines all the basic math operations (in addition to some not-so-basic ones). Listing 1–6 shows the BigInteger version of `computeIterativelyFaster`.

> **TIP:** The `java.math` package also defines `BigDecimal` in addition to `BigInteger`, while `java.lang.Math` provides math constant and operations. If your application does not need double precision, use Android's `FloatMath` instead of `Math` for performance (although gains may vary depending on platform).

Listing 1–6. *BigInteger Version of Fibonacci.computeIterativelyFaster*

```java
public class Fibonacci {
    public static BigInteger computeIterativelyFasterUsingBigInteger (int n)
    {
        if (n > 1) {
            BigInteger a, b = BigInteger.ONE;
            n--;
            a = BigInteger.valueOf(n & 1);
            n /= 2;
            while (n-- > 0) {
                a = a.add(b);
                b = b.add(a);
            }
            return b;
        }
        return (n == 0) ? BigInteger.ZERO : BigInteger.ONE;
    }
}
```

That implementation guarantees correctness as overflows can no longer occur. However, it is not without problems because, again, it is quite slow: a call to computeIterativelyFasterUsingBigInteger(50000) takes about 1.3 seconds to complete. The lackluster performance can be explained by three things:

- BigInteger is immutable.

- BigInteger is implemented using BigInt and native code.

- The larger the numbers, the longer it takes to add them together.

Since BigInteger is immutable, we have to write "a = a.add(b)" instead of simply "a.add(b)". Many would assume "a.add(b)" is the equivalent of "a += b" and many would be wrong: it is actually the equivalent of "a + b". Therefore, we have to write "a = a.add(b)" to assign the result. That small detail is extremely significant as "a.add(b)" creates a new BigInteger object that holds the result of the addition.

Because of BigInteger's current internal implementation, an additional BigInt object is created for every BigInteger object that is allocated. This results in twice as many objects being allocated during the execution of computeIterativelyFasterUsingBigInteger: about 100,000 objects are created when calling computeIterativelyFasterUsingBigInteger (50000) (and all of them but one will become available for garbage collection almost immediately). Also, BigInt is implemented using native code and calling native code from Java (using JNI) has a certain overhead.

The third reason is that very large numbers do not fit in a single, long 64-bit value. For example, the 50,000[th] Fibonacci number is 34,7111–bit long.

> **NOTE:** BigInteger's internal implementation (BigInteger.java) may change in future Android releases. In fact, internal implementation of any class can change.

For performance reasons, memory allocations should be avoided whenever possible in critical paths of the code. Unfortunately, there are some cases where allocations are needed, for example when working with immutable objects like BigInteger. The next optimization focuses on reducing the number of allocations by switching to a different algorithm. Based on the Fibonacci Q-matrix, we have the following:

$$F_{2n-1} = F_n^2 + F_{n-1}^2$$

$$F_{2n} = (2F_{n-1} + F_n) * F_n$$

This can be implemented using BigInteger again (to guarantee correct results), as shown in Listing 1–7.

Listing 1–7. *Faster Recursive Implementation of Fibonacci Series Using BigInteger*

```java
public class Fibonacci {
    public static BigInteger computeRecursivelyFasterUsingBigInteger (int n)
    {
        if (n > 1) {
            int m = (n / 2) + (n & 1); // not obvious at first - wouldn't it be great to
have a better comment here?
            BigInteger fM = computeRecursivelyFasterUsingBigInteger(m);
            BigInteger fM_1 = computeRecursivelyFasterUsingBigInteger(m - 1);
            if ((n & 1) == 1) {
                // F(m)^2 + F(m-1)^2
                return fM.pow(2).add(fM_1.pow(2)); // three BigInteger objects created
            } else {
                // (2*F(m-1) + F(m)) * F(m)
                return fM_1.shiftLeft(1).add(fM).multiply(fM); // three BigInteger
objects created
            }
        }
        return (n == 0) ? BigInteger.ZERO : BigInteger.ONE; // no BigInteger object
created
    }

    public static long computeRecursivelyFasterUsingBigIntegerAllocations(int n)
    {
        long allocations = 0;
        if (n > 1) {
            int m = (n / 2) + (n & 1);
            allocations += computeRecursivelyFasterUsingBigIntegerAllocations(m);
            allocations += computeRecursivelyFasterUsingBigIntegerAllocations(m - 1);

            // 3 more BigInteger objects allocated
            allocations += 3;
        }
        return allocations; // approximate number of BigInteger objects allocated when
computeRecursivelyFasterUsingBigInteger(n) is called
    }
}
```

A call to computeRecursivelyFasterUsingBigInteger(50000) returns in about 1.6 seconds. This shows this latest implementation is actually slower than the fastest iterative implementation we have so far. Again, the number of allocations is the culprit as around 200,000 objects were allocated (and almost immediately marked as eligible for garbage collection).

> **NOTE:** The actual number of allocations is less than what computeRecursivelyFasterUsingBigIntegerAllocations would return. Because BigInteger's implementation uses preallocated objects such as BigInteger.ZERO, BigInteger.ONE, or BigInteger.TEN, there may be no need to allocate a new object for some operations. You would have to look at Android's BigInteger implementation to know exactly how many objects are allocated.

This implementation is slower, but it is a step in the right direction nonetheless. The main thing to notice is that even though we need to use BigInteger to guarantee correctness, we don't have to use BigInteger for every value of n. Since we know the primitive type long can hold results for n less than or equal to 92, we can slightly modify the recursive implementation to mix BigInteger and primitive type, as shown in Listing 1–8.

Listing 1–8. *Faster Recursive Implementation of Fibonacci Series Using BigInteger and long Primitive Type*

```
public class Fibonacci {
    public static BigInteger computeRecursivelyFasterUsingBigIntegerAndPrimitive(int n)
    {
        if (n > 92) {
            int m = (n / 2) + (n & 1);
            BigInteger fM = computeRecursivelyFasterUsingBigIntegerAndPrimitive(m);
            BigInteger fM_1 = computeRecursivelyFasterUsingBigIntegerAndPrimitive(m -
1);
            if ((n & 1) == 1) {
                return fM.pow(2).add(fM_1.pow(2));
            } else {
                return fM_1.shiftLeft(1).add(fM).multiply(fM); // shiftLeft(1) to
multiply by 2
            }
        }
        return BigInteger.valueOf(computeIterativelyFaster(n));
    }

    private static long computeIterativelyFaster(int n)
    {
        // see Listing 1-5 for implementation
    }
}
```

A call to computeRecursivelyFasterUsingBigIntegerAndPrimitive(50000) returns in about 73 milliseconds and results in about 11,000 objects being allocated: a small modification in the algorithm yields results about 20 times faster and about 20 times fewer objects being allocated. Quite impressive! It is possible to improve the performance even further by reducing the number of allocations, as shown in Listing 1–9. Precomputed results can be quickly generated when the Fibonacci class is first loaded, and these results can later be used directly.

Listing 1–9. *Faster Recursive Implementation of Fibonacci Series Using BigInteger and Precomputed Results*

```java
public class Fibonacci {
    static final int PRECOMPUTED_SIZE= 512;
    static BigInteger PRECOMPUTED[] = new BigInteger[PRECOMPUTED_SIZE];

    static {
        PRECOMPUTED[0] = BigInteger.ZERO;
        PRECOMPUTED[1] = BigInteger.ONE;
        for (int i = 2; i < PRECOMPUTED_SIZE; i++) {
            PRECOMPUTED[i] = PRECOMPUTED[i-1].add(PRECOMPUTED[i-2]);
        }
    }

    public static BigInteger computeRecursivelyFasterUsingBigIntegerAndTable(int n)
    {
        if (n > PRECOMPUTED_SIZE - 1) {
            int m = (n / 2) + (n & 1);
            BigInteger fM = computeRecursivelyFasterUsingBigIntegerAndTable (m);
            BigInteger fM_1 = computeRecursivelyFasterUsingBigIntegerAndTable (m - 1);
            if ((n & 1) == 1) {
                return fM.pow(2).add(fM_1.pow(2));
            } else {
                return fM_1.shiftLeft(1).add(fM).multiply(fM);
            }
        }
        return PRECOMPUTED[n];
    }
}
```

The performance of this implementation depends on PRECOMPUTED_SIZE: the bigger, the faster. However, memory usage may become an issue since many BigInteger objects will be created and remain in memory for as long as the Fibonacci class is loaded. It is possible to merge the implementations shown in Listing 1–8 and Listing 1–9, and use a combination of precomputed results and computations with primitive types. For example, terms 0 to 92 could be computed using computeIterativelyFaster, terms 93 to 127 using precomputed results and any other term using recursion. As a developer, you are responsible for choosing the best implementation, which may not always be the fastest. Your choice will be based on various factors, including:

- What devices and Android versions your application target

- Your resources (people and time)

As you may have already noticed, optimizations tend to make the source code harder to read, understand, and maintain, sometimes to such an extent that you would not recognize your own code weeks or months later. For this reason, it is important to carefully think about what optimizations you really need and how they will affect your application development, both in the short term and in the long term. It is always recommended you first implement a working solution before you think of optimizing it (and make sure you save a copy of the working solution). After all, you may realize optimizations are not needed at all, which could save you a lot of time. Also, make sure you include comments in your code for everything that is not obvious to a person with ordinary skill in the art. Your coworkers will thank you, and you may give yourself a pat on the back as well when you stumble on some of your old code. My poor comment in Listing 1–7 is proof.

> **NOTE:** All implementations disregard the fact that n could be negative. This was done intentionally to make a point, but your code, at least in all public APIs, should throw an IllegalArgumentException whenever appropriate.

Caching Results

When computations are expensive, it may be a good idea to remember past results to make future requests faster. Using a cache is quite simple as it typically translates to the pseudo-code shown in Listing 1–10.

Listing 1–10. *Using a Cache*

```
result = cache.get(n); // input parameter n used as key
if (result == null) {
    // result was not in the cache so we compute it and add it
    result = computeResult(n);
    cache.put(n, result); // n is the key, result is the value
}
return result;
```

The faster recursive algorithm to compute Fibonacci terms yields many duplicate calculations and could greatly benefit from memoization. For example, computing the 50,000[th] term requires computing the 25,000[th] and 24,999[th] terms. Computing the 25,000[th] term requires computing the 12,500[th] and 12,499[th] terms, while computing the 24,999[th] term requires computing... the same 12,500[th] and 12,499[th] terms again! Listing 1–11 shows a better implementation using a cache.

If you are familiar with Java, you may be tempted to use a HashMap as your cache, and it would work just fine. However, Android defines SparseArray, a class that is intended to be more efficient than HashMap when the key is an integer value: HashMap would require the key to be of type java.lang.Integer, while SparseArray uses the primitive type int for keys. Using HashMap would therefore trigger the creation of many Integer objects for the keys, which SparseArray simply avoids.

Listing 1–11. *Faster Recursive Implementation Using BigInteger, long Primitive TypeAnd Cache*

```
public class Fibonacci {
    public static BigInteger computeRecursivelyWithCache (int n)
    {
        SparseArray<BigInteger> cache = new SparseArray<BigInteger>();
        return computeRecursivelyWithCache(n, cache);
    }

    private static BigInteger computeRecursivelyWithCache (int n,
SparseArray<BigInteger> cache)
    {
        if (n > 92) {
            BigInteger fN = cache.get(n);
```

```
            if (fN == null) {
                int m = (n / 2) + (n & 1);
                BigInteger fM = computeRecursivelyWithCache(m, cache);
                BigInteger fM_1 = computeRecursivelyWithCache(m - 1, cache);
                if ((n & 1) == 1) {
                    fN = fM.pow(2).add(fM_1.pow(2));
                } else {
                    fN = fM_1.shiftLeft(1).add(fM).multiply(fM);
                }
                cache.put(n, fN);
            }
            return fN;
        }
        return BigInteger.valueOf(iterativeFaster(n));
    }

    private static long iterativeFaster (int n) { /* see Listing 1-5 for implementation
*/ }
}
```

Measurements showed `computeRecursivelyWithCache(50000)` takes about 20 milliseconds to complete, or about 50 fewer milliseconds than a call to `computeRecursivelyFasterUsingBigIntegerAndPrimitive(50000)`. Obviously, the difference is exacerbated as n grows: when n equals 200,000 the two methods complete in 50 and 330 milliseconds respectively.

Because many fewer `BigInteger` objects are allocated, the fact that `BigInteger` is immutable is not as big of a problem when using the cache. However, remember that three `BigInteger` objects are still created (two of them being very short-lived) when fN is computed, so using mutable big integers would still improve performance.

Even though using `HashMap` instead of `SparseArray` may be a little slower, it would have the benefit of making the code Android-independent, that is, you could use the exact same code in a non-Android environment (without `SparseArray`).

> **NOTE:** Android defines multiple types of sparse arrays: `SparseArray` (to map integers to objects), `SparseBooleanArray` (to map integers to booleans), and `SparseIntArray` (to map integers to integers).

android.util.LruCache<K, V>

Another class worth mentioning is `android.util.LruCache<K, V>`, introduced in Android 3.1 (codename Honeycomb MR1), which makes it easy to define the maximum size of the cache when it is allocated. Optionally, you can also override the `sizeOf()` method to change how the size of each cache entry is computed. Because it is only available in Android 3.1 and later, you may still end up having to use a different class to implement a cache in your own application if you target Android revisions older than 3.1. This is a very likely scenario considering Android 3.1 as of today represents only a very small portion of the Android devices in use. An alternative solution is to extend java.util.LinkedHashMap and override removeEldestEntry. An LRU cache (for Least Recently Used) discards the least recently used items first. In some applications, you may need exactly the opposite, that is, a cache that discards the most recently used items first. Android does not define such an MruCache class for now, which is not surprising considering MRU caches are not as commonly used.

Of course, a cache can be used to store information other than computations. A common use of a cache is to store downloaded data such as pictures and still maintain tight control over how much memory is consumed. For example, override LruCache's sizeOf method to limit the size of the cache based on a criterion other than simply the number of entries in the cache. While we briefly discussed the LRU and MRU strategies, you may want to use different replacement strategies for your own cache to maximize cache hits. For example, your cache could first discard the items that are not costly to recreate, or simply randomly discard items. Follow a pragmatic approach and design your cache accordingly. A simple replacement strategy such as LRU can yield great results and allow you to focus your resources on other, more important problems.

We've looked at several different techniques to optimize the computation of Fibonacci numbers. While each technique has its merits, no one implementation is optimal. Often the best results are achieved by combining multiple various techniques instead of relying on only one of them. For example, an even faster implementation would use precomputations, a cache mechanism, and maybe even slightly different formulas. (Hint: what happens when n is a multiple of 4?) What would it take to compute $F_{Integer.MAX\_VALUE}$ in less than 100 milliseconds?

API Levels

The LruCache class mentioned above is a good example of why you need to know what API level you are going to target. A new version of Android is released approximately every six months, with new APIs only available from that release. Any attempt to call an API that does not exist results in a crash, bringing not only frustration for the user but also shame to the developer. For example, calling Log.wtf(TAG, "Really?") on an Android 1.5 device crashes the application, as Log.wtf was introduced in Android 2.2 (API level 8). What a terrible failure indeed that would be. Table 1–1 shows the performance improvements made in the various Android versions.

Table 1–1. *Android Versions*

API level	Version	Name	Significant performance improvements
1	1.0	Base	
2	1.1	Base 1.1	
3	1.5	Cupcake	Camera start-up time, image capture time, faster acquisition of GPS location, NDK support
4	1.6	Donut	
5	2.0	Éclair	Graphics
6	2.0.1	Éclair 0.1	
7	2.1	Éclair MR1	
8	2.2	Froyo	V8 Javascript engine (browser), JIT compiler, memory management
9	2.3.0	Gingerbread	Concurrent garbage collector, event distribution, better OpenGL drivers
	2.3.1		
	2.3.2		
10	2.3.3	Gingerbread MR1	
	2.3.4		
11	3.0	Honeycomb	Renderscript, animations, hardware-accelerated 2D graphics, multicore support
12	3.1	Honeycomb MR1	LruCache, partial invalidates in hardware-accelerated views, new Bitmap.setHasAlpha() API
13	3.2	Honeycomb MR2	
14	4.0	Ice Cream Sandwich	Media effects (transformation filters), hardware-accelerated 2D graphics (required)

However, your decision to support a certain target should normally not be based on which API you want to use, but instead on what market you are trying to reach. For example, if your target is primarily tablets and not cell phones, then you could target Honeycomb. By doing so, you would limit your application's audience to a small subset of Android devices, because Honeycomb represents only about 2.4% as of December 2011, and not all tablets support Honeycomb. (For example, Barnes & Noble's Nook uses Android 2.2 while Amazon's Kindle Fire uses Android 2.3.) Therefore, supporting older Android versions could still make sense.

The Android team understood that problem when they released the Android Compatibility package, which is available through the SDK Updater. This package contains a static library with some of the new APIs introduced in Android 3.0, namely the fragment APIs. Unfortunately, this compatibility package contains only the fragment APIs and does not address the other APIs that were added in Honeycomb. Such a compatibility package is the exception, not the rule. Normally, an API introduced at a specific API level is not available at lower levels, and it is the developer's responsibility to choose APIs carefully.

To get the API level of the Android platform, you can use Build.VERSION.SDK_INT. Ironically, this field was introduced in Android 1.6 (API level 4), so trying to retrieve the version this way would also result in a crash on Android 1.5 or earlier. Another option is to use Build.VERSION.SDK, which has been present since API level 1. However, this field is now deprecated, and the version strings are not documented (although it would be pretty easy to understand how they have been created).

> **TIP:** Use reflection to check whether the SDK_INT field exists (that is, if the platform is Android 1.6 or later). See Class.forName("android.os.Build$VERSION").getField("SDK").

Your application's manifest file should use the `<uses-sdk>` element to specify two important things:

- The minimum API level required for the application to run (android:minSdkVersion)
- The API level the application targets (android:targetSdkVersion)

It is also possible to specify the maximum API level (android:maxSdkVersion), but using this attribute is not recommended. Specifying maxSdkVersion could even lead to applications being uninstalled automatically after Android updates. The target API level is the level at which your application has been explicitly tested.

By default, the minimum API level is set to 1 (meaning the application is compatible with all Android versions). Specifying an API level greater than 1 prevents the application from being installed on older devices. For example, android:minSdkVersion="4" guarantees Build.VERSION.SDK_INT can be used without risking any crash. The minimum API level does not have to be the highest API level you are using in your application as long as you make sure you call only a certain API when the API actually exists, as shown in Listing 1–12.

Listing 1–12. *Calling a SparseArray Method Introduced in Honeycomb (API Level 11)*

```
if (Build.VERSION.SDK_INT >= Build.VERSION_CODES.HONEYCOMB) {
    sparseArray.removeAt(1); // API level 11 and above
} else {
    int key = sparseArray.keyAt(1); // default implementation is slower
    sparseArray.remove(key);
}
```

This kind of code is more frequent when trying to get the best performance out of your Android platform since you want to use the best API for the job while you still want your application to be able to run on an older device (possibly using slower APIs).

Android also uses these attributes for other things, including determining whether the application should run in screen compatibility mode. Your application runs in screen compatibility mode if minSdkVersion is set to 3 or lower, and targetSdkVersion is not set to 4 or higher. This would prevent your application from displaying in full screen on a tablet, for example, making it much harder to use. Tablets have become very popular only recently, and many applications have not been updated yet, so it is not uncommon to find applications that do not display properly on a big screen.

> **NOTE:** Android Market uses the minSdkVersion and maxSdkVersion attributes to filter applications available for download on a particular device. Other attributes are used for filtering as well. Also, Android defines two versions of screen compatibility mode, and their behaviors differ. Refer to "Supporting Multiple Screens" on http://d.android.com/guide for a complete description.

Instead of checking the version number, as shown in Listing 1–12, you can use reflection to find out whether a particular method exists on the platform. While this is a cleaner and safer implementation, reflection can make your code slower; therefore you should try to avoid using reflection where performance is critical. One possible approach is to call Class.forName() and Class.getMethod() to find out if a certain method exists in the static initialization block, and then only call Method.invoke() where performance is important.

Fragmentation

The high number of Android versions, 14 API levels so far, makes your target market quite fragmented, possibly leading to more and more code like the one in Listing 1–12. However, in practice, a few Android versions represent the majority of all the devices. As of December 2011, Android 2.x versions represent more than 95% of the devices connecting to Android Market. Even though Android 1.6 and earlier devices are still in operation, today it is quite reasonable not to spend additional resources to optimize for these platforms.

The number of available devices running Android is even greater, with currently close to 200 phones listed on www.google.com/phone, including 80 in the United States alone. While the listed devices are all phones or tablets, they still differ in many ways: screen resolutions, presence of physical keyboard, hardware-accelerated graphics, processors. Supporting the various configurations, or even only a subset, makes application development more challenging. Therefore it is important to have a good knowledge of the market you are targeting in order to focus your efforts on important features and optimizations.

> **NOTE:** Not all existing Android devices are listed on www.google.com/phone as some countries are not listed yet, for example India and its dual-SIM Spice MI270 running Android 2.2.

Google TV devices (first released in 2010 by Logitech and Sony in the United States) are technically not so different from phones or tablets. However, the way people interact with these devices differs. When supporting these TV devices, one of your main challenges will be to understand how your application could be used on a TV. For example, applications can provide a more social experience on a TV: a game could offer a simultaneous multiplayer mode, a feature that would not make much sense on a phone.

Data Structures

As the various Fibonacci implementations demonstrated, good algorithms and good data structures are keys to a fast application. Android and Java define many data structures you should have good knowledge of to be able to quickly select the right ones for the right job. Consider choosing the appropriate data structures one of your highest priorities.

The most common data structures from the java.util package are shown in Figure 1.1.

To those data structures Android adds a few of its own, usually to solve or improve performance of common problems.

- LruCache
- SparseArray
- SparseBooleanArray
- SparseIntArray
- Pair

> **NOTE:** Java also defines the Arrays and Collections classes. These two classes contain only static methods, which operate on arrays and collections respectively. For example, use Arrays.sort to sort an array and Arrays.binarySearch to search for a value in a sorted array.

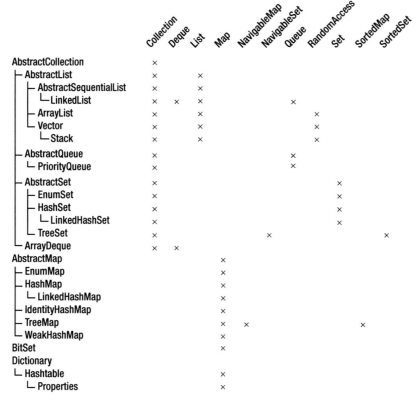

	Collection	Deque	List	Map	NavigableMap	NavigableSet	Queue	RandomAccess	Set	SortedMap	SortedSet
AbstractCollection	×										
├ AbstractList	×		×								
│ ├ AbstractSequentialList	×		×								
│ │ └ LinkedList	×	×	×				×				
│ ├ ArrayList	×		×					×			
│ └ Vector	×		×					×			
│ └ Stack	×		×					×			
├ AbstractQueue	×						×				
│ └ PriorityQueue	×						×				
├ AbstractSet	×								×		
│ ├ EnumSet	×								×		
│ ├ HashSet	×								×		
│ │ └ LinkedHashSet	×								×		
│ └ TreeSet	×					×					×
└ ArrayDeque	×	×									
AbstractMap				×							
├ EnumMap				×							
├ HashMap				×							
│ └ LinkedHashMap				×							
├ IdentityHashMap				×							
├ TreeMap				×	×					×	
└ WeakHashMap				×							
BitSet				×							
Dictionary											
└ Hashtable				×							
└ Properties				×							

Figure 1–1. *Data structures in the java.util package*

While one of the Fibonacci implementations used a cache internally (based on a sparse array), that cache was only temporary and was becoming eligible for garbage collection immediately after the end result was computed. It is possible to also use an LruCache to save end results, as shown in Listing 1–13.

Listing 1–13. *Using an LruCache to Remember Fibonacci Terms*

```
int maxSize = 4 * 8 * 1024 * 1024; // 32 megabits
LruCache<Integer, BigInteger> cache = new LruCache<Integer, BigInteger> (maxSize) {
    protected int sizeOf (Integer key, BigInteger value) {
        return value.bitLength(); // close approximation of object's size, in bits
    }
};
...
int n = 100;
BigInteger fN = cache.get(n);
if (fN == null) {
    fN = Fibonacci. computeRecursivelyWithCache(n);
    cache.put(n, fN);
}
```

Whenever you need to select a data structure to solve a problem, you should be able to narrow down your choice to only a few classes since each class is usually optimized for a specific purpose or provides a specific service. For example, choose `ArrayList` over `Vector` if you don't need the operations to be synchronized. Of course, you may always create your own data structure class, either from scratch (extending `Object`) or extending an existing one.

> **NOTE:** Can you explain why LruCache is not a good choice for computeRecursivelyWithCache's internal cache as seen in Listing 1–11?

If you use one of the data structures that rely on hashing (e.g. HashMap) and the keys are of a type you created, make sure you override the equal and hashCode methods. A poor implementation of hashCode can easily nullify the benefits of using hashing.

> **TIP:** Refer to `http://d.android.com/reference/java/lang/Object.html` for a good example of an implementation of `hashCode()`.

Even though it is often not natural for many embedded application developers, don't hesitate to consider converting one data structure into another in various parts of your application: in some cases, the performance increase can easily outweigh the conversion overhead as better algorithms can be applied. A common example is the conversion of a collection to an array, possibly sorted. Such a conversion would obviously require memory as a new object needs to be created. On memory-constrained devices, such allocation may not always be possible, resulting in an OutOfMemoryError exception. The Java Language Specification says two things:

- The class `Error` and its subclasses are exceptions from which ordinary programs are not ordinarily expected to recover.
- Sophisticated programs may wish to catch and attempt to recover from Error exceptions.

If your memory allocation is only part of an optimization and you, as a sophisticated application developer, can provide a fallback mechanism (for example, an algorithm, albeit slower, using the original data structure) then catching the OutOfMemoryError exception can make sense as it allows you to target more devices. Such optional optimizations make your code harder to maintain but give you a greater reach.

> **NOTE:** Counterintuitively, not all exceptions are subclasses of Exception. All exceptions are subclasses of `Throwable` (from which Exception and Error are the only direct subclasses).

In general, you should have very good knowledge of the java.util and android.util packages since they are the toolbox virtually all components rely on. Whenever a new Android version is released, you should pay special attention to the modifications in these packages (added classes, changed classes) and refer to the *API Differences*

Report on `http://d.android.com/sdk`. More data structures are discussed in java.util.concurrent, and they will be covered in Chapter 5.

Responsiveness

Performance is not only about raw speed. Your application will be perceived as being fast as long as it appears fast to the user, and to appear fast your application must be responsive. As an example, to appear faster, your application can defer allocations until objects are needed, a technique known as lazy initialization, and during the development process you most likely want to detect when slow code is executed in performance-sensitive calls.

The following classes are the cornerstones of most Android Java applications:

- `Application`
- `Activity`
- `Service`
- `ContentProvider`
- `BroadcastReceiver`
- `Fragment` (Android 3.0 and above)
- `View`

Of particular interest in these classes are all the `onSomething()` methods that are called from the main thread, such as `onStart()` and `onFocusChanged()`. The main thread, also referred to as the UI thread, is basically the thread your application runs in. It is possible, though not recommended, to run all your code in the main thread. The main thread is where, among other things:

- Key events are received (for example, `View.onKeyDown()` and `Activity.onKeyLongPress()`).
- Views are drawn (`View.onDraw()`).
- Lifecycle events occur (for example, `Activity.onCreate()`).

> **NOTE:** Many methods are called from the main thread by design. When you override a method, verify how it will be called. The Android documentation does not always specify whether a method is called from the main thread.

In general, the main thread keeps receiving notifications of what is happening, whether the events are generated from the system itself or from the user. Your application has only one main thread, and all events are therefore processed sequentially. That being said, it becomes easy now to see why responsiveness could be negatively affected: the first event in the queue has to be processed before the subsequent events can be handled, one at a time. If the processing of an event takes too long to complete, then other events have to wait longer for their turn.

An easy example would be to call computeRecursivelyWithCache from the main thread. While it is reasonably fast for low values of n, it is becoming increasingly slower as n grows. For very large values of n you would most certainly be confronted with Android's infamous Application Not Responding (ANR) dialog. This dialog appears when Android detects your application is unresponsive, that is when Android detects an input event has not been processed within 5 seconds or a BroadcastReceiver hasn't finished executing within 10 seconds. When this happens, the user is given the option to simply wait or to "force close" the application (which could be the first step leading to your application being uninstalled).

It is important for you to optimize the startup sequence of all the activities, which consists of the following calls:

- onCreate
- onStart
- onResume

Of course, this sequence occurs when an activity is created, which may actually be more often than you think. When a configuration change occurs, your current activity is destroyed and a new instance is created, resulting in the following sequence of calls:

- onPause
- onStop
- onDestroy
- onCreate
- onStart
- onResume

The faster this sequence completes, the faster the user will be able to use your application again. One of the most common configuration changes is the orientation change, which signifies the device has been rotated.

> **NOTE:** Your application can specify which configuration changes each of its activities wants to handle itself with the activity element's android:configChanges attribute in its manifest. This would result in onConfigurationChanged() being called instead of having the activity destroyed.

Your activities' onCreate() methods will most likely contain a call to setContentView or any other method responsible for inflating resources. Because inflating resources is a relatively expensive operation, you can make the inflation faster by reducing the complexity of your layouts (the XML files that define what your application looks like). Steps to simplify the complexity of your layouts include:

- Use RelativeLayout instead of nested LinearLayouts to keep layouts as "flat" as possible. In addition to reducing the number of objects allocated, it will also make processing of events faster.

- Use ViewStub to defer creation of objects (see the section on lazy initialization).

> **NOTE:** Pay special attention to your layouts in ListView as there could be many items in the list. Use the SDK's layoutopt tool to analyze your layouts.

The basic rule is to keep anything that is done in the main thread as fast as possible in order to keep the application responsive. However, this often translates to doing as little as possible in the main thread. In most cases, you can achieve responsiveness simply by moving operations to another thread or deferring operations, two techniques that typically do not result in code that is much harder to maintain. Before moving a task to another thread, make sure you understand why the task is too slow. If this is due to a bad algorithm or bad implementation, you should fix it since moving the task to another thread would merely be like sweeping dust under a carpet.

Lazy initializations

Procrastination does have its merits after all. A common practice is to perform all initializations in a component's onCreate() method. While this would work, it means onCreate() takes longer to return. This is particularly important in your application's activities: since onStart() won't be called until after onCreate() returns (and similarly onResume() won't be called until after onStart() returns), any delay will cause the application to take longer to start, and the user may end up frustrated.

For example, Android uses the lazy initialization concept with android.view.ViewStub, which is used to lazily inflate resources at runtime. When the view stub is made visible, it is replaced by the matching inflated resources and becomes eligible for garbage collection.

Since memory allocations take time, waiting until an object is really needed to allocate it can be a good option. The benefits of lazily allocating an object are clear when an object is unlikely to be needed at all. An example of lazy initialization is shown in Listing 1–14, which is based on Listing 1–13. To avoid always having to check whether the object is null, consider the factory method pattern.

Listing 1–14. *Lazily Allocating the Cache*

```
int n = 100;
if (cache == null) {
    // createCache allocates the cache object, and may be called from many places
    cache = createCache();
}
BigInteger fN = cache.get(n);
if (fN == null) {
    fN = Fibonacci. computeRecursivelyWithCache(n);
    cache.put(n, fN);
}
```

Refer to Chapter 8 to learn how to use and android.view.ViewStub in an XML layout and how to lazily inflate a resource.

StrictMode

You should always assume the following two things when writing your application:

- The network is slow (and the server you are trying to connect to may not even be responding).
- File system access is slow.

As a consequence, you should always try not to perform any network or file system access in your application's main thread as slow operations may affect responsiveness. While your development environment may never experience any network issue or any file system performance problem, your users may not be as lucky as you are.

> **NOTE:** SD cards do not all have the same "speed". If your application depends heavily on the performance of external storage then you should make sure you test your application with various SD cards from different manufacturers.

Android provides a utility to help you detect such defects in your application. StrictMode is a tool that does its best to detect bad behavior. Typically, you would enable StrictMode when your application is starting, i.e when its onCreate() method is called, as shown in Listing 1–15.

Listing 1–15. *Enabling StrictMode in Your Application*

```java
public class MyApplication extends Application {
    @Override
    public void onCreate ()
    {
        super.onCreate();

        StrictMode.setThreadPolicy(new StrictMode.ThreadPolicy.Builder()
        .detectCustomSlowCalls() // API level 11, to use with StrictMode.noteSlowCode
        .detectDiskReads()
        .detectDiskWrites()
        .detectNetwork()
        .penaltyLog()
        .penaltyFlashScreen() // API level 11
        .build());

        // not really performance-related, but if you use StrictMode you might as well
define a VM policy too
        StrictMode.setVmPolicy(new StrictMode.VmPolicy.Builder()
        .detectLeakedSqlLiteObjects()
        .detectLeakedClosableObjects() // API level 11
        .setClassInstanceLimit(Class.forName("com.apress.proandroid.SomeClass"), 100) //
API level 11
        .penaltyLog()
        .build());
```

```
        }
    }
```

StrictMode was introduced in Android 2.3, with more features added in Android 3.0, so you should make sure you target the correct Android version and make sure your code is executed only on the appropriate platforms, as shown in Listing 1–12.

Noteworthy methods introduced in Android 3.0 include `detectCustomSlowCall()` and `noteSlowCall()`, both being used to detect slow, or potentially slow, code in your application. Listing 1–16 shows how to mark your code as potentially slow code.

Listing 1–16. *Marking Your Own Code as Potentially Slow*

```java
public class Fibonacci {
    public static BigInteger computeRecursivelyWithCache(int n)
    {
        StrictMode.noteSlowCall("computeRecursivelyWithCache"); // message can be
anything
        SparseArray<BigInteger> cache = new SparseArray<BigInteger>();
        return computeRecursivelyWithCache(n, cache);
    }
    …
}
```

A call to `computeRecursivelyWithCache` from the main thread that takes too long to execute would result in the following log if the StrictMode Thread policy is configured to detect slow calls:

```
StrictMode policy violation; ~duration=21121 ms:
android.os.StrictMode$StrictModeCustomViolation: policy=31 violation=8 msg=
computeRecursivelyWithCache
```

Android provides some helper methods to make it easier to allow disk reads and writes from the main thread temporarily, as shown in Listing 1–17.

Listing 1–17. *Modifying the Thread Policy to Temporarily Allow Disk Reads*

```java
    StrictMode.ThreadPolicy oldPolicy = StrictMode.allowThreadDiskReads();
    // read something from disk
    StrictMode.setThreadPolicy(oldPolicy);
```

There is no method for temporarily allowing network access, but there is really no reason to allow such access even temporarily in the main thread as there is no reasonable way to know whether the access will be fast. One could argue there is also no reasonable way to know the disk access will be fast, but that's another debate.

> **NOTE:** Enable StrictMode only during development, and remember to disable it when you deploy your application. This is always true, but even more true if you build the policies using the `detectAll()` methods as future versions of Android may detect more bad behaviors.

SQLite

Most applications won't be heavy users of SQLite, and therefore you very likely won't have to worry too much about performance when dealing with databases. However, you need to know about a few concepts in case you ever need to optimize your SQLite-related code in your Android application:

- SQLite statements
- Transactions
- Queries

> **NOTE:** This section is not intended to be a complete guide to SQLite but instead provides you with a few pointers to make sure you use databases efficiently. For a complete guide, refer to www.sqlite.org and the Android online documentation.

The optimizations covered in this section do not make the code harder to read and maintain, so you should make a habit of applying them.

SQLite Statements

At the origin, SQL statements are simple strings, for example:

- CREATE TABLE cheese (name TEXT, origin TEXT)
- INSERT INTO cheese VALUES ('Roquefort', 'Roquefort-sur-Soulzon')

The first statement would create a table named "cheese" with two columns named "name" and "origin". The second statement would insert a new row in the table. Because they are simply strings, the statements have to be interpreted, or compiled, before they can be executed. The compilation of the statements is performed internally when you call for example SQLiteDatabase.execSQL, as shown in Listing 1–18.

Listing 1–18. *Executing Simple SQLite Statements*

```
SQLiteDatabase db = SQLiteDatabase.create(null); // memory-backed database
db.execSQL("CREATE TABLE cheese (name TEXT, origin TEXT)");
db.execSQL("INSERT INTO cheese VALUES ('Roquefort', 'Roquefort-sur-Soulzon')");
db.close(); // remember to close database when you're done with it
```

> **NOTE:** Many SQLite-related methods can throw exceptions.

As it turns out, executing SQLite statements can take quite some time. In addition to the compilation, the statements themselves may need to be created. Because String is also immutable, this could lead to the same performance issue we had with the high number of `BigInteger` objects being allocated in `computeRecursivelyFasterUsingBigInteger`. We are now going to focus on the performance of the insert statement. After all, a table should be created only once, but many rows could be added, modified, or deleted.

If we want to build a comprehensive database of cheeses (who wouldn't?), we would end up with many insert statements, as shown in Listing 1–19. For every insert statement, a String would be created and execSQL would be called, the parsing of the SQL statement being done internally for every cheese added to the database.

Listing 1–19. *Building a Comprehensive Cheeses Database*

```java
public class Cheeses {
    private static final String[] sCheeseNames = {
        "Abbaye de Belloc",
        "Abbaye du Mont des Cats",
        ...
        "Vieux Boulogne"
    };
    private static final String[] sCheeseOrigins = {
        "Notre-Dame de Belloc",
        "Mont des Cats",
        ...
        "Boulogne-sur-Mer"
    };
    private final SQLiteDatabase db;
    public Cheeses () {
        db = SQLiteDatabase.create(null); // memory-backed database
        db.execSQL("CREATE TABLE cheese (name TEXT, origin TEXT)");
    }
    public void populateWithStringPlus () {
        int i = 0;
        for (String name : sCheeseNames) {
            String origin = sCheeseOrigins[i++];
            String sql = "INSERT INTO cheese VALUES(\"" + name + "\",\"" + origin +
"\")";
            db.execSQL(sql);
        }
    }
}
```

Adding 650 cheeses to the memory-backed database took 393 milliseconds on a Galaxy Tab 10.1, or 0.6 microsecond per row.

An obvious improvement is to make the creation of the sql string, the statement to execute, faster. Using the + operator to concatenate strings is not the most efficient method in this case, and it is possible to improve performance by either using a `StringBuilder` object or calling `String.format`. The two new methods are shown in Listing 1–20. As they simply optimize the building of the string to pass to execSQL, these two optimizations are not SQL-related per se.

Listing 1–20. *Faster Ways to Create the SQL Statement Strings*

```java
public void populateWithStringFormat () {
    int i = 0;
    for (String name : sCheeseNames) {
        String origin = sCheeseOrigins[i++];
```

```
            String sql = String.format("INSERT INTO cheese VALUES(\"%s\",\"%s\")", name,
origin);
            db.execSQL(sql);
        }
    }

    public void populateWithStringBuilder () {
        StringBuilder builder = new StringBuilder();
        builder.append("INSERT INTO cheese VALUES(\"");
        int resetLength = builder.length();
        int i = 0;
        for (String name : sCheeseNames) {
            String origin = sCheeseOrigins[i++];
            builder.setLength(resetLength); // reset position
            builder.append(name).append("\",\"").append(origin).append("\")"); // chain
calls
            db.execSQL(builder.toString());
        }
    }
```

The `String.format` version took 436 milliseconds to add the same number of cheeses, while the `StringBuilder` version returned in only 371 milliseconds. The `String.format` version is therefore slower than the original one, while the `StringBuilder` version is only marginally faster.

Even though these three methods differ in the way they create Strings, they all have in common the fact that they call `execSQL`, which still has to do the actual compilation (parsing) of the statement. Because all the statements are very similar (they only differ by the name and origin of the cheese), we can use `compileStatement` to compile the statement only once, outside the loop. This implementation is shown in Listing 1–21.

Listing 1–21. *Compilation of SQLite Statement*

```
    public void populateWithCompileStatement () {
        SQLiteStatement stmt = db.compileStatement("INSERT INTO cheese VALUES(?,?)");
        int i = 0;
        for (String name : sCheeseNames) {
            String origin = sCheeseOrigins[i++];
            stmt.clearBindings();
            stmt.bindString(1, name); // replace first question mark with name
            stmt. bindString(2, origin); // replace second question mark with origin
            stmt.executeInsert();
        }
    }
```

Because the compilation of the statement is done only once instead of 650 times and because the binding of the values is a more lightweight operation than the compilation, the performance of this method is significantly faster as it builds the database in only 268 milliseconds. It also has the advantage of making the code easier to read.

Android also provides additional APIs to insert values in a database using a `ContentValues` object, which basically contains the binding information between column names and values. The implementation, shown in Listing 1–22, is actually very close to `populateWithCompileStatement`, and the "INSERT INTO cheese VALUES" string does not even appear as this part of the insert statement is implied by the call to `db.insert()`.

However, the performance of this implementation is below what we achieved with populateWithCompileStatement since it takes 352 milliseconds to complete.

Listing 1–22. *Populating the Database Using ContentValues*

```
public void populateWithContentValues () {
    ContentValues values = new ContentValues();
    int i = 0;
    for (String name : sCheeseNames) {
        String origin = sCheeseOrigins[i++];
        values.clear();
        values.put("name", name);
        values.put("origin", origin);
        db.insert("cheese", null, values);
    }
}
```

The fastest implementation is also the most flexible one as it allows more options in the statement. For example, you could use "INSERT OR FAIL" or "INSERT OR IGNORE" instead of simply "INSERT".

> **NOTE:** Many changes were made in Android 3.0's android.database and android.database.sqlite packages. For instance, the managedQuery, startManagingCursor, and stopManagingCursor methods in the Activity class are all deprecated in favor of CursorLoader.

Android also defines a few classes that can improve performance. For example, you can use DatabaseUtils.InsertHelper to insert multiple rows in a database while compiling the SQL insert statement only once. It is currently implemented the same way we implemented populateWithCompileStatement although it does not offer the same flexibility as far as options are concerned (for example, FAIL or ROLLBACK).

Not necessarily related to performance, you may also use the static methods in the DatabaseUtils class to simplify your implementation.

Transactions

The examples above did not explicitly create any transaction, however one was automatically created for every insertion and committed immediately after each insertion. Creating a transaction explicitly allows for two basic things:

- Atomic commit
- Better performance

The first feature is important but not from a performance point of view. Atomic commit means either all or none of the modifications to the database occur. A transaction cannot be only partially committed. In our example, we can consider the insertion of all 650 cheeses as one transaction. Either we succeed at building the complete list of cheeses or we don't, but we are not interested in a partial list. The implementation is shown in Listing 1–23.

Listing 1–23. *Insertion of All Cheeses in a Single Transaction*

```
public void populateWithCompileStatementOneTransaction () {
    try {
        db.beginTransaction();
        SQLiteStatement stmt = db.compileStatement("INSERT INTO cheese
VALUES(?,?)");
        int i = 0;
        for (String name : sCheeseNames) {
            String origin = sCheeseOrigins[i++];
            stmt.clearBindings();
            stmt.bindString(1, name); // replace first question mark with name
            stmt. bindString(2, origin); // replace second question mark with origin
            stmt.executeInsert();
        }
        db.setTransactionSuccessful(); // remove that call and none of the changes
will be committed!
    } catch (Exception e) {
        // handle exception here
    } finally {
        db.endTransaction(); // this must be in the finally block
    }
}
```

This new implementation took 166 milliseconds to complete. While this is quite an improvement (about 100 milliseconds faster), one could argue both implementations were probably acceptable for most applications as it is quite unusual to insert so many rows so quickly. Indeed, most applications would typically access rows only once in a while, possibly as a response to some user action. The most important point is that the database was memory-backed and not saved to persistent storage (SD card or internal Flash memory). When working with databases, a lot of time is spent on accessing persistent storage (read/write), which is much slower than accessing volatile memory. By creating the database in internal persistent storage, we can verify the effect of having a single transaction. The creation of the database in persistent storage is shown in Listing 1–24.

Listing 1–24. *Creation of Database On Storage*

```
public Cheeses (String path) {
    // path could have been created with getDatabasePath("fromage.db")

    // you could also make sure the path exists with a call to mkdirs
    // File file = new File(path);
    // File parent = new File(file.getParent());
    // parent.mkdirs();

    db = SQLiteDatabase.openOrCreateDatabase(path, null);
    db.execSQL("CREATE TABLE cheese (name TEXT, origin TEXT)");
}
```

When the database is on storage and not in memory, the call to populateWithCompileStatement takes almost 34 seconds to complete (52 milliseconds per row), while the call to populateWithCompileStatementOneTransaction takes less than

200 milliseconds. Needless to say, the one-transaction approach is a much better solution to our problem. These figures obviously depend on the type of storage being used. Storing the database on an external SD card would make it even slower and therefore would make the one-transaction approach even more appealing.

> **NOTE:** Make sure the parent directory exists when you create a database on storage. See `Context.getDatabasePath` and `File.mkdirs` for more information. For convenience, use SQLiteOpenHelper instead of creating databases manually.

Queries

The way to make queries faster is to also limit the access to the database, especially on storage. A database query simply returns a `Cursor` object, which can then be used to iterate through the results. Listing 1–25 shows two methods to iterate through all the rows. The first method creates a cursor that gets both columns in the database whereas the second method's cursor retrieves only the first column.

Listing 1–25. *Iterating Through All the Rows*

```
public void iterateBothColumns () {
    Cursor c = db.query("cheese", null, null, null, null, null, null);
    if (c.moveToFirst()) {
        do {
        } while (c.moveToNext());
    }
    c.close(); // remember to close cursor when you are done (or else expect an
exception at some point)
}

public void iterateFirstColumn () {
    Cursor c = db.query("cheese", new String[]{"name"}, null, null, null, null,
null); // only difference
    if (c.moveToFirst()) {
        do {
        } while (c.moveToNext());
    }
    c.close();
}
```

As expected, because it does not have to read data from the second column at all, the second method is faster: 23 milliseconds vs. 61 milliseconds (when using multiple transactions). Iterating through all the rows is even faster when all the rows are added as one transaction: 11 milliseconds for `iterateBothColumns` vs. 7 milliseconds for `iterateFirstColumn`. As you can see, you should only read the data you care about. Choosing the right parameters in calls to query can make a substantial difference in performance. You can reduce the database access even more if you only need up to a certain number of rows, and specify the limit parameter in the call to query.

TIP: Consider using the FTS (full-text search) extension to SQLite for more advanced search features (using indexing). Refer to www.sqlite.org/fts3.html for more information.

Summary

Years ago, Java had a bad reputation for performance, but today this is no longer true. The Dalvik virtual machine, including its Just-In-Time compiler, improves with every new release of Android. Your code can be compiled into native code that takes advantage of the latest CPU architectures without you having to recompile anything. While implementation is important, your highest priority should be to carefully select data structures and algorithms. Good algorithms can be pretty forgiving and perform quite well even without you optimizing anything. On the other hand, a bad algorithm almost always gives poor results, no matter how hard you work on its implementation.

Finally, never sacrifice responsiveness. It may make your application development a little bit more difficult, but the success of your application depends on it.

Chapter 2

Getting Started With the NDK

The Android Native Development Kit (NDK) is a companion to the SDK and is what you use when you want part or all of your Android application to use native code. While bytecode needs to be interpreted by a virtual machine, native code can be directly executed by the device's processor without any intermediate step, making execution faster, and sometimes much faster. The Dalvik Just-In-Time (JIT) compiler is compiling the bytecode into native code, making your applications faster by having to interpret the code less often (and ideally, only once) since it will use the native code it generated whenever it is available. When you use the NDK, the compilation into native code occurs on your development environment and not on the Android device. You may be wondering why you would need to worry about the NDK since the Dalvik JIT compiler can generate native code dynamically and therefore you could write your application in Java using the SDK. This chapter covers the reasons why you may need to use the NDK and the various ways to use it.

There are essentially two ways to use native code and the NDK:

- You can write one part of your application in Java and the other part in C/C++.

- You can write the whole application in C/C++.

> **NOTE:** NDK support was added in Android 1.5. Today very few devices run Android versions older than 1.5, and it is therefore safe to use the NDK to write part of your application in C/C++. However, writing your entire application in C/C++ requires Android 2.3 or later.

This chapter starts by showing you what the NDK is made of. Then, we will take a look at how to mix C/C++ code with Java code in an Android application, and how to make sure the code is optimized for all platforms you want to target. Finally, we'll delve into a new class, NativeActivity, introduced in Android 2.3 that allows you to write your whole application in C/C++, and we'll show you a simple example of using sensors in your C/C++ code.

What Is In the NDK?

The NDK is a set of tools you use to develop native code for your application. Everything is in a single directory, which you download as an archive file from `http://d.android.com/sdk/ndk`. For example, the Windows version of the NDK revision 6b contains these directories:

- build
- docs
- platforms
- samples
- sources
- tests
- toolchains

A few files are also located at the root of the NDK directory:

- documentation.html
- GNUmakefile
- ndk-build
- ndk-gdb
- ndk-stack
- README.txt
- RELEASE.txt

The NDK documentation is nowhere near as thorough as the SDK on `http://d.android.com`, so start by opening documentation.html with your favorite web browser. The README text file is also begging you so go ahead and oblige.

The NDK is a collection of six components:

- Documentation
- Header files
- C/C++ files
- Precompiled libraries
- Tools to compile, link, analyze, and debug your code
- Sample applications

Native code is, by definition, specific to a certain architecture. For example, an Intel CPU would not understand ARM instructions, and vice versa. Therefore, the NDK includes precompiled libraries for multiple platforms as well as different versions of tools. NDK revision 7 supports three Application Binary Interfaces (ABIs):

- armeabi
- armeabi-v7a
- x86

NOTE: The NDK does not support the ARMv6 ABI.

Most of you are already familiar with the x86 name as it refers to the Intel architecture, a name that is practically ubiquitous. The armeabi and armeabi-v7a names may not sound familiar, but you can find ARM-based chips in many products, from washing machines to DVD players, so chances are you used an ARM-based device long before you even heard of Android. Close to 2 billion ARM-based chips were shipped in the second quarter of 2011 alone: 1.1 billion in mobile phones and tablets, and 0.8 billion in other consumer and embedded devices.

The term "armeabi" stands for ARM Embedded Application Binary Interface, while v5 and v7a refer to two different architectures. ARM architectures started with v1, and the latest one is v7. Each architecture is used by a family of processor cores, with v5 being used by some ARM7, ARM9, and ARM10 cores, and v7 by the Cortex family. The Cortex series includes A5, A8, A9, and soon A15, with the majority of today's smartphones and tablets using A8 and A9 cores.

The Android NDK does not support the ARMv6 architecture, which is used by the ARM11 family of processor cores, even though some Android devices use ARM11-based chipsets. Table 2–1 shows a list of Android devices.

Table 2–1. *Some Android Devices and Their Architectures*

Device	Manufacturer	CPU	Processor family
Blade	ZTE	Qualcomm MSM7227	ARM11
LePhone	Lenovo	Qualcomm Snapdragon	Based on Cortex A8
Nexus S	Samsung	Samsung Hummingbird	Cortex A8
Xoom	Motorola	Nvidia Tegra 2	Cortex A9 (dual core)
Galaxy Tab (7'')	Samsung	Samsung Hummingbird	Cortex A8
Galaxy Tab 10.1	Samsung	Nvidia Tegra 2	Cortex A9 (dual core)
Revue (set-top box)	Logitech	CE4150 (Sodaville)	Intel Atom
NSZ-GT1 (Blu-ray player)	Sony	CE4170 (Sodaville)	Intel Atom

While MIPS Technologies announced that a MIPS-based smartphone running Android 2.2 passed the Android CTS back in June 2011, the Android NDK still does not support the MIPS ABI. As of today, ARM is still the dominant architecture in Android devices.

> **NOTE:** All Google TV devices released in 2010 (Logitech set-top box, Sony TVs, and Blu-ray player) are based on the Intel CE4100. However, the Google TV platform currently does not support the NDK.

As the NDK is frequently updated, you should always try to use the latest revision. New revisions may improve performance, for example by providing better compilers or more optimized precompiled libraries. New revisions can also fix bugs from previous revisions. When publishing an update to your application, consider rebuilding your C/C++ code with the latest NDK even if you modified only the Java part of your application. However, make sure you always run tests on the C/C++ code! Table 2–2 shows the NDK revisions.

Table 2–2. *Android NDK Revisions*

Revision	Date	Features
1	June 2009	Android 1.5 NDK, Release 1
		Supports ARMv5TE instructions
		GCC 4.2.1
2	September 2009	Android 1.6 NDK, Release 1
		Adds OpenGL ES 1.1 native library support
3	March 2010	Adds OpenGL ES 2.0 native library support
		GCC 4.4.0
4b	June 2010	Simplifies build system with ndk-build tool
		Simplifies debugging with ndk-gdb tool
		Adds supports for armeabi-v7a (Thumb-2, VFP, NEON Advanced SIMD)
		Adds API for accessing pixel buffers of Bitmap objects from native code
5c	June 2011	Many more native APIs (really, many!)
		Adds support for prebuilt libraries
		GCC 4.4.3
		Fixes issues from revisions 5 (December 2010) and 5b (January 2011).

Revision	Date	Features
6b	August 2011	Adds support for x86 ABI
		New ndk-stack tool for debugging
		Fixes issues from revision 6 (July 2011).
7	November 2011	Native multimedia APIs based on OpenMAX AL 1.0.1
		Native audio APIs based on OpenSL 1.0.1
		New C++ runtimes (gabi++ and gnustl_shared)
		Support for RTTI in STLport

Mixing Java and C/C++ Code

Calling a C/C++ function from Java is actually quite easy but requires several steps:

1. The native method must be declared in your Java code.

2. The Java Native Interface (JNI) glue layer needs to be implemented.

3. Android makefiles have to be created.

4. The native method must be implemented in C/C++.

5. The native library must be compiled.

6. The native library must be loaded.

It really is easy in its own twisted way. We will go through each one of these steps, and by the end of this section, you will know the basics of mixing Java and C/C++. We will discuss the more intricate details of the Android makefiles, which allow you to optimize your code even more, in later sections. Since the Android NDK exists for Linux, MacOS X, and Windows (with Cygwin, or without when using NDK revision 7), the specific steps may vary slightly although the overall operations will remain the same. The following steps assume an Android project is already created and you now want to add native code to it.

Declaring the Native Method

The first step is shown in Listing 2–1 and is rather trivial.

Listing 2–1. *Declaration of the Native Method in Fibonacci.java*

```
public class Fibonacci {
    public static native long recursiveNative (int n); // note the 'native' keyword
}
```

The native method is simply declared with the native keyword, and no implementation is provided in Java. The method shown above is public, but native methods can be public, protected, private, or package-private, just like any other Java method. Similarly, native methods don't have to be static methods, and don't have to use primitive types only. From the caller's point of view, a native method is just like any other method. Once it is declared, you can start adding calls to this method in your Java code, and everything will compile just fine. However, if your application runs and calls `Fibonacci.recursiveNative`, it will crash with an `UnsatisfiedLinkError` exception. This is expected because you really haven't done much so far other than declare a function, and the actual implementation of the function does not exist yet.

Once your native method is declared, you can start writing the JNI glue layer.

Implementing the JNI Glue Layer

Java uses the JNI framework to call methods from libraries written in C/C++. The Java Development Kit (JDK) on your development platform can help you with building the JNI glue layer. First, you need a header file that defines the function you are going to implement. You don't have to write this header file yourself as you can (and should) use the JDK's javah tool for that.

In a terminal, simply change directories to your application directory, and call javah to create the header file you need. You create this header file in your application's jni directory. Since the jni directory does not exist initially, you have to create it explicitly before you create the header file. Assuming your project is saved in ~/workspace/MyFibonacciApp, the commands to execute are:

```
cd ~/workspace/MyFibonacciApp
mkdir jni
javah -classpath bin -jni -d jni com.apress.proandroid.Fibonacci
```

> **NOTE:** You have to provide the fully qualified name of the class. If javah returns a "Class com.apress.proandroid.Fibonacci not found" error, make sure you specified the right directory with -classpath, and the fully qualified name is correct. The -d option is to specify where the header file should be created. Since javah will need to use Fibonacci.class, make sure your Java application has been compiled before you execute the command.

You should now have a header file only a mother could love called com_apress_proandroid_Fibonacci.h in ~/workspace/MyFibonacciApp/jni, as shown in Listing 2–2. You shouldn't have to modify this file directly. If you need a new version of the file (for example, if you decide to rename the native method in your Java file or add a new one), you can use javah to create it.

Listing 2–2. *JNI Header File*

```
/* DO NOT EDIT THIS FILE - it is machine generated */
#include <jni.h>
/* Header for class com_apress_proandroid_Fibonacci */

#ifndef _Included_com_apress_proandroid_Fibonacci
#define _Included_com_apress_proandroid_Fibonacci
#ifdef __cplusplus
```

```
extern "C" {
#endif
/*
 * Class:       com_apress_proandroid_Fibonacci
 * Method:      recursiveNative
 * Signature: (I)J
 */
JNIEXPORT jlong JNICALL
Java_com_apress_proandroid_Fibonacci_recursiveNative
  (JNIEnv *, jclass, jint);

#ifdef __cplusplus
}
#endif
#enddif
```

A C header file alone won't do you any good though. You now need the implementation of the Java_com_apress_proandroid_Fibonacci_recursiveNative function in a file you will create, com_apress_proandroid_Fibonacci.c, as shown in Listing 2–3.

Listing 2–3. *JNI C Source File*

```
#include "com_apress_proandroid_Fibonacci.h"

/*
 * Class:       com_apress_proandroid_Fibonacci
 * Method:      recursiveNative
 * Signature: (I)J
 */
jlong JNICALL
Java_com_apress_proandroid_Fibonacci_recursiveNative
  (JNIEnv *env, jclass clazz, jint n)
{
    return 0; // just a stub for now, let's return 0
}
```

All functions in the JNI layer have something in common: their first argument is always of type JNIEnv* (pointer to a JNIEnv object). The JNIEnv object is the JNI environment itself that you use to interact with the virtual machine (should you need to). The second argument is of type jclass when the method is declared as static, or jobject when it is not.

> **TIP:** Try javah with the –stubs option to generate the C file (javah –classpath bin –stubs com_apress_proandroid_Fibonacci –d jni). It may work if you are using an old JDK, although it is likely you'll get this error message: "Error: JNI does not require stubs, please refer to the JNI documentation".

Creating the Makefiles

At that point, you most certainly could compile this C++ file into a library using the NDK's GCC compiler, but the NDK provides a tool, ndk-build, that can do that for you. To know what to do, the ndk-build tool uses two files that you create:

- Application.mk (optional)
- Android.mk

You should create both files in the application's jni directory (where the JNI header and source files are already located). As a source of inspiration when creating these two files, simply refer to existing projects that already define these files. The NDK contains examples of applications using native code in the samples directory, hello-jni being the simplest one. Since Application.mk is an optional file, you won't find it in every single sample. You should start by using very simple Application.mk and Android.mk files to build your application as fast as possible without worrying about performance for now. Even though Application.mk is optional and you can do without it, a very basic version of the file is shown in Listing 2–4.

Listing 2–4. *Basic Application.mk File Specifying One ABI*

```
APP_ABI := armeabi-v7a
```

This Application.mk specifies only one version of the library should be built, and this version should target the Cortex family of processors. If no Application.mk is provided, a single library targeting the armeabi ABI (ARMv5) will be built, which would be equivalent to defining an Application.mk file, as shown in Listing 2–5.

Listing 2–5. *Application.mk File Specifying armeabi As Only ABI*

```
APP_ABI := armeabi
```

Android.mk in its simplest form is a tad more verbose as its syntax is dictated, in part, by the tools that will be used to eventually compile the library. Listing 2–6 shows a basic version of Android.mk.

Listing 2–6. *Basic Android.mk*

```
LOCAL_PATH := $(call my-dir)

include $(CLEAR_VARS)

LOCAL_MODULE := fibonacci

LOCAL_SRC_FILES := com_apress_proandroid_Fibonacci.c

include $(BUILD_SHARED_LIBRARY)
```

The file must start with the definition of the local path, where Android.mk is located. The Android NDK provides several macros you can use in your makefiles, and here we use the my-dir macro, which returns the path of the last included makefile. In our case, the last included makefile is simply Android.mk in ~/workspace/MyFibonacciApp/jni, and therefore LOCAL_PATH will be set to ~/workspace/MyFibonacciApp.

The second line is simply to clear all the LOCAL_XXX variables, except LOCAL_PATH. If you forget that line, the variables could be defined incorrectly. You want your build to start in a predictable state, and therefore you should never forget to include that line in Android.mk before you define a module.

LOCAL_MODULE simply defines the name of a module, which will be used to generate the name of the library. For example, if LOCAL_MODULE is set to fibonacci, then the shared library will be libfibonacci.so. LOCAL_SRC_FILES then lists all the files to be compiled, in this case only com_apress_proandroid_Fibonacci.c (the JNI glue layer) as we haven't implemented the actual Fibonacci function yet. Whenever you add a new file, always remember to add it to LOCAL_SRC_FILES or it won't be compiled into the library.

Finally, when all the variables are defined, you need to include the file that contains the rule to actually build the library. In this case, we want to build a shared library, and therefore we include $(BUILD_SHARED_LIBRARY).

While this may seem convoluted, at first you will only need to worry about defining LOCAL_MODULE and LOCAL_SRC_FILES as the rest of the file is pretty much boilerplate.

For more information about these makefiles, refer to the Application.mk and Android.mk sections of this chapter.

Implementing the Native Function

Now that the makefiles are defined, we need to complete the C implementation by creating fibonacci.c, as shown in Listing 2–7, and calling the newly implemented function from the glue layer, as shown in Listing 2–8. Because the function implemented in fibonacci.c needs to be declared before it can be called, a new header file is also created, as shown in Listing 2–9. You will also need to add fibonacci.c to the list of files to compile in Android.mk.

Listing 2–7. *Implementation of the New Function in* fibonacci.c

```
#include "fibonacci.h"

uint64_t recursive (unsigned int n)
{
    if (n > 1) return recursive(n-2) + recursive(n-1);
    return n;
}
```

Listing 2–8. *Calling the Function From the Glue Layer*

```
#include "com_apress_proandroid_Fibonacci.h"
#include "fibonacci.h"

/*
 * Class:      com_apress_proandroid_Fibonacci
 * Method:     recursiveNative
 * Signature: (I)J
 */
```

```
jlong JNICALL
Java_com_apress_proandroid_Fibonacci_recursiveNative
  (JNIEnv *env, jclass clazz, jint n)
{
    return recursive(n);
}
```

Listing 2–9. *Header File* `fibonacci.h`

```
#ifndef _FIBONACCI_H_
#define _FIBONACCI_H_

#include <stdint.h>

extern uint64_t recursive (unsigned int n);

#endif
```

NOTE: Make sure you use the right types in your C/C++ code as jlong is 64-bit. Use well-defined types such as uint64_t or int32_t when size matters.

Some may argue that using multiple files creates unnecessary complexity, and everything could be implemented in the glue layer, that is, in a single file instead of three or four (`fibonacci.h`, `fibonacci.c`, `com_apress_proandroid_Fibonacci.c`, and possibly even `com_apress_proandroid_Fibonacci.h`). While this is technically feasible, as shown in Listing 2–10, it is not recommended. Doing this would tightly couple the glue layer with the implementation of the native function, making it harder to reuse the code in a non-Java application. For example, you may want to reuse the same header and C/C++ files in an iOS application. Keep the glue layer JNI-specific, and JNI-specific only.

While you may also be tempted to remove the inclusion of the JNI header file, keeping it as it guarantees your functions are consistent with what is defined in the Java layer (assuming you remember to recreate the header file with the `javah` tool whenever there is a relevant change in Java).

Listing 2–10. *All Three Files Combined Into One*

```
#include "com_apress_proandroid_Fibonacci.h"
#include <stdint.h>

static uint64_t recursive (unsigned int n)
{
    if (n > 1) return recursive(n-2) + recursive(n-1);
    return n;
}

/*
 * Class:       com_apress_proandroid_Fibonacci
 * Method:      recursiveNative
 * Signature: (I)J
 */
jlong JNICALL
Java_com_apress_proandroid_Fibonacci_recursiveNative
  (JNIEnv *env, jclass clazz, jint n)
```

```
{
    return recursive(n);
}
```

Compiling the Native Library

Now that the C implementation is complete, we can finally build the shared library by calling ndk-build from the application's jni directory.

> **TIP:** Modify your PATH environment variable to include the NDK directory so you can call ndk-build and other scripts easily without having to specify the command's full path.

The result is a shared library called libfibonacci.so in the lib/armeabi directory. You may have to refresh the project in Eclipse to show the newly created libraries. If you compile and run the application, and the application calls Fibonacci.recursiveNative, it will again crash with an UnsatisfiedLinkError exception. This is a typical error as many developers simply forget to explicitly load the shared library from the Java code: the virtual machine is not clairvoyant yet and needs to be told what library to load. This is achieved by a call to System.loadLibrary(), as shown in Listing 2–11.

Listing 2–11. *Loading the Library in Static Initialization Block*

```
public class Fibonacci {
    static {
        System.loadLibrary("fibonacci"); // to load libfibonacci.so
    }

    public static native long recursiveNative (int n);
}
```

Loading the Native Library

Calling System.loadLibrary from within a static initialization block is the easiest way to load a library. The code in such a block is executed when the virtual machine loads the class and before any method is called. A potential, albeit quite uncommon, performance issue is if you have several methods in your class, and not all of them require everything to be initialized (for example, shared libraries loaded). In other words, the static initialization block can add significant overhead that you would want to avoid for certain functions, as shown in Listing 2–12.

Listing 2–12. *Loading the Library in the Static Initialization Block*

```
public class Fibonacci {
    static {
        System.loadLibrary("fibonacci"); // to load libfibonacci.so
        // do more time-consuming things here, which would delay the execution of
superFast
    }
```

```
    public static native long recursiveNative (int n);

    public long superFast (int n) {
        return 42;
    }
}
```

> **NOTE:** The time it takes to load a library also depends on the library itself (its size and number of methods, for example).

So far, we have seen the basics of mixing Java and C/C++. While native code can improve performance, the difference is in part due to how the C/C++ code is compiled. In fact, many compilation options exist, and the result may vary greatly depending on which options are used.

The following two sections tell you more about the options you can define in the Application.mk and Android.mk makefiles, which until now were very basic.

Application.mk

The Application.mk file shown in Listing 2–4 is one of the simplest of its kind. However, this file can specify quite a few more things, and you may need to define many of them in your application. Table 2–3 shows the different variables you can define in Application.mk.

Table 2–3. *Variables in Application.mk*

Variable	Meaning
APP_PROJECT_PATH	Project path
APP_MODULES	List of modules to compile
APP_OPTIM	Defined as "release" or "debug"
APP_CFLAGS	Compiler flags for C and C++ files
APP_CXXFLAGS	Obsolete, use APP_CPPFLAGS instead
APP_CPPFLAGS	Compiler flags for C++ files only
APP_BUILD_SCRIPT	To use a build script other than jni/Android.mk
APP_ABI	List of ABIs to compile code for
APP_STL	The C++ Standard Library to use, defined as "system," "stlport_static," "stlport_shared," or "gnustl_static"
STLPORT_FORCE_REBUILD	To build the STLport library from scratch instead of using the precompiled one, set to true

You will focus on these variables when fine-tuning your application for performance:

- APP_OPTIM
- APP_CFLAGS
- APP_CPPFLAGS
- APP_STL
- APP_ABI

APP_OPTIM is optional and can be set to either "release" or "debug." If it is not defined, it will be automatically set based on whether your application is debuggable (android:debuggable set to true in the application's manifest): if the application is debuggable, then APP_OPTIM would be set to "debug"; otherwise, it would be set to "release." Since it makes sense to build libraries in debug mode when you want to debug your application, the default behavior should be deemed acceptable for most cases, and therefore most of the time you would not need or want to explicitly define APP_OPTIM in your Application.mk.

APP_CFLAGS (C/C++) and APP_CPPFLAGS (C++ only) define the flags passed to the compiler. They don't necessarily specify flags to optimize the code as they could simply be used to include a path to follow to find include files (for example, APP_CFLAGS += -I$(LOCAL_PATH)/myincludefiles). Refer to the gcc documentation for an exhaustive list of flags. The most typical performance-related flags would be the –Ox series, where x specifies the optimization level, from 0 for no optimization to 3, or –Os. However, in most cases, simply defining APP_OPTIM to release, or not defining APP_OPTIM at all should be sufficient as it will choose an optimization level for you, which should produce acceptable results.

APP_STL is used to specify which standard library the application should use. For example, four possible values are defined in NDK revision 6:

- system
- stlport_static
- stlport_shared
- gnustl_static

Each library has its pros and cons. For example:

- Only gnustl_static supports C++ exceptions and Run-Time Type Information (RTTI). Support for RTTI in STLport library was added in NDK r7.

- Use stlport_shared if multiple shared native libraries use the C++ library. (Remember to load the library explicitly with a call to System.loadLibrary("stlport_shared").)

- Use stlport_static if you have only one shared native library in your application (to avoid loading the library dynamically).

You can enable C++ exceptions and RTTI by adding –fexceptions and –frtti to APP_CPPFLAGS respectively.

Optimizing For (Almost) All Devices

If the performance of your application depends heavily on the performance of the C++ library, test your application with different libraries and choose the best one. The choice may not be solely based on performance though, as you have to consider other parameters too, such as the final size of your application or the features you need from the C++ library (for example, RTTI).

The library we compiled above (libfibonacci.so) was built for the armeabi ABI. Two issues now surface:

- While the native code is compatible with the armeabi-v7a ABI, it is not optimized for the Cortex family of processors.

- The native code is not compatible with the x86 ABI.

The Cortex family of processors is more powerful than the processors based on the older ARMv5 architecture. One of the reasons it is more powerful is because new instructions were defined in the ARMv7 architecture, which a library built for ARMv5 will not even use. As the compiler was targeting the armeabi ABI, it made sure it would not use any instruction that an ARMv5-based processor would not understand. Even though your library would be compatible with a Cortex-based device, it would not fully take advantage of the CPU and therefore would not realize its full performance potential.

> **NOTE:** There are many reasons why the ARMv7 architecture is more powerful than ARMv5, and the instruction set is only one of them. Visit the ARM website (http://www.arm.com) for more information about their various architectures.

The second issue is even more serious as a library built for an ARM ABI simply could not be used on an x86-based device. If the native code is mandatory for the application to function, then your application won't work on any Intel-based Android device. In our case, System.loadLibrary("fibonacci") would fail with an UnsatisfiedLinkError exception, meaning the library could not be loaded.

These two issues can easily be fixed though, as APP_ABI can be defined as a list of ABIs to compile native code for, as shown in Listing 2–12. By specifying multiple ABIs, you can guarantee the native code will not only be generated for all these architectures, but also optimized for each one of them.

Listing 2–12. *Application.mk Specifying Three ABIs*

```
APP_ABI := armeabi armeabi-v7a x86
```

After recompiling your application with this new Application.mk, the lib directory will contain three sub-directories. In addition to armeabi, it will contain two new sub-directories named armeabi-v7a and x86. As you will have easily guessed, the two new directories refer to the two new ABIs the application now supports. Each of these three directories contains a file called `libfibonacci.so`.

> **TIP:** Use `ndk-build -B  V=1` after you edit Application.mk or Android.mk to force a rebuild of your libraries and display the build commands. This way you can always verify your changes have the desired effect on the build process.

The application file is much bigger now because it contains three instances of the "same" library, each targeting a different ABI. The Android package manager will determine which one of these libraries to install when the application is installed on the device. The Android system defines a primary ABI and, optionally, a secondary ABI. The primary ABI is the preferred ABI, that is, the package manager will first install libraries that target the primary ABI. If a secondary ABI is defined, it will then install the libraries that target the secondary ABI and for which there is no equivalent library targeting the primary ABI. For example, a Cortex-based Android device should define the primary ABI as armeabi-v7a and the secondary ABI as armeabi. Table 2–4 shows the primary and secondary ABIs for all devices.

Table 2–4. *Primary and Secondary ABIs*

Android system	Primary ABI	Secondary ABI
ARMv5-based	armeabi	not defined
ARMv7-based	armeabi-v7a	armeabi
x86-based	x86	not defined

The secondary ABI provides a means for newer Android devices to maintain compatibility with older applications as the ARMv7 ABI is fully backward compatible with ARMv5.

> **NOTE:** An Android system may define more than primary and secondary ABIs in the future, for example if ARM designs a new ARMv8 architecture that is backward compatible with ARMv7 and ARMv5.

Supporting All Devices

An issue remains though. Despite the fact that the application now supports all the ABIs supported by the NDK, Android can (and most certainly will) be ported onto new architectures. For example, we mentioned a MIPS cellphone earlier. While Java's premise is "write once, run everywhere" (the bytecode is target-agnostic, and one does not need to recompile the code to support new platforms), native code is target-specific, and none of the three libraries we generated would be compatible with a MIPS-based Android system. There are two ways to solve this problem:

- You can compile the new library and publish an update to your application as soon as an NDK supports a new ABI.

- You can provide a default Java implementation to be used when the package manager fails to install the native code.

The first solution is rather trivial as it only involves installing the new NDK, modifying your application's Application.mk, recompiling your application, and publishing the update (for example, on Android Market). However, the official Android NDK may not always support all ABIs Android has already been ported on or will be ported on. As a consequence, it is recommended you also implement the second solution; in other words, a Java implementation should also be provided.

> **NOTE:** MIPS Technologies provides a separate NDK, which allows you to build libraries for the MIPS ABI. Visit http://developer.mips.com/android for more information.

Listing 2–13 shows how a default Java implementation can be provided when loading the library fails.

Listing 2–13. *Providing a Default Java Implementation*

```
public class Fibonacci {
    private static final boolean useNative;
    static {
        boolean success;
        try {
            System.loadLibrary("fibonacci"); // to load libfibonacci.so
            success = true;
        } catch (Throwable e) {
            success = false;
        }
        useNative = success;
    }

    public static long recursive (int n) {
        if (useNative) return recursiveNative(n);
        return recursiveJava(n);
    }

    private static long recursiveJava (int n) {
        if (n > 1) return recursiveJava(n-2) + recursiveJava(n-1);
        return n;
    }

    private static native long recursiveNative (int n);
}
```

An alternative design is to use the Strategy pattern:

- Define a strategy interface.

- Define two classes that both implement the interface (one using native code, the other one using only Java).

- Instantiate the right class based on the result of `System.loadLibrary()`.

Listing 2–14 shows an implementation of this alternative design.

Listing 2–14. *Providing a Default Java Implementation Using the Strategy Pattern*

```java
// FibonacciInterface.java

public interface FibonacciInterface {
    public long recursive (int n);
}

// Fibonacci.java

public final class FibonacciJava implements FibonacciInterface {
    public long recursive(int n) {
        if (n > 1) return recursive(n-2)+recursive(n-1);
        return n;
    }
}

// FibonacciNative.java

public final class FibonacciNative implements FibonacciInterface {
    static {
        System.loadLibrary("fibonacci");
    }

    public native long recursive (int n);
}

// Fibonacci.java

public class Fibonacci {
    private static final FibonacciInterface fibStrategy;
    static {
        FibonacciInterface fib;
        try {
            fib = new FibonacciNative();
        } catch (Throwable e) {
            fib = new FibonacciJava();
        }
        fibStrategy = fib;
    }

    public static long recursive (int n) {
        return fibStrategy.recursive(n);
    }
}
```

> **NOTE:** Since the native function is now declared in `FibonacciNative.java` instead of `Fibonacci.java`, you will have to create the native library again, this time using `com_apress_proandroid_FibonacciNative.c` and `com_apress_proandroid_FibonacciNative.h`. (`Java_com_apress_proandroid_FibonacciNative_recursiveNative` would be the name of the function called from Java.) Using the previous library would trigger an `UnsatisfiedLinkError` exception.

While there are minor differences between the two implementations as far as performance is concerned, they are irrelevant enough to be safely ignored:

- The first implementation requires a test every single time the `recursive()` method is called.

- The second implementation requires an object allocation in the static initialization block and a call to a virtual function when `recursive()` is called.

From a design point of view though, it is recommended you use the Strategy pattern:

- You only have to select the right strategy once, and you don't take the risk of forgetting an "`if (useNative)`" test.

- You can easily change strategy by modifying only a couple of lines of code.

- You keep strategies in different files, making maintenance easier.

- Adding a method to the strategy interface forces you to implement the methods in all implementations.

As you can see, configuring Application.mk is not necessarily a trivial task. However, you will quickly realize that you are using the same parameters most of the time for all your applications, and simply copying one of your existing Application.mk to your new application will often do the trick.

Android.mk

While Application.mk allows you to specify variables common to your whole application, Android.mk is used to specify what modules you want to build and how to build them, all of this in excruciating detail. Table 2–5 lists the available variables in NDK revision 6.

Table 2–5. *Variables You Can Define in Android.mk*

Variable	Meaning
LOCAL_PATH	Path of Android.mk, can be set to $(call my-dir)
LOCAL_MODULE	Name of the module
LOCAL_MODULE_FILENAME	Redefinition of library name (optional)
LOCAL_SRC_FILES	Files to compile in module
LOCAL_CPP_EXTENSION	Redefinition of file extension of C++ source files (default is .cpp)
LOCAL_C_INCLUDES	List of paths to append to the include search path
LOCAL_CFLAGS	Compiler flags for C and C++ files
LOCAL_CXXFLAGS	Obsolete, use LOCAL_CPPFLAGS instead
LOCAL_CPPFLAGS	Compiler flags for C++ files only
LOCAL_STATIC_LIBRARIES	List of static libraries to link to module
LOCAL_SHARED_LIBRARIES	List of shared libraries the module depends on at runtime
LOCAL_WHOLE_STATIC_LIBRARIES	Similar to LOCAL_STATIC_LIBRARIES, but uses the --whole-archive flag
LOCAL_LDLIBS	List of additional linker flags (for example, –lGLESv2 to link with the OpenGL ES 2.0 library)
LOCAL_ALLOW_UNDEFINED_SYMBOLS	Allow undefined symbols by setting this variable to true (default is false)
LOCAL_ARM_MODE	The mode (ARM or Thumb) the binaries will be compiled in
LOCAL_ARM_NEON	Allow the use of NEON Advanced SIMD instructions/intrinsics
LOCAL_DISABLE_NO_EXECUTE	Disable NX bit (default is false, that is NX enabled)
LOCAL_EXPORT_CFLAGS LOCAL_EXPORT_CPPFLAGS LOCAL_EXPORT_C_INCLUDES LOCAL_EXPORT_LDLIBS	Used to export the variables to modules depending on this module (that is, list the module in LOCAL_STATIC_LIBRARY or LOCAL_SHARED_LIBRARY)
LOCAL_FILTER_ASM	Allow a shell command to be executed on assembly files

Once again, we are going to focus on the few variables that have an impact on performance:

- LOCAL_CFLAGS
- LOCAL_CPPFLAGS
- LOCAL_ARM_MODE
- LOCAL_ARM_NEON
- LOCAL_DISABLE_NO_EXECUTE

`LOCAL_CFLAGS` and `LOCAL_CPPFLAGS` are similar to `APP_CFLAGS` and `APP_CPPFLAGS`, but apply only to the current module, whereas the flags defined in Application.mk are for all the modules. It is recommended you actually don't set optimization levels in Android.mk but instead rely on `APP_OPTIM` in Application.mk.

`LOCAL_ARM_MODE` can be used to force the binaries to be generated in ARM mode, that is, using 32–bit instructions. While code density may suffer compared to Thumb mode (16-bit instructions), performance may improve as ARM code tends to be faster than Thumb code. For example, Android's own Skia library is explicitly compiled in ARM mode. Obviously, this only applies to ARM ABIs, that is, armeabi and armeabi-v7a. If you want to compile only specific files using ARM mode, you can list them in `LOCAL_SRC_FILES` with the .arm suffix, for example, `file.c.arm` instead of `file.c`.

`LOCAL_ARM_NEON` specifies whether you can use Advanced SIMD instruction or intrinsics in your code, and whether the compiler can generate NEON instructions in the native code. While the performance can be dramatically improved with NEON instructions, NEON was only introduced in the ARMv7 architecture and is an optional component. Consequently, NEON is not available on all devices. For example, the Samsung Galaxy Tab 10.1 does not support NEON but the Samsung Nexus S does. Like `LOCAL_ARM_MODE`, support for NEON can be for individual files, and the .neon suffix is used. Chapter 3 covers the NEON extension and provides sample code.

> **TIP:** You can combine the .arm and .neon suffixes in `LOCAL_SRC_FILES`, for example, `file.c.arm.neon`. If both suffixes are used, make sure .arm is used first or else it won't compile.

The `LOCAL_DISABLE_NO_EXECUTE` does not have any impact on performance in itself. However, expert developers may be interested in disabling the NX bit when code is generated dynamically (most likely to achieve much better performance). This is not a common thing to do, and you probably won't ever have to specify that flag in your Android.mk as the NX bit is enabled by default. Disabling the NX bit is also considered a security risk.

Android.mk can specify multiple modules, and each module can use different flags and different source files. Listing 2–15 shows such an Android.mk file, compiling two modules with different flags for each.

Listing 2–15. *Two Modules Specified In Android.mk*

```
LOCAL_PATH := $(call my-dir)

include $(CLEAR_VARS)
LOCAL_MODULE := fibonacci
LOCAL_ARM_MODE := thumb
LOCAL_SRC_FILES := com_apress_proandroid_Fibonacci.c fibonacci.c
include $(BUILD_SHARED_LIBRARY)

include $(CLEAR_VARS)
LOCAL_MODULE := fibonarmcci
LOCAL_ARM_MODE := arm
LOCAL_SRC_FILES := com_apress_proandroid_Fibonacci.c fibonacci.c
include $(BUILD_SHARED_LIBRARY)
```

Like Application.mk, Android.mk can be configured in many ways. Choosing the right values for variables in these two files can be the key to achieving good performance without having recourse to more advanced and complicated optimizations. With the NDK always evolving, you should refer to the latest online documentation as new variables can be added in new releases while others may become deprecated. When a new NDK is released, it is recommended you recompile your application and publish an update, especially when the new release comes with a new compiler.

> **NOTE:** Test your application again after you have recompiled it with a different tool chain (that is, the new SDK or NDK).

Performance Improvements With C/C++

Now that you know how to combine Java and C/C++ code, you may think that C/C++ is always preferred over Java to achieve best performance. This is not true, and native code is not the answer to all your performance problems. Actually, you may sometimes experience a performance degradation when calling native code. While this may sound surprising, it really shouldn't as switching from Java space to native space is not without any cost. The Dalvik JIT compiler will also produce native code, which may be equivalent to or possibly even better than your own native code.

Let's consider the `Fibonacci.computeIterativelyFaster()` method from Chapter 1 and its C implementation, as shown in Listing 2–16.

Listing 2–16. *Iterative C Implementation of Fibonacci Series*

```
uint64_t computeIterativelyFaster (unsigned int n)
{
    if (n > 1) {
        uint64_t a, b = 1;
        n--;
        a = n & 1;
        n /= 2;
        while (n-- > 0) {
            a += b;
```

```
            b += a;
        }
        return b;
    }
    return n;
    }
}
```

As you can see, the C implementation is very similar to the Java implementation, except for the use of unsigned types. You can also observe the Dalvik bytecode shown in Listing 2–17 looks similar to the ARM native code shown in Listing 2–18, generated with the NDK's objdump tool. Among other things, the objdump NDK tool allows you to disassemble a binary file (object file, library, or executable) and display the assembler mnemonics. This tool is very much like dexdump, which basically performs the same operations but on .dex files (for example, an application's classes.dex file).

> **NOTE:** Use objdump's –d option to disassemble a file, for example, objdump –d
> libfibonacci.so. Execute objdump without any option or parameter to see the list of all supported options. The NDK comes with different versions of objdump: one for the ARM ABIs and one for the x86 ABI.

Listing 2–17. *Dalvik Bytecode of* Fibonacci.iterativeFaster

```
0008e8:                   |[0008e8] com.apress.proandroid.Fibonacci.iterativeFaster:(I)J
0008f8: 1215              |0000: const/4 v5, #int 1 // #1
0008fa: 3758 1600         |0001: if-le v8, v5, 0017 // +0016
0008fe: 1602 0100         |0003: const-wide/16 v2, #int 1 // #1
000902: d808 08ff         |0005: add-int/lit8 v8, v8, #int -1 // #ff
000906: dd05 0801         |0007: and-int/lit8 v5, v8, #int 1 // #01
00090a: 8150              |0009: int-to-long v0, v5
00090c: db08 0802         |000a: div-int/lit8 v8, v8, #int 2 // #02
000910: 0184              |000c: move v4, v8
000912: d808 04ff         |000d: add-int/lit8 v8, v4, #int -1 // #ff
000916: 3c04 0400         |000f: if-gtz v4, 0013 // +0004
00091a: 0425              |0011: move-wide v5, v2
00091c: 1005              |0012: return-wide v5
00091e: bb20              |0013: add-long/2addr v0, v2
000920: bb02              |0014: add-long/2addr v2, v0
000922: 0184              |0015: move v4, v8
000924: 28f7              |0016: goto 000d // -0009
000926: 8185              |0017: int-to-long v5, v8
000928: 28fa              |0018: goto 0012 // -0006
```

Listing 2–18. *ARM Assembly Code of C Implementation of* iterativeFaster

```
00000410 <iterativeFaster>:
 410:   e3500001    cmp     r0, #1   ; 0x1
 414:   e92d0030    push    {r4, r5}
 418:   91a02000    movls   r2, r0
 41c:   93a03000    movls   r3, #0   ; 0x0
 420:   9a00000e    bls     460 <iterativeFaster+0x50>
 424:   e2400001    sub     r0, r0, #1      ; 0x1
 428:   e1b010a0    lsrs    r1, r0, #1
 42c:   03a02001    moveq   r2, #1   ; 0x1
```

```
430:    03a03000    moveq    r3, #0   ; 0x0
434:    0a000009    beq      460 <iterativeFaster+0x50>
438:    e3a02001    mov      r2, #1   ; 0x1
43c:    e3a03000    mov      r3, #0   ; 0x0
440:    e0024000    and      r4, r2, r0
444:    e3a05000    mov      r5, #0   ; 0x0
448:    e0944002    adds     r4, r4, r2
44c:    e0a55003    adc      r5, r5, r3
450:    e0922004    adds     r2, r2, r4
454:    e0a33005    adc      r3, r3, r5
458:    e2511001    subs     r1, r1, #1       ; 0x1
45c:    1afffff9    bne      448 <iterativeFaster+0x38>
460:    e1a01003    mov      r1, r3
464:    e1a00002    mov      r0, r2
468:    e8bd0030    pop      {r4, r5}
46c:    e12fff1e    bx       lr
```

> **NOTE:** Refer to `http://infocenter.arm.com` for a complete documentation of the ARM instruction set.

The assembly code is what is going to be executed by the CPU. Since the Dalvik bytecode looks a lot like the assembly code (even though the assembly code is more compact), one could infer that the native code the Dalvik Just-In-Time compiler will generate should be pretty close to the native code shown in Listing 2–18. Also, if the bytecode were significantly different from the assembly code, the Dalvik JIT compiler may still generate native code very similar to the assembly code the NDK generated.

Now, to be able to compare these methods, we need to run some tests. Actual performance evaluation needs empirical evidence, and we are going to test and compare four items:

- Java implementation without JIT compiler
- Java implementation with JIT compiler
- Native implementation (debug)
- Native implementation (release)

The test skeleton (found in `Fibonacci.java`) is shown in Listing 2–19, and results are shown in Figure 2–1 and Figure 2–2.

Listing 2–19. *Test Skeleton*

```
static {
    System.loadLibrary("fibonacci_release"); // we use two libraries
    System.loadLibrary("fibonacci_debug");
}

private static final int ITERATIONS = 1000000;

private static long testFibonacci (int n)
{
    long time = System.currentTimeMillis();
```

```
        for (int i = 0; i < ITERATIONS; i++) {
            // call iterativeFaster(n), iterativeFasterNativeRelease(n) or
interativeFasterNativeDebug(n)
            callFibonacciFunctionHere(n);
        }
        time = System.currentTimeMillis() - time;
        Log.i("testFibonacci", String.valueOf(n) + " >> Total time: " + time + "
milliseconds");
    }

    private static void testFibonacci ()
    {
        for (int i = 0; i < 92; i++) {
            testFibonacci(i);
        }
    }
}

    private static native long iterativeFasterNativeRelease (int n);

    private static native long iterativeFasterNativeDebug (int n);
```

Figure 2–1 shows the duration of the test in milliseconds for each of the four
implementations listed above. Figure 2–2 shows the relative performance of the four
implementations with the baseline being the Java implementation with JIT compiler
enabled.

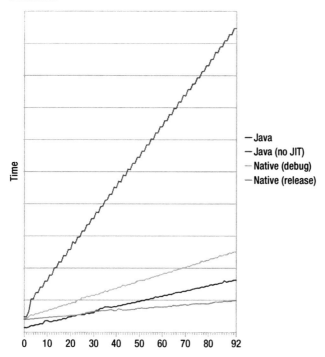

Figure 2–1. *The performance of different implementations of* iterativeFaster()

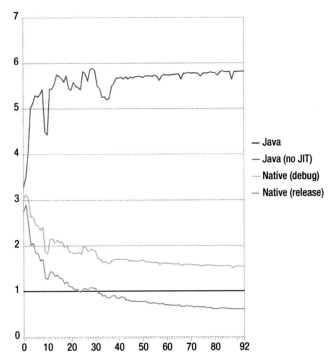

Figure 2–2. *The performance of different implementations of* `iterativeFaster()` *relative to a JIT-enabled Java implementation*

We can draw a few conclusions:

- The Dalvik JIT compiler can increase performance significantly. (The JIT-enabled version is 3 to 6 times faster than JIT-disabled version.)

- The native implementation is not always faster than the JIT-enabled Java version.

- The more time spent in the native space, the more diluted the Java/native transition cost is.

Google's own tests showed the Dalvik JIT compiler could improve performance by a factor of 5 with CPU-intensive code, and our own results here confirm that. The performance gain will depend on the code though, so you should not always assume such a ratio. This is important to measure if you still target older devices running a JIT-less version of Android (Android 2.1 or earlier). In some cases, using native code is the only option to provide an acceptable user experience on older devices.

More About JNI

The JNI glue layer we used was extremely simple as all it did was to call another C function. Unfortunately, it won't be as easy all the time as things get more complicated when non-primitive types are used and when the native code needs to access fields or methods from the Java object or class. On the plus side, everything you do in the JNI glue layer will be quite mechanical.

Strings

Working with strings in both Java and C/C++ can often lead to performance problems. Java's String uses 16-bit Unicode characters (UTF-16) while many C/C++ functions simply use char* to refer to strings (that is, strings in C/C++ are most of the time ASCII or UTF-8). Nostalgic developers may even use the EBCDIC encoding for obfuscation purposes. That being said, Java strings have to be converted to C/C++ strings before they can be used. A simple example is shown in Listing 2–20.

Listing 2–20. *Java Native Method Using String and JNI Glue Layer*

```
// Java (in Myclass.java)
public class MyClass {
    public static native void doSomethingWithString (String s);
}

// JNI glue layer (in C file)
void JNICALL
Java_com_apress_proandroid_MyClass_doSomethingWithString
  (JNIEnv *env, jclass clazz, jstring s)
{
    const char* str = (*env)->GetStringUTFChars(env, s, NULL);
    if (str != NULL) {
        // do something with str string here

        // remember to release the string to avoid memory leaks galore
        (*env)->ReleaseStringUTFChars(env, s, str);
    }
}
```

The JNI offers multiple methods to work with strings, and they all pretty much work the same way:

- The Java String must be converted to a C/C++ string.

- C/C++ string must be released.

Table 2–6 shows the various string get/release methods the JNI provides, together with a short description.

Table 2–6. *JNI Get/Release String Methods*

Get	Release	Description
GetStringChars	ReleaseStringChars	Gets a pointer to a UTF-16 string (may require memory allocation)
GetStringUTFChars	ReleaseStringUTFChars	Gets a pointer to a UTF-8 string (may require memory allocation)
GetStringCritical	ReleaseStringCritical	Gets a pointer to a UTF-16 string (may require memory allocation, restrictions on what you can do between calls to GetStringCritical and ReleaseStringCritical)
GetStringRegion	n/a	Copies part of a string to a pre-allocated buffer (UTF-16 format, no memory allocation)
GetStringUTFRegion	n/a	Copies part of a string to a pre-allocated buffer (UTF-8 format, no memory allocation)

Since memory allocations are never free, you should favor the `GetStringRegion` and `GetStringUTFRegion` in your code whenever possible. By doing so, you:

- Avoid possible memory allocations.
- Copy only the part of the String you need in a pre-allocated buffer (possibly in the stack).
- Avoid having to release the string, and avoid forgetting about releasing the string.

> **NOTE:** Refer to the online JNI documentation and the NDK's `jni.h` header file for more information about other String functions.

Accessing Fields or Methods

You can access fields and methods from Java objects or classes from within the JNI glue layer, however it is not as simple as accessing a field or calling a function of a C++ object or class. Fields and methods of Java objects or classes are accessed by id. To access a field or call a method, you need to:

- Get the id of this field or method.
- Use a JNI function to set/get the field or call the method.

An example is shown in Listing 2–21.

Listing 2–21. *Modifying a Field and Calling a Method From the JNI Glue Layer*

```java
// Java (in MyClass.java)

public class MyClass {
    static {
        System.loadLibrary("mylib");
    }

    public static int someInteger = 0;

    public static native void sayHelloToJNI();

    public static void helloFromJNI() {
        Log.i("MyClass", "Greetings! someInteger=" + someInteger);
    }
}
```

```c
// JNI glue layer (in C file)

void JNICALL
Java_com_apress_proandroid_MyClass_sayHelloToJNI
  (JNIEnv *env, jclass clazz)
{
    // we get the ids for the someInteger field and helloFromJNI method
    jfieldID someIntegerId = (*env)->GetStaticFieldID(env, clazz, "someInteger", "I");
    jfieldID helloFromJNIId = (*env)->GetStaticMethodID(env, clazz, "helloFromJNI",
"()V");

    // we increment someInteger
    jint value = (*env)->GetStaticIntField(env, clazz, someIntegerId);
    (*env)->SetStaticIntField(env, clazz, value + 1);

    // we call helloFromJNI
    (*env)->CallStaticVoidMethod(env, clazz, helloFromJNIId);
}
```

For performance reasons, you don't want to retrieve the field or method ids every single time you need to access a field or call a method. The field and method ids are set when the class is loaded by the virtual machine and are valid only as long as the class is still loaded. If the class is unloaded by the virtual machine and reloaded again, the new ids may be different from the old ones. That being said, an efficient approach is to retrieve the ids when the class is loaded, that is, in the static initialization block, as shown in Listing 2–22.

Listing 2–22. *Retrieving Field/Method Ids Only Once*

```java
// Java (in MyClass.java)

public class MyClass {
    static {
        System.loadLibrary("mylib");
        getIds(); // we get the ids only once when the class is loaded
    }

    public static int someInteger = 0;
```

```
    public static native void sayHelloToJNI();

    public static void helloFromJNI() {
        Log.i("MyClass", "Greetings! someInteger=" + someInteger);
    }

    private static native void getIds();
}

// JNI glue layer (in C file)

static jfieldID someIntegerId;
static jfieldID helloFromJNIId;

void JNICALL
Java_com_apress_proandroid_MyClass_sayHelloToJNI
  (JNIEnv *env, jclass clazz)
{
    // we do not need to get the ids here anymore

    // we increment someInteger
    jint value = (*env)->GetStaticIntField(env, clazz, someIntegerId);
    (*env)->SetStaticIntField(env, clazz, value + 1);

    // we call helloFromJNI
    (*env)->CallStaticVoidMethod(env, clazz, helloFromJNIId);
}

void JNICALL
Java_com_apress_proandroid_MyClass_getIds
  (JNIEnv *env, jclass clazz)
{
    // we get the ids for the someInteger field and helloFromJNI method
    someIntegerId = (*env)->GetStaticFieldID(env, clazz, "someInteger", "I");
    helloFromJNIId = (*env)->GetStaticMethodID(env, clazz, "helloFromJNI", "()V");
}
```

The JNI defines tons of functions you can use to access fields and call methods. For example, accessing an integer field and accessing a Boolean field are two operations that are done with two different functions. Similarly, different functions are defined to call a static method and a non-static method.

NOTE: Refer to the online JNI documentation and the NDK's jni.h header file for a complete list of functions you can use.

Android defines its own set of functions and data structures to access the most common classes used in native code. For example, the APIs defined in android/bitmap.h (introduced in NDK release 4b) allow access to the pixel buffers of bitmap objects:

- AndroidBitmap_getInfo
- AndroidBitmap_lockPixels
- AndroidBitmap_unlockPixels

NDK revision 5 introduced many new APIs application developers can use from native code to access parts of the Android Java framework, without relying on JNI idiosyncrasies (JNIEnv, jclass, jobject, for example).

Native Activity

So far, we have seen how to mix Java and C/C++ in a single application. Android 2.3 goes one step further and defines the NativeActivity class, which allows you to write the whole application in C/C++ but does not force you to, as you still have access to the whole Android Java framework through JNI.

> **NOTE:** You do not have to use NativeActivity for all activities in your application. For example, you could write an application with two activities: one NativeActivity and one ListActivity.

If you prefer to read source files or header files in lieu of more formal documentation, you are in for a treat. In fact, most of the documentation is contained in the header files, which you can find in the NDK's platforms/android-9/arch-arm/usr/include/android directory. The list of header files is shown in Table 2–7.

Table 2–7. *Header Files That Native Activities Will Use*

Header file	Content
api-level.h	Definition of __ANDROID_API__
asset_manager.h	Asset Manager APIs
asset_manager_jni.h	API to convert Java object (AssetManager) to native object
bitmap.h	Bitmap APIs
configuration.h	Configuration APIs
input.h	Input APIs (devices, keys, gestures, etc)
keycodes.h	Definition of all key codes (e.g. AKEYCODE_SEARCH)
log.h	Log APIs
looper.h	Convenience APIs to handle events
native_activity.h	Where many things start
native_window.h	Window APIs

Header file	Content
native_window_jni.h	API to convert Java object (Surface) to native object
obb	Opaque Binary Blob APIs (see Java's StorageManager)
rect	Definition of ARect type
sensor	Sensor APIs (accelerometer, gyroscope, etc)
storage_manager.h	Storage Manager APIs
window.h	Window flags (see Java's WindowManager.LayoutParams)

Creating a native activity is quite simple. The first step is to define your application's manifest file to let Android know you are going to use a native activity. For that you need to specify two things in your application's AndroidManifest.xml for each native activity:

- The class to instantiate
- The library to load and its entry point

The first item is actually no different from other non-native activities. When your activity is created, Android needs to instantiate the right class, and this is what android:name is for inside the <activity> tag. In most cases there is no need for your application to extend the NativeActivity class, so you will almost always use android.app.NativeActivity as the class to instantiate. Nothing prevents you from instantiating a class of your creation that extends NativeActivity though.

The second item is for Android to know what library contains your activity's native code so that it can be loaded automatically when the activity is created. That piece of information is given to Android as metadata as a name/value pair: the name has to be set to android.app.lib_name, and the value specifies the name of the library without the lib prefix or .so suffix. Optionally, you can also specify the library's entry point as name/value metadata, the name being set to android.app.func_name, and the value to the function name. By default, the function name is set to ANativeActivity_onCreate.

An example of a manifest file is shown in Listing 2–23. The minimum SDK version is set to 9 as NativeActivity was introduced in Android 2.3, and the activity's native code is in libmyapp.so.

Listing 2–23. *The Native Application's AndroidManifest.xml*

```
<?xml version="1.0" encoding="utf-8"?>
<manifest xmlns:android="http://schemas.android.com/apk/res/android"
package="com.apress.proandroid"
      android:versionCode="1"
      android:versionName="1.0">
    <uses-sdk android:minSdkVersion="9" />

    <application android:icon="@drawable/icon"
                android:label="@string/app_name"
```

```
                      android:hasCode="false">
        <activity android:name="android.app.NativeActivity"
                  android:label="@string/app_name">
          <meta-data android:name="android.app.lib_name"
                     android:value="myapp" />
          <meta-data android:name="android.app.func_name"
                     android:value="ANativeActivity_onCreate" />
          <intent-filter>
              <action android:name="android.intent.action.MAIN" />
              <category android:name="android.intent.category.LAUNCHER" />
          </intent-filter>
        </activity>
    </application>
</manifest>
```

> **NOTE:** Optionally, if your application does not contain any Java code, you can set
> android:hasCode to false in the <application> tag.

Launching this application now would result in a runtime error as the libmyapp.so does not exist yet. Consequently, the next step is to build this missing library. This is done as usual using the NDK's ndk-build tool.

Building the Missing Library

You have to define your Application.mk file as well as your Android.mk file. When using native activities, the difference lies in Android.mk, as shown in Listing 2–24. You also need a file that contains the actual implementation of the application, myapp.c (shown in Listing 2–25).

Listing 2–24. *The Native Application's Android.mk*

```
LOCAL_PATH := $(call my-dir)

include $(CLEAR_VARS)

LOCAL_MODULE     := myapp
LOCAL_SRC_FILES  := myapp.c
LOCAL_LDLIBS     := -llog -landroid
LOCAL_STATIC_LIBRARIES := android_native_app_glue

include $(BUILD_SHARED_LIBRARY)

$(call import-module,android/native_app_glue)
```

The differences between this Android.mk and the one we previously used are:

- The shared libraries to link with
- The static library to link with

Since your native activity is going to use the Android native application APIs, you need to add -landroid to LOCAL_LDLIBS. You may need to link with more libraries depending on what you are going to use. For example, -llog is for linking with the logging library to allow you to use the logcat debugging facility.

The Android NDK provides a simpler way to create a native application, which is implemented in the NDK's native_app_glue module. To use this module you need to not only add it to LOCAL_STATIC_LIBRARIES, but also import it into your project by using the import-module function macro, as indicated by the last line in Listing 2–24.

> **NOTE:** The native_app_glue module is implemented in the NDK, and the source code is located in the android-ndk-r7/sources/android/native_app_glue directory. You are free to modify the implementation and compile your application using your own modified version as the library is linked statically.

Listing 2–25 shows an example of an application, implemented in a single file myapp.c, which listens to the following events:

- Application events (similar to methods like onStart in Java)
- Input events (key, motion)
- Accelerometer
- Gyroscope (callback-based)

This application does not do anything meaningful other than enabling sensors and showing you how to process sensor events. In this particular case, the sensor values are displayed with a call to __android_log_print. Use this application as the skeleton for your own needs.

Listing 2–25. *Implementation of myapp.c*

```
#include <android_native_app_glue.h>
#include <android/sensor.h>
#include <android/log.h>

#define TAG "myapp"

typedef struct {
    // accelerometer
    const ASensor* accelerometer_sensor;
    ASensorEventQueue* accelerometer_event_queue;
    // gyroscope
    const ASensor* gyroscope_sensor;
    ASensorEventQueue* gyroscope_event_queue;
} my_user_data_t;

static int32_t on_key_event (struct android_app* app, AInputEvent* event)
{
    // use AKeyEvent_xxx APIs
    return 0; // or 1 if you have handled the event
}

static int32_t on_motion_event (struct android_app* app, AInputEvent* event)
```

```c
{
    // use AMotionEvent_xxx APIs
    return 0; // or 1 if you have handled the event
}

// this simply checks the event type and calls the appropriate function
static int32_t on_input_event (struct android_app* app, AInputEvent* event)
{
    int32_t type = AInputEvent_getType(event);
    int32_t handled = 0;

    switch (type) {
        case AINPUT_EVENT_TYPE_KEY:
            handled = on_key_event(app, event);
            break;

        case AINPUT_EVENT_TYPE_MOTION:
            handled = on_motion_event(app, event);
            break;
    }

    return handled;
}

// some functions not yet implemented
static void on_input_changed (struct android_app* app) {}
static void on_init_window (struct android_app* app) {}
static void on_term_window (struct android_app* app) {}
static void on_window_resized (struct android_app* app) {}
static void on_window_redraw_needed (struct android_app* app) {}
static void on_content_rect_changed (struct android_app* app) {}

// we enable the sensors here
static void on_gained_focus (struct android_app* app)
{
    my_user_data_t* user_data = app->userData;
    if (user_data->accelerometer_sensor != NULL) {
        ASensorEventQueue_enableSensor(
            user_data->accelerometer_event_queue,
            user_data->accelerometer_sensor);
        ASensorEventQueue_setEventRate(
            user_data->accelerometer_event_queue,
            user_data->accelerometer_sensor, 1000000L/60);
    }
    if (user_data->gyroscope_sensor != NULL) {
        ASensorEventQueue_enableSensor(
            user_data->gyroscope_event_queue,
            user_data->gyroscope_sensor);
        ASensorEventQueue_setEventRate(
            user_data->gyroscope_event_queue,
            user_data->gyroscope_sensor, 1000000L/60);
    }
}

// we disable the sensors when focus is lost
static void on_lost_focus (struct android_app* app)
{
```

```
    my_user_data_t* user_data = app->userData;
    if (user_data->accelerometer_sensor != NULL) {
        ASensorEventQueue_disableSensor(
            user_data->accelerometer_event_queue,
            user_data->accelerometer_sensor);
    }
    if (user_data->gyroscope_sensor != NULL) {
        ASensorEventQueue_disableSensor(
            user_data->gyroscope_event_queue,
            user_data->gyroscope_sensor);
    }
}

// more functions to implement here…
static void on_config_changed (struct android_app* app) {}
static void on_low_memory (struct android_app* app) {}
static void on_start (struct android_app* app) {}
static void on_resume (struct android_app* app) {}
static void on_save_state (struct android_app* app) {}
static void on_pause (struct android_app* app) {}
static void on_stop (struct android_app* app) {}
static void on_destroy (struct android_app* app) {}

// this simply checks the command and calls the right function
static void on_app_command (struct android_app* app, int32_t cmd) {
    switch (cmd) {
        case APP_CMD_INPUT_CHANGED:
            on_input_changed(app);
            break;

        case APP_CMD_INIT_WINDOW:
            on_init_window(app);
            break;

        case APP_CMD_TERM_WINDOW:
            on_term_window(app);
            break;

        case APP_CMD_WINDOW_RESIZED:
            on_window_resized(app);
            break;

        case APP_CMD_WINDOW_REDRAW_NEEDED:
            on_window_redraw_needed(app);
            break;

        case APP_CMD_CONTENT_RECT_CHANGED:
            on_content_rect_changed(app);
            break;

        case APP_CMD_GAINED_FOCUS:
            on_gained_focus(app);
            break;

        case APP_CMD_LOST_FOCUS:
            on_lost_focus(app);
            break;
```

```
            case APP_CMD_CONFIG_CHANGED:
                on_config_changed(app);
                break;

            case APP_CMD_LOW_MEMORY:
                on_low_memory(app);
                break;

            case APP_CMD_START:
                on_start(app);
                break;

            case APP_CMD_RESUME:
                on_resume(app);
                break;

            case APP_CMD_SAVE_STATE:
                on_save_state(app);
                break;

            case APP_CMD_PAUSE:
                on_pause(app);
                break;

            case APP_CMD_STOP:
                on_stop(app);
                break;

            case APP_CMD_DESTROY:
                on_destroy(app);
                break;
        }
}

// user-defined looper ids
#define LOOPER_ID_USER_ACCELEROMETER    (LOOPER_ID_USER + 0)
#define LOOPER_ID_USER_GYROSCOPE                (LOOPER_ID_USER + 1)

// we'll be able to retrieve up to 8 events at a time
#define NB_SENSOR_EVENTS 8

static int gyroscope_callback (int fd, int events, void* data)
{
    // not really a good idea to log anything here as you may get more than you wished
for…
    __android_log_write(ANDROID_LOG_INFO, TAG, "gyroscope_callback");
    return 1;
}

static void list_all_sensors (ASensorManager* sm)
{
    ASensorList list;
    int i, n;
    n = ASensorManager_getSensorList(sm, & list);
    for (i = 0; i < n; i++) {
        const ASensor* sensor = list[i];
```

```
        const char* name = ASensor_getName(sensor);
        const char* vendor = ASensor_getVendor(sensor);
        int type = ASensor_getType(sensor);
        int min_delay = ASensor_getMinDelay(sensor);
        float resolution = ASensor_getResolution(sensor);

        __android_log_print(
            ANDROID_LOG_INFO, TAG, "%s (%s) %d %d %f",name, vendor, type, min_delay,
resolution);
    }
}

// where things start...
void android_main (struct android_app* state)
{
    my_user_data_t user_data;
    ASensorManager* sm = ASensorManager_getInstance();

    app_dummy(); // don't forget that call

    // we simply list all the sensors on the device
    list_all_sensors(sm);

    state->userData = & user_data;
    state->onAppCmd = on_app_command;
    state->onInputEvent = on_input_event;

    // accelerometer
    user_data.accelerometer_sensor =
        ASensorManager_getDefaultSensor(sm, ASENSOR_TYPE_ACCELEROMETER);
    user_data.accelerometer_event_queue = ASensorManager_createEventQueue(
        sm, state->looper, LOOPER_ID_USER_ACCELEROMETER, NULL, NULL);

    // gyroscope (callback-based)
    user_data.gyroscope_sensor =
        ASensorManager_getDefaultSensor(sm, ASENSOR_TYPE_GYROSCOPE);
    user_data.gyroscope_event_queue = ASensorManager_createEventQueue(
        sm, state->looper, LOOPER_ID_USER_GYROSCOPE, gyroscope_callback, NULL);

    while (1) {
        int ident;
        int events;
        struct android_poll_source* source;

        while ((ident = ALooper_pollAll(-1, NULL, &events, (void**)&source)) >= 0) {

            // "standard" events first
            if ((ident == LOOPER_ID_MAIN) || (ident == LOOPER_ID_INPUT)) {
                // source should not be NULL but we check anyway
                if (source != NULL) {
                    // this will call on_app_command or on_input_event
                    source->process(source->app, source);
                }
            }

            // accelerometer events
            if (ident == LOOPER_ID_USER_ACCELEROMETER) {
```

```
                          ASensorEvent sensor_events[NB_SENSOR_EVENTS];
                          int i, n;
                          while ((n = ASensorEventQueue_getEvents(
                              user_data.accelerometer_event_queue, sensor_events,
NB_SENSOR_EVENTS)) > 0) {

                              for (i = 0; i < n; i++) {
                                  ASensorVector* vector = & sensor_events[i].vector;
                                  __android_log_print(
                                      ANDROID_LOG_INFO, TAG,
                                      "%d accelerometer x=%f y=%f z=%f", i, vector->x, vector->y,
vector->z);
                              }
                          }
                      }

                      // process other events here

                      // don't forget to check whether it's time to return
                      if (state->destroyRequested != 0) {
                          ASensorManager_destroyEventQueue(sm,
user_data.accelerometer_event_queue);
                          ASensorManager_destroyEventQueue(sm, user_data.gyroscope_event_queue);
                          return;
                      }
                  }

                  // do your rendering here when all the events have been processed
              }
}
```

Alternative

Another way to create a native application is to implement your native version of onCreate in which you not only initialize your application but also define all your other callbacks (that is, the equivalent of onStart, onResume, to name just a few). This is exactly what the native_app_glue module implements for you to simplify your own development. Also, the native_app_glue module guarantees certain events are handled in a separate thread, allowing your application to remain responsive. Should you decide to define your own onCreate implementation, you would not need to link with the native_app_glue library, and instead of implementing android_main, you would implement ANativeActivity_onCreate, as shown in Listing 2.26.

Listing 2–26. *Implementation of ANativeActivity_onCreate*

```
#include <android/native_activity.h>

void ANativeActivity_onCreate (ANativeActivity* activity, void* savedState, size_t
savedStateSize)
{
    // set all callbacks here
    activity->callbacks->onStart = my_on_start;
    activity->callbacks->onResume = my_on_resume;
    …
```

```
// set activity->instance to some instance-specific data
activity->instance = my_own_instance; // similar to userData

// no event loop here, it simply returns and NativeActivity will then call the
callbacks you defined
}
```

While this may appear simpler, it becomes more complicated when you start listening to some other events (such as sensors) and draw things on the screen.

> **TIP:** Do not change the name of the library's entry point in your manifest file if you are using the native_app_glue module as it implements ANativeActivity_onCreate.

The new NativeActivity class in itself does not improve performance. It is simply a mechanism to make native application development easier. In fact, you could implement that same mechanism in your own application to write native applications on older Android versions. Despite the fact that your application is, or can be, fully written in C/C++, it still runs in the Dalvik virtual machine, and it still relies on the NativeActivity Java class.

Summary

We have seen how the use of native code can improve performance. Even though carefully crafted native code rarely results in a degradation of performance, performance is not the only reason why you should use the NDK. The following are all good reasons why you should use it:

- You want to reuse existing code instead of having to rewrite everything in Java.

- You want to write new code to use on other platforms that don't support Java.

- You want to target older Android devices that do not have a Just-In-Time compiler (Android 2.1 and earlier), and native code is the only way to offer a good user experience.

- Using native code in your application makes the user experience better, even on Android devices with a JIT compiler.

The first two reasons are so important you may actually be willing to sacrifice performance in some cases (although make sure the user experience does not suffer, or at least does not suffer beyond an acceptable threshold). Like many developers, your resources are limited, yet you want to reach as many people as possible with your applications. Limiting yourself to a single platform won't maximize your investments.

Chapter 3

Advanced NDK

Chapter 2 showed you how to set up a project using the Android NDK and how you could use C or C++ code in your Android application. In many cases, this is as far as you will need to go. However, there may be times when digging a little deeper is required to find what can be optimized even more.

In this chapter, you will get your hands dirty and learn how you can use a low-level language to take advantage of all the bells and whistles the CPU has to offer, which may not be possible to use from plain C or C++ code. The first part of the chapter shows you several examples of how you can optimize functions using the assembly language and gives you an overview of the ARM instruction set. The second part covers some of the C extensions the GCC compiler supports that you can take advantage of to improve your application's performance. Finally, the chapter concludes with a few very simple tips for optimizing code relatively quickly.

While the latest Android NDK supports the armeabi, armeabi-v7a, and x86 ABIs, this chapter will focus on the first two as Android is mostly deployed on ARM-based devices. If you plan on writing assembly code, then ARM should be your first target. While the first Google TV devices were Intel-based, Google TV does not yet support the NDK.

Assembly

The NDK allows you to use C and C++ in your Android applications. Chapter 2 showed you what native code would look like after the C or C++ code is compiled and how you could use objdump -d to disassemble a file (object file or library). For example, the ARM assembly code of computeIterativelyFaster is shown again in Listing 3–1.

Listing 3–1. *ARM Assembly Code of C Implementation of* computeIterativelyFaster

```
00000410 < computeIterativelyFaster>:
 410:   e3500001        cmp     r0, #1  ; 0x1
 414:   e92d0030        push    {r4, r5}
 418:   91a02000        movls   r2, r0
 41c:   93a03000        movls   r3, #0  ; 0x0
 420:   9a00000e        bls     460 <computeIterativelyFaster+0x50>
```

```
424:   e2400001     sub     r0, r0, #1        ; 0x1
428:   e1b010a0     lsrs    r1, r0, #1
42c:   03a02001     moveq   r2, #1   ; 0x1
430:   03a03000     moveq   r3, #0   ; 0x0
434:   0a000009     beq     460 < computeIterativelyFaster+0x50>
438:   e3a02001     mov     r2, #1   ; 0x1
43c:   e3a03000     mov     r3, #0   ; 0x0
440:   e0024000     and     r4, r2, r0
444:   e3a05000     mov     r5, #0   ; 0x0
448:   e0944002     adds    r4, r4, r2
44c:   e0a55003     adc     r5, r5, r3
450:   e0922004     adds    r2, r2, r4
454:   e0a33005     adc     r3, r3, r5
458:   e2511001     subs    r1, r1, #1        ; 0x1
45c:   1afffff9     bne     448 < computeIterativelyFaster+0x38>
460:   e1a01003     mov     r1, r3
464:   e1a00002     mov     r0, r2
468:   e8bd0030     pop     {r4, r5}
46c:   e12fff1e     bx      lr
```

In addition to allowing you to use C or C++ in your application, the Android NDK also lets you to write assembly code directly. Strictly speaking, such a feature is not NDK-specific as assembly code is supported by the GCC compiler, which is used by the Android NDK. Consequently, almost everything you learn in this chapter can also be applied to other projects of yours, for example in applications targeting iOS devices like the iPhone.

As you can see, assembly code can be quite difficult to read, let alone write. However, being able to understand assembly code will allow you to more easily identify bottlenecks and therefore more easily optimize your applications. It will also give you bragging rights.

To familiarize yourself with assembly, we will look at three simple examples:

■ Computation of the greatest common divisor

■ Conversion from one color format to another

■ Parallel computation of average of 8-bit values

These examples are simple enough to understand for developers who are new to assembly, yet they exhibit important principles of assembly optimization. Because these examples introduce you to only a subset of the available instructions, a more complete introduction to the ARM instruction set will follow as well as a brief introduction to the überpowerful ARM SIMD instructions. Finally, you will learn how to dynamically check what CPU features are available, a mandatory step in your applications that target features not available on all devices.

Greatest Common Divisor

The greatest common divisor (gcd) of two non-zero integers is the largest positive integer that divides both numbers. For example, the greatest common divisor of 10 and

55 is 5. An implementation of a function that computes the greatest common divisor of two integers is shown in Listing 3–2.

Listing 3–2. *Greatest Common Divisor Simple Implementation*

```
unsigned int gcd (unsigned int a, unsigned int b)
{
    // a and b must be different from zero (else, hello infinite loop!)

    while (a != b) {
        if (a > b) {
            a -= b;
        } else {
            b -= a;
        }
    }

    return a;
}
```

If you define APP_ABI in your Application.mk file such that x86, armeabi, and armeabi-v7 architectures are supported in your application, then you will have three different libraries. Disassembling each library will result in three different pieces of assembly code. However, since you have the option to compile in either ARM or Thumb mode with the armeabi and armeabi-v7a ABIs, there are actually a total of five pieces of code you can review.

> **TIP:** Instead of specifying each individual ABI you want to compile a library for, you can define APP_ABI as "all" (APP_ABI := all) starting with NDK r7. When a new ABI is supported by the NDK you will only have to execute ndk-build without having to modify Application.mk.

Listing 3–3 shows the resulting x86 assembly code while Listing 3–4 and Listing 3–5 show the ARMv5 and ARMv7 assembly code respectively. Because different versions of compilers can output different code, the code you will observe may be slightly different than the that shown here. The generated code will also depend on the optimization level and other options you may have defined.

Listing 3–3. *x86 Assembly Code*

```
00000000 <gcd>:
   0:   8b 54 24 04      mov    0x4(%esp),%edx
   4:   8b 44 24 08      mov    0x8(%esp),%eax
   8:   39 c2            cmp    %eax,%edx
   a:   75 0a            jne    16 <gcd+0x16>
   c:   eb 12            jmp    20 <gcd+0x20>
   e:   66 90            xchg   %ax,%ax
  10:   29 c2            sub    %eax,%edx
  12:   39 d0            cmp    %edx,%eax
  14:   74 0a            je     20 <gcd+0x20>
  16:   39 d0            cmp    %edx,%eax
  18:   72 f6            jb     10 <gcd+0x10>
  1a:   29 d0            sub    %edx,%eax
  1c:   39 d0            cmp    %edx,%eax
```

```
1e:    75 f6          jne    16 <gcd+0x16>
20:    f3 c3          repz ret
```

If you are familiar with the x86 mnemonics, you can see that this code makes heavy use of the jump instructions (jne, jmp, je, jb). Also, while most instructions are 16-bit (for example, "f3 c3"), some are 32-bit.

> **NOTE:** Make sure you use the right version of objdump to disassemble object files and libraries. For example, using the ARM version of objdump to attempt to disassemble an x86 object file will result in the following message:
>
> arm-linux-androideabi-objdump: Can't disassemble for architecture UNKNOWN!

Listing 3–4. *ARMv5 Assembly Code (ARM Mode)*

```
00000000 <gcd>:
   0:    e1500001          cmp    r0, r1
   4:    e1a03000          mov    r3, r0
   8:    0a000004          beq    20 <gcd+0x20>
   c:    e1510003          cmp    r1, r3
  10:    30613003          rsbcc  r3, r1, r3
  14:    20631001          rsbcs  r1, r3, r1
  18:    e1510003          cmp    r1, r3
  1c:    1afffffa          bne    c <gcd+0xc>
  20:    e1a00001          mov    r0, r1
  24:    e12fff1e          bx     lr
```

Listing 3–5. *ARMv7a Assembly Code (ARM Mode)*

```
00000000 <gcd>:
   0:    e1500001          cmp    r0, r1
   4:    e1a03000          mov    r3, r0
   8:    0a000004          beq    20 <gcd+0x20>
   c:    e1510003          cmp    r1, r3
  10:    30613003          rsbcc  r3, r1, r3
  14:    20631001          rsbcs  r1, r3, r1
  18:    e1510003          cmp    r1, r3
  1c:    1afffffa          bne    c <gcd+0xc>
  20:    e1a00001          mov    r0, r1
  24:    e12fff1e          bx     lr
```

As it turns out, the GCC compiler generates the same code for the armeabi and armeabi-v7a ABIs when the code shown in Listing 3–2 is compiled in ARM mode. This won't always be the case though as the compiler usually takes advantage of new instructions defined in newer ABIs.

Because you could decide to compile the code in Thumb mode instead of ARM mode, let's also review the code that would be generated in Thumb mode. Listing 3–6 shows the ARMv5 assembly code (armeabi ABI in Application.mk) while Listing 3–7 shows the ARMv7 assembly code (armeabi-v7a ABI in Application.mk).

Listing 3–6. *ARMv5 Assembly Code (Thumb Mode)*

```
00000000 <gcd>:
   0:   1c03          adds    r3, r0, #0
   2:   428b          cmp     r3, r1
   4:   d004          beq.n   10 <gcd+0x10>
   6:   4299          cmp     r1, r3
   8:   d204          bcs.n   14 <gcd+0x14>
   a:   1a5b          subs    r3, r3, r1
   c:   428b          cmp     r3, r1
   e:   d1fa          bne.n    6 <gcd+0x6>
  10:   1c08          adds    r0, r1, #0
  12:   4770          bx      lr
  14:   1ac9          subs    r1, r1, r3
  16:   e7f4          b.n      2 <gcd+0x2>
```

All instructions in Listing 3–6 are 16-bit (that is, "e7f4," the last instruction of the listing) and the twelve instructions therefore require 24 bytes of space.

Listing 3–7. *ARMv7 Assembly Code (Thumb Mode)*

```
00000000 <gcd>:
   0:   4288          cmp     r0, r1
   2:   4603          mov     r3, r0
   4:   d007          beq.n   16 <gcd+0x16>
   6:   4299          cmp     r1, r3
   8:   bf34          ite     cc
   a:   ebc1 0303     rsbcc   r3, r1, r3
   e:   ebc3 0101     rsbcs   r1, r3, r1
  12:   4299          cmp     r1, r3
  14:   d1f7          bne.n    6 <gcd+0x6>
  16:   4608          mov     r0, r1
  18:   4770          bx      lr
  1a:   bf00          nop
```

This time, the two listings are different. While the ARMv5 architecture uses the Thumb instruction set (all 16-bit instructions), the ARMv7 architecture supports the Thumb2 instruction set and instructions can be 16- or 32-bit.

As a matter of fact, Listing 3–7 looks a lot like Listing 3–5. The main difference is with the use of the ite (if-then-else) instruction in Listing 3–7, and the fact that the ARM code is 40-byte long while the Thumb2 code is only 28-byte long.

> **NOTE:** Even though the ARM architecture is the dominant one, being able to read x86 assembly code cannot hurt.

Usually, the GCC compiler does a pretty good job and you won't have to worry too much about the generated code. However, if a piece of code you wrote in C or C++ turns out to be one of the bottlenecks of your application, you should carefully review the assembly code the compiler generated and determine whether you could do better by writing the assembly code yourself. Very often the compiler will generate high-quality code and you won't be able to do better. That being said, there are cases where, armed with both an intimate knowledge of the instruction set and a slight taste for suffering, you can achieve better results than the compiler.

> **NOTE:** Consider modifying the C/C++ code to achieve better performance as it is often much easier than writing assembly code.

The gcd function can indeed be implemented differently, resulting in code not only faster but also more compact, as shown in Listing 3–8.

Listing 3–8. *Hand-crafted Assembly Code*

```
.global gcd_asm
.func gcd_asm

gcd_asm:
    cmp    r0, r1
    subgt  r0, r0, r1
    sublt  r1, r1, r0
    bne    gcd_asm
    bx     lr
.endfunc
.end
```

Not including the final instruction to return from the function, the core of the algorithm is implemented in only four instructions. Measurements also showed this implementation as being faster. Note the single call to the CMP instruction in Listing 3–8 compared with the two calls in Listing 3–7.

This code can be copied in a file called gcd_asm.S and added to the list of files to compile in Android.mk. Because this file is using ARM instructions, it obviously won't compile if the target ABI is x86. Consequently, your Android.mk file should make sure the file is only part of the list of files to compile when it is compatible with the ABI. Listing 3–9 shows how to modify Android.mk accordingly.

Listing 3–9. *Android.mk*

```
LOCAL_PATH := $(call my-dir)

include $(CLEAR_VARS)
LOCAL_MODULE := chapter3
LOCAL_SRC_FILES := gcd.c

ifeq ($(TARGET_ARCH_ABI),armeabi)
LOCAL_SRC_FILES += gcd_asm.S
endif

ifeq ($(TARGET_ARCH_ABI),armeabi-v7a)
LOCAL_SRC_FILES += gcd_asm.S
endif

include $(BUILD_SHARED_LIBRARY)
```

Because gcd_asm.S is already written using assembly code, the resulting object file should look extremely similar to the source file. Listing 3–10 shows the disassembled code and indeed, the disassembled code is virtually identical to the source.

Listing 3–10. *Disassembled gcd_asm Code*

```
00000000 <gcd_asm>:
   0:   e1500001            cmp     r0, r1
   4:   c0400001            subgt   r0, r0, r1
   8:   b0411000            sublt   r1, r1, r0
   c:   1afffffb            bne     0 <gcd_asm>
  10:   e12fff1e            bx      lr
```

> **NOTE:** The assembler may in some cases substitute some instructions for others so you may still observe slight differences between the code you wrote and the disassembled code.

By simplifying the assembly code, we achieved better results without dramatically making maintenance more complicated.

Color Conversion

A common operation in graphics routines is to convert a color from one format to another. For example, a 32-bit value representing a color with four 8-bit channels (alpha, red, green, and blue) could be converted to a 16-bit value representing a color with three channels (5 bits for red, 6 bits for green, 5 bits for blue, no alpha). The two formats would typically be referred to as ARGB8888 and RGB565 respectively.

Listing 3–11 shows a trivial implementation of such a conversion.

Listing 3–11. *Implementation of Color Conversion Function*

```c
unsigned int argb888_to_rgb565 (unsigned int color)
{
    /*
        input:  aaaaaaaarrrrrrrrggggggggbbbbbbbb
        output: 0000000000000000rrrrrggggggbbbbb
    */

    return
        /* red   */ ((color >> 8) & 0xF800) |
        /* green */ ((color >> 5) & 0x07E0) |
        /* blue  */ ((color >> 3) & 0x001F);
}
```

Once again, five pieces of assembly code can be analyzed. Listing 3–12 shows the x86 assembly code, Listing 3–13 shows the ARMv5 assembly code in ARM mode, Listing 3–14 shows the ARMv7 assembly code in ARM mode, Listing 3–15 shows the ARMv5 assembly code in Thumb mode, and finally Listing 3–16 shows the ARMv7 assembly code in Thumb mode.

Listing 3–12. *x86 Assembly Code*

```
00000000 <argb8888_to_rgb565>:
   0:   8b 54 24 04          mov    0x4(%esp),%edx
   4:   89 d0                mov    %edx,%eax
   6:   89 d1                mov    %edx,%ecx
   8:   c1 e8 05             shr    $0x5,%eax
   b:   c1 e9 08             shr    $0x8,%ecx
   e:   25 e0 07 00 00       and    $0x7e0,%eax
  13:   81 e1 00 f8 00 00    and    $0xf800,%ecx
  19:   c1 ea 03             shr    $0x3,%edx
  1c:   09 c8                or     %ecx,%eax
  1e:   83 e2 1f             and    $0x1f,%edx
  21:   09 d0                or     %edx,%eax
  23:   c3                   ret
```

Listing 3–13. *ARMv5 Assembly Code (ARM Mode)*

```
00000000 <argb8888_to_rgb565>:
   0:   e1a022a0             lsr    r2, r0, #5
   4:   e1a03420             lsr    r3, r0, #8
   8:   e2022e7e             and    r2, r2, #2016     ; 0x7e0
   c:   e2033b3e             and    r3, r3, #63488    ; 0xf800
  10:   e1a00c00             lsl    r0, r0, #24
  14:   e1823003             orr    r3, r2, r3
  18:   e1830da0             orr    r0, r3, r0, lsr #27
  1c:   e12fff1e             bx     lr
```

Listing 3–14. *ARMv7 Assembly Code (ARM Mode)*

```
00000000 <argb8888_to_rgb565>:
   0:   e7e431d0             ubfx   r3, r0, #3, #5
   4:   e1a022a0             lsr    r2, r0, #5
   8:   e1a00420             lsr    r0, r0, #8
   c:   e2022e7e             and    r2, r2, #2016     ; 0x7e0
  10:   e2000b3e             and    r0, r0, #63488    ; 0xf800
  14:   e1820000             orr    r0, r2, r0
  18:   e1800003             orr    r0, r0, r3
  1c:   e12fff1e             bx     lr
```

Listing 3–15. *ARMv5 Assembly Code (Thumb Mode)*

```
00000000 <argb8888_to_rgb565>:
   0:   23fc                 movs   r3, #252
   2:   0941                 lsrs   r1, r0, #5
   4:   00db                 lsls   r3, r3, #3
   6:   4019                 ands   r1, r3
   8:   23f8                 movs   r3, #248
   a:   0a02                 lsrs   r2, r0, #8
   c:   021b                 lsls   r3, r3, #8
   e:   401a                 ands   r2, r3
  10:   1c0b                 adds   r3, r1, #0
  12:   4313                 orrs   r3, r2
  14:   0600                 lsls   r0, r0, #24
  16:   0ec2                 lsrs   r2, r0, #27
  18:   1c18                 adds   r0, r3, #0
  1a:   4310                 orrs   r0, r2
  1c:   4770                 bx     lr
  1e:   46c0                 nop            (mov r8, r8)
```

Listing 3–16. *ARMv7 Assembly Code (Thumb Mode)*

```
00000000 <argb888_to_rgb565>:
   0:    0942            lsrs    r2, r0, #5
   2:    0a03            lsrs    r3, r0, #8
   4:    f402 62fc       and.w   r2, r2, #2016      ; 0x7e0
   8:    f403 4378       and.w   r3, r3, #63488     ; 0xf800
   c:    4313            orrs    r3, r2
   e:    f3c0 00c4       ubfx    r0, r0, #3, #5
  12:    4318            orrs    r0, r3
  14:    4770            bx      lr
  16:    bf00            nop
```

Simply looking at how many instructions are generated, the ARMv5 code in Thumb mode seems to be the least efficient. That being said, counting the number of instructions is not an accurate way of determining how fast or how slow a piece of code is going to be. To get a closer estimate of the duration, one would have to count how many cycles each instruction will need to complete. For example, the "orr r3, r2" instruction needs only one cycle to execute. Today's CPUs make it quite hard to compute how many cycles will ultimately be needed as they can execute several instructions per cycle and in some cases even execute instructions out of order to maximize throughput.

> **NOTE:** For example, refer to the Cortex-A9 Technical Reference Manual to learn more about the cycle timings of instructions.

Now, it is possible to write a slightly different version of the same conversion function using the UBFX and BFI instructions, as shown in Listing 3–17.

Listing 3–17. *Hand-crafted Assembly Code*

```
.global argb8888_ro_rgb565_asm
.func argb8888_ro_rgb565_asm

argb8888_ro_rgb565_asm:
    // r0=aaaaaaaarrrrrrrrggggggggbbbbbbbb
    // r1=undefined (scratch register)

    ubfx r1, r0, #3, #5

    // r1=000000000000000000000000000bbbbb

    lsr r0, r0, #10

    // r0=0000000000aaaaaaaarrrrrrrrgggggg

    bfi r1, r0, #5, #6

    // r1=0000000000000000000000gggggbbbbb

    lsr r0, r0, #9

    // r0=00000000000000000000aaaaaaaarrrrr
```

```
    bfi r1, r0, #11, #5

    // r1=0000000000000000rrrrrgggggggbbbbb

    mov r0, r1

    // r0=0000000000000000rrrrrgggggggbbbbb

    bx    lr
.endfunc
.end
```

Since this code uses the UBFX and BFI instructions (both introduced in the ARMv6T2 architecture), it won't compile for the armeabi ABI (ARMv5). Obviously it won't compile for the x86 ABI either.

Similar to what was shown in Listing 3–9, your Android.mk should make sure the file is only compiled with the right ABI. Listing 3–18 shows the addition of the rgb.c and rgb_asm.S files to the build.

Listing 3–18. *Android.mk*

```
LOCAL_PATH := $(call my-dir)

include $(CLEAR_VARS)
LOCAL_MODULE := chapter3
LOCAL_SRC_FILES := gcd.c rgb.c

ifeq ($(TARGET_ARCH_ABI),armeabi)
LOCAL_SRC_FILES += gcd_asm.S
endif

ifeq ($(TARGET_ARCH_ABI),armeabi-v7a)
LOCAL_SRC_FILES += gcd_asm.S rgb_asm.S
endif

include $(BUILD_SHARED_LIBRARY)
```

If you add rgb_asm.S to the list of files to compile with the armeabi ABI, you will then get the following errors:

```
        Error: selected processor does not support `ubfx r1,r0,#3,#5'
        Error: selected processor does not support `bfi r1,r0,#5,#6'
        Error: selected processor does not support `bfi r1,r0,#11,#5'
```

Parallel Computation of Average

In this example, we want to treat each 32-bit value as four independent 8-bit values and compute the byte-wise average between two such values. For example, the average of 0x10FF3040 and 0x50FF7000 would be 0x30FF5020 (average of 0x10 and 0x50 is 0x30, average of 0xFF and 0xFF is 0xFF).

An implementation of such function is shown in Listing 3–19.

Listing 3–19. *Implementation of Parallel Average Function*

```
unsigned int avg8 (unsigned int a, unsigned int b)
{
    return
        ((a >> 1) & 0x7F7F7F7F) +
        ((b >> 1) & 0x7F7F7F7F) +
        (a & b & 0x01010101);
}
```

Like with the two previous examples, five pieces of assembly code are shown in Listings 3–20 to 3–24.

Listing 3–20. *x86 Assembly Code*

```
00000000 <avg8>:
   0:   8b 54 24 04             mov     0x4(%esp),%edx
   4:   8b 44 24 08             mov     0x8(%esp),%eax
   8:   89 d1                   mov     %edx,%ecx
   a:   81 e1 01 01 01 01       and     $0x1010101,%ecx
  10:   d1 ea                   shr     %edx
  12:   21 c1                   and     %eax,%ecx
  14:   81 e2 7f 7f 7f 7f       and     $0x7f7f7f7f,%edx
  1a:   d1 e8                   shr     %eax
  1c:   8d 14 11                lea     (%ecx,%edx,1),%edx
  1f:   25 7f 7f 7f 7f          and     $0x7f7f7f7f,%eax
  24:   8d 04 02                lea     (%edx,%eax,1),%eax
  27:   c3                      ret
```

Listing 3–21. *ARMv5 Assembly Code (ARM mode)*

```
00000000 <avg8>:
   0:   e59f301c        ldr     r3, [pc, #28]   ; 24 <avg8+0x24>
   4:   e59f201c        ldr     r2, [pc, #28]   ; 28 <avg8+0x28>
   8:   e0003003        and     r3, r0, r3
   c:   e0033001        and     r3, r3, r1
  10:   e00200a0        and     r0, r2, r0, lsr #1
  14:   e0830000        add     r0, r3, r0
  18:   e00220a1        and     r2, r2, r1, lsr #1
  1c:   e0800002        add     r0, r0, r2
  20:   e12fff1e        bx      lr
  24:   01010101        .word   0x01010101
  28:   7f7f7f7f        .word   0x7f7f7f7f
```

Because the ARMv5 MOV instruction cannot simply copy the value to the register, an LDR instruction is used instead to copy 0x01010101 to register r3. Similarly, an LDR instruction is used to copy 0x7f7f7f7f to r2.

Listing 3–22. *ARMv7 Assembly Code (ARM Mode)*

```
00000000 <avg8>:
   0:   e3003101        movw    r3, #257      ; 0x101
   4:   e3072f7f        movw    r2, #32639    ; 0x7f7f
   8:   e3403101        movt    r3, #257      ; 0x101
   c:   e3472f7f        movt    r2, #32639    ; 0x7f7f
  10:   e0003003        and     r3, r0, r3
  14:   e00200a0        and     r0, r2, r0, lsr #1
  18:   e0033001        and     r3, r3, r1
  1c:   e00220a1        and     r2, r2, r1, lsr #1
  20:   e0830000        add     r0, r3, r0
```

```
    24:    e0800002              add    r0, r0, r2
    28:    e12fff1e              bx     lr
```

Instead of using an LDR instruction to copy 0x01010101 to r3, the ARMv7 code uses two MOV instructions: the first one, MOVW, is to copy a 16-bit value (0x0101) to the bottom 16 bits of r3 while the second one, MOVT, is to copy 0x0101 to the top 16 bits of r3. After these two instructions, r3 will indeed contain the 0x01010101 value. The rest of the assembly code looks like the ARMv5 assembly code.

Listing 3–23. *ARMv5 Assembly Code (Thumb Mode)*

```
00000000 <avg8>:
    0:    b510              push   {r4, lr}
    2:    4c05              ldr    r4, [pc, #20]    (18 <avg8+0x18>)
    4:    4b05              ldr    r3, [pc, #20]    (1c <avg8+0x1c>)
    6:    4004              ands   r4, r0
    8:    0840              lsrs   r0, r0, #1
    a:    4018              ands   r0, r3
    c:    400c              ands   r4, r1
    e:    1822              adds   r2, r4, r0
   10:    0848              lsrs   r0, r1, #1
   12:    4003              ands   r3, r0
   14:    18d0              adds   r0, r2, r3
   16:    bd10              pop    {r4, pc}
   18:    01010101          .word  0x01010101
   1c:    7f7f7f7f          .word  0x7f7f7f7f
```

Since this code makes use of the r4 register, it needs to be saved onto the stack and later restored

Listing 3–24. *ARMv7 Assembly Code (Thumb Mode)*

```
00000000 <avg8>:
    0:    f000 3301         and.w  r3, r0, #16843009    ; 0x1010101
    4:    0840              lsrs   r0, r0, #1
    6:    400b              ands   r3, r1
    8:    f000 307f         and.w  r0, r0, #2139062143  ; 0x7f7f7f7f
    c:    0849              lsrs   r1, r1, #1
    e:    1818              adds   r0, r3, r0
   10:    f001 317f         and.w  r1, r1, #2139062143  ; 0x7f7f7f7f
   14:    1840              adds   r0, r0, r1
   16:    4770              bx     lr
```

The Thumb2 assembly code is more compact as only one instruction is needed to copy 0x01010101 and 0x7f7f7f7f to r3 and r0.

Before deciding to write optimized assembly code, you may stop and think a little bit about how the C code itself could be optimized. After a little bit of thinking, you may end up with the code shown in Listing 3–25.

Listing 3–25. *Faster Implementation of Parallel Average Function*

```
unsigned int avg8_faster (unsigned int a, unsigned int b)
{
    return (((a ^ b) & 0xFEFEFEFE) >> 1) + (a & b);
}
```

The C code is more compact that the first version and would appear to be faster. The first version used two >>, four &, and two + operations (total of eight "basic" operations) while the new version uses only five "basic" operations. Intuitively, the second implementation should be faster. And it is indeed.

Listing 3–26 shows the ARMv7 Thumb resulting assembly code.

Listing 3–26. *ARMv7 Assembly Code (Thumb Mode)*

```
00000000 <avg8_faster>:
   0:   ea81 0300   eor.w   r3, r1, r0
   4:   4001        ands    r1, r0
   6:   f003 33fe   and.w   r3, r3, #4278124286   ; 0xfefefefe
   a:   eb01 0053   add.w   r0, r1, r3, lsr #1
   e:   4770        bx      lr
```

This faster implementation results in faster and more compact code (not including the instruction to return from the function, four instructions instead of eight).

While this may sound terrific, a closer look at the ARM instruction set reveals the UHADD8 instruction, which would perform an unsigned byte-wise addition, halving the results. This happens to be exactly what we want to compute. Consequently, an even faster implementation can easily be implemented and is shown in Listing 3–27.

Listing 3–27. *Hand-crafted Assembly Code*

```
.global avg8_asm
.func avg8_asm

avg8_asm:
    uhadd8 r0, r0, r1
    bx     lr
.endfunc
.end
```

Other "parallel instructions" exist. For example, UHADD16 would be like UHADD8 but instead of performing byte-wise additions it would perform halfword-wise additions. These instructions can improve performance significantly but because compilers have a hard time generating code that uses them, you will often find yourself having to write the assembly code manually in order to take advantage of them.

> **NOTE:** Parallel instructions were introduced in the ARMv6 architecture so you won't be able to use them when compiling for the armeabi ABI (ARMv5).

Writing whole functions using assembly code can quickly become tedious. In many cases, only parts of a routine would benefit from using assembly code while the rest can be written in C or C++. The GCC compiler lets you mix assembly with C/C++, as shown in Listing 3–28.

Listing 3–28. *Assembly Code Mixed With C Code*

```
unsigned int avg8_fastest (unsigned int a, unsigned int b)
{
#if defined(__ARM_ARCH_7A__)
    unsigned int avg;

    asm("uhadd8 %[average], %[val1], %[val2]"
        : [average] "=r" (avg)
        : [val1] "r" (a), [val2] "r" (b));

    return avg;
#else
    return (((a ^ b) & 0xFEFEFEFE) >> 1) + (a & b); // default generic implementation
#endif
}
```

> **NOTE:** Visit http://gcc.gnu.org/onlinedocs/gcc/Extended-Asm.html for more
> information about extended asm and
> http://gcc.gnu.org/onlinedocs/gcc/Constraints.html for details about the
> constraints. A single asm() statement can include multiple instructions.

The updated Android.mk is shown in Listing 3–29.

Listing 3–29. *Android.mk*

```
LOCAL_PATH := $(call my-dir)

include $(CLEAR_VARS)
LOCAL_MODULE := chapter3
LOCAL_SRC_FILES := gcd.c rgb.c avg8.c

ifeq ($(TARGET_ARCH_ABI),armeabi)
LOCAL_SRC_FILES += gcd_asm.S
endif

ifeq ($(TARGET_ARCH_ABI),armeabi-v7a)
LOCAL_SRC_FILES += gcd_asm.S rgb_asm.S avg8_asm.S
endif

include $(BUILD_SHARED_LIBRARY)
```

This example shows that sometimes, good knowledge of the instruction set is needed to achieve the best performance. Since Android devices are mostly based on ARM architectures, you should focus your attention on the ARM instruction set. The ARM documentation available on the ARM website (infocenter.arm.com) is of great quality so make sure you use it.

ARM Instructions

ARM instructions are plentiful. While the goal is not to document in great detail what each one does, Table 3–1 shows the list of available ARM instructions, each one with a brief description.

As you become familiar with them, you will learn that some of them are used much more often than others, albeit the more obscure ones are often the ones that can dramatically improve performance. For example, the ADD and MOV are practically ubiquitous while the SETEND instruction is not going to be used very often (yet it is a great instruction when you need to access data of different endianness).

> **NOTE:** For detailed information about these instructions, refer to the ARM Compiler Toolchain Assembler Reference document available at http://infocenter.arm.com.

Table 3–1. *ARM Instructions*

Mnemonic	Description
ADC	Add with carry
ADD	Add
ADR	Generate PC- or register-relative address
ADRL (pseudo-instruction)	Generate PC- or register-relative address
AND	Logical AND
ASR	Arithmetic Shift Right
B	Branch
BFC	Bit Field Clear
BFI	Bit Field Insert
BIC	Bit Clear
BKPT	Breakpoint
BL	Branch with Link
BLX	Branch with Link, change instruction set
BX	Branch, change instruction set

Mnemonic	Description
BXJ	Branch, change to Jazelle
CBZ	Compare and Branch if Zero
CBNZ	Compare and Branch if Not Zero
CDP	Coprocessor Data Processing
CDP2	Coprocessor Data Processing
CHKA	Check Array
CLREX	Clear Exclusive
CLZ	Count Leading Zeros
CMN	Compare Negative
CMP	Compare
CPS	Change Processor State
DBG	Debug Hint
DMB	Data Memory Barrier
DSB	Data Synchronization Barrier
ENTERX	Change state to ThumbEE
EOR	Exclusive OR
HB	Handler Branch
HBL	Handler Branch
HBLP	Handler Branch
HBP	Handler Branch
ISB	Instruction Synchronization Barrier
IT	If-Then
LDC	Load Coprocessor

Mnemonic	Description
LDC2	Load Coprocessor
LDM	Load Multiple registers
LDR	Load Register
LDR (pseudo-instruction)	Load Register
LDRB	Load Register with Byte
LDRBT	Load Register with Byte, user mode
LDRD	Load Registers with two words
LDREX	Load Register, Exclusive
LDREXB	Load Register with Byte, Exclusive
LDREXD	Load Registers with two words, Exclusive
LDREXH	Load Registers with Halfword, Exclusive
LDRH	Load Register with Halfword
LDRHT	Load Register with Halfword, user mode
LDRSB	Load Register with Signed Byte
LDRSBT	Load Register with Signed Byte, user mode
LDRSH	Load Register with Signed Halfword
LDRT	Load Register, user mode
LEAVEX	Exit ThumbEE state
LSL	Logical Shift Left
LSR	Logical Shift Right
MAR	Move from Registers to 40-bit Accumulator
MCR	Move from Register to Coprocessor
MCR2	Move from Register to Coprocessor

Mnemonic	Description
MCRR	Move from Registers to Coprocessor
MCRR2	Move from Registers to Coprocessor
MIA	Multiply with Internal Accumulate
MIAPH	Multiply with Internal Accumulate, Packed Halfwords
MIAxy	Multiply with Internal Accumulate, Halfwords
MLA	Multiply and Accumulate
MLS	Multiply and Subtract
MOV	Move
MOVT	Move Top
MOV32 (pseudo)	Move 32-bit value to register
MRA	Move from 40-bit Accumulators to Registers
MRC	Move from Coprocessor to Register
MRC2	Move from Coprocessor to Register
MRRC	Move from Coprocessor to Registers
MRRC2	Move from Coprocessor to Registers
MRS	Move from PSR to Register
MRS	Move from system Coprocessor to Register
MSR	Move from Register to PSR
MSR	Move from Register to system Coprocessor
MUL	Multiply
MVN	Move Not
NOP	No Operation
ORN	Logical OR NOT

Mnemonic	Description
ORR	Logical OR
PKHBT	Pack Halfwords (Bottom + Top)
PKHTB	Pack Halfwords (Top + Bottom)
PLD	Preload Data
PLDW	Preload Data with intent to Write
PLI	Preload Instructions
POP	Pop registers from stack
PUSH	Push registers to stack
QADD	Signed Add, Saturate
QADD8	Parallel Signed Add (4 x 8-bit), Saturate
QADD16	Parallel Signed Add (2 x 16-bit), Saturate
QASX	Exchange Halfwords, Signed Add and Subtract, Saturate
QDADD	Signed Double and Add, Saturate
QDSUB	Signed Double and Subtract, Saturate
QSAX	Exchange Halfwords, Signed Subtract and Add, Saturate
QSUB	Signed Subtract, Saturate
QSUB8	Parallel Signed Subtract (4 x 8-bit), Saturate
QSUB16	Parallel Signed Subtract (2 x 16-bit), Saturate
RBIT	Reverse Bits
REV	Reverse bytes (change endianness)
REV16	Reverse bytes in halfwords
REVSH	Reverse bytes in bottom halfword and sign extend
RFE	Return From Exception

Mnemonic	Description
ROR	Rotate Right
RRX	Rotate Right with Extend
RSB	Reverse Subtract
RSC	Reverse Subtract with Carry
SADD8	Parallel Signed Add (4 x 8-bit)
SADD16	Parallel Signed Add (2 x 16-bit)
SASX	Exchange Halfwords, Signed Add and Subtract
SBC	Subtract with Carry
SBFX	Signed Bit Field Extract
SDIV	Signed Divide
SEL	Select bytes
SETEND	Set Endianness for memory access
SEV	Set Event
SHADD8	Signed Add (4 x 8-bit), halving the results
SHADD16	Signed Add (2 x 16-bit), halving the results
SHASX	Exchange Halfwords, Signed Add and Subtract, halving the results
SHSAX	Exchange Halfwords, Signed Subtract and Add, halving the results
SHSUB8	Signed Subtract (4 x 8-bit), halving the results
SHSUB16	Signed Subtract (2 x 16-bit), halving the results
SMC	Secure Monitor Call
SMLAxy	Signed Multiply with Accumulate
SMLAD	Dual Signed Multiply Accumulate
SMLAL	Signed Multiply Accumulate

Mnemonic	Description
SMLALxy	Signed Multiply Accumulate
SMLALD	Dual Signed Multiply Accumulate Long
SMLAWy	Signed Multiply with Accumulate
SMLSD	Dual Signed Multiply Subtract Accumulate
SMLSLD	Dual Signed Multiply Subtract Accumulate Long
SMMLA	Signed top word Multiply with Accumulate
SMMLS	Signed top word Multiply with Subtract
SMMUL	Signed top word Multiply
SMUAD	Dual Signed Multiply and Add
SMULxy	Signed Multiply
SMULL	Signed Multiply
SMULWy	Signed Multiply
SMUSD	Dual Signed Multiply and Subtract
SRS	Store Return State
SSAT	Signed Saturate
SSAT16	Signed Saturate, parallel halfwords
SSAX	Exchange Halfwords, Signed Subtract and Add
SSUB8	Signed Byte-wise subtraction
SSUB16	Signed Halfword-wise subtraction
STC	Store Coprocessor
STC2	Store Coprocessor
STM	Store Multiple Registers (see LDM)
STR	Store Register (see LDR)

Mnemonic	Description
STRB	Store Register with byte
STRBT	Store Register with byte, user mode
STRD	Store Registers with two words
STREX	Store Register, Exclusive (see LDREX)
STREXB	Store Register with Byte, Exclusive
STREXD	Store Register with two words, Exclusive
STREXH	Store Register with Halfword, Exclusive
STRH	Store Register with Halfword
STRHT	Store Register with Halfword, user mode
STRT	Store Register, user mode
SUB	Subtract
SUBS	Exception Return, no stack
SVC	Supervisor Call
SWP	Swap Registers and Memory (deprecated in v6)
SWPB	Swap Registers and Memory (deprecated in v6)
SXTAB	Sign Extend Byte and Add
SXTAB16	Sign Extend two 8-bit values to two 16-bit values and Add
SXTAH	Sign Extend Halfword and Add
SXTB	Sign Extend Byte
SXTB16	Sign Extend two 8-bit values to two 16-bit values
SXTH	Sign Extend Halfword
SYS	Execute system coprocessor instruction
TBB	Table Branch Byte

Mnemonic	Description
TBH	Table Branch Halfword
TEQ	Test Equivalence
TST	Test
UADD8	Parallel Unsigned Add (4 x 8-bit)
UADD16	Parallel Unsigned Add (2 x 16-bit)
UASX	Exchange Halfwords, Unsigned Add and Subtract
UBFX	Unsigned Bit Field Extract
UDIV	Unsigned Divide
UHADD8	Unsigned Add (4 x 8-bit), halving the results
UHADD16	Unsigned Add (2 x 16-bit), halving the results
UHASX	Exchange Halfwords, Unsigned Add and Subtract, halving the results
UHSAX	Exchange Halfwords, Unsigned Subtract and Add, halving the results
UHSUB8	Unsigned Subtract (4 x 8-bit), halving the results
UHSUB16	Unsigned Subtract (2 x 16-bit), halving the results
USAD8	Unsigned Sum of Absolute Difference
USADA8	Accumulate Unsigned Sum of Absolute Difference
USAT	Unsigned Saturate
USAT16	Unsigned Saturate, parallel halfwords
USAX	Exchange Halfwords, Unsigned Subtract and Add
USUB8	Unsigned Byte-wise subtraction
USUB16	Unsigned Halfword-wise subtraction
UXTB	Zero Extend Byte
UXTB16	Zero Extend two 8-bit values to two 16-bit values

Mnemonic	Description
UXTH	Zero Extend, Halfword
WFE	Wait For Event
WFI	Wait For Interrupt
YIELD	Yield

ARM NEON

NEON is a 128-bit SIMD (Single Instruction, Multiple Data) extension to the Cortex A family of processors. If you understood what the UHADD8 instruction was doing in Listing 3–27, then you will easily understand NEON.

NEON registers are seen as vectors. For example, a 128-bit NEON register can be seen as four 32-bit integers, eight 16-bit integers, or even sixteen 8-bit integers (the same way the UHADD8 instruction interprets a 32-bit register as four 8-bit values). A NEON instruction would then perform the same operation on all elements.

NEON has several important features:

- Single instruction can perform multiple operations (after all, this is the essence of SIMD instructions)
- Independent registers
- Independent pipeline

Many NEON instructions will look similar to ARM instructions. For example, the VADD instruction will add corresponding elements in two vectors, which is similar to what the ADD instruction does (although the ADD instruction simply adds two 32-bit registers and does not treat them as vectors). All NEON instructions start with the letter V, so identifying them is easy.

There are basically two ways to use NEON in your code:

- You can use NEON instructions in hand-written assembly code.
- You can use NEON intrinsics defined in arm-neon.h, a header file provided in the NDK.

The NDK provides sample code for NEON (hello-neon), so you should first review this code. While using NEON can greatly increase performance, it may also require you to modify your algorithms a bit to fully take advantage of vectorization.

To use NEON instructions, make sure you add the .neon suffix to the file name in Android.mk's LOCAL_SRC_FILES. If all files need to be compiled with NEON support, you can set LOCAL_ARM_NEON to true in Android.mk.

A great way to learn about NEON is to look at the Android source code itself. For example, SkBlitRow_opts_arm.cpp (in the external/skia/src/opts directory) contains several routines using NEON instructions, using asm() or intrinsics. In the same directory you will also find SkBlitRow_opts_SSE2.cpp, which contains optimized routines using x86 SIMD instructions. The Skia source code is also available online at http://code.google.com/p/skia.

CPU Features

As you have seen already, not all CPUs are the same. Even within the same family of processors (for example, ARM Cortex family), not all processors support the same features as some are optional. For example, not all ARMv7 processors support the NEON extension or the VFP extension. For this reason, Android provides functions to help you query what kind of platform the code is running on. These functions are defined in cpu-features.h, a header file provided in the NDK, and Listing 3–30 shows you how to use these functions to determine whether a generic function should be used or one that takes advantage of the NEON instruction set.

Listing 3–30. *Checking CPU Features*

```
#include <cpu-features.h>

static inline int has_features(uint64_t features, uint64_t mask)
{
    return ((features & mask) == mask);
}

static void (*my_function)(int* dst, const int* src, int size); // function pointer

extern void neon_function(int* dst, const int* src, int size); // defined in some other file
extern void default_function(int* dst, const int* src, int size);

int init () {
    AndroidCpuFamily cpu = android_getCpuFamily();

    uint64_t features = android_getCpuFeatures();

    int count = android_getCpuCount(); // ignore here

    if (cpu == ANDROID_CPU_FAMILY_ARM) {
        if (has_features(features,
                        ANDROID_CPU_ARM_FEATURE_ARMv7|
                        ANDROID_CPU_ARM_FEATURE_NEON))
        {
            my_function = neon_function;
        }
        else
        {
            // use default functions here
            my_function = default_function; // generic function
        }
    }
    else
```

```
    {
        my_function = default_function; // generic function
    }
}

void call_function(int* dst, const int* src, int size)
{
    // we assume init() was called earlier to set the my_function pointer

    my_function(dst, src, size);
}
```

To use the CPU features functions, you will have to do two things in your Android.mk:

- Add "cpufeatures" to the list of static libraries to link with (LOCAL_STATIC_LIBRARIES := cpufeatures).

- Import the android/cpufeatures module by adding $(call import-module,android/cpufeatures) at the end of Android.mk.

Typically, probing the capabilities of the platform will be one of the first tasks you will have to perform in order to use the best possible functions.

If your code depends on the presence of the VFP extension, you may have to check also whether NEON is supported. The ANDROID_CPU_ARM_FEATURE_VFPv3 flag is for the minimum profile of the extension with sixteen 64-bit floating-point registers (D0 to D15). If NEON is supported, then thirty-two 64-bit floating-point registers are available (D0 to D31). Registers are shared between NEON and VFP and registers are aliased:

- Q0 (128-bit) is an alias for D0 and D1 (both 64-bit).

- D0 is an alias for S0 and S1 (S registers are single-precision 32-bit registers).

The fact that registers are shared and aliased is a very important detail, so make sure you use registers carefully when hand-writing assembly code.

> **NOTE:** Refer to the NDK's documentation and more particularly to CPU-FEATURES.html for more information about the APIs.

C Extensions

The Android NDK comes with the GCC compiler (version 4.4.3 in release 7 of the NDK). As a consequence, you are able to use the C extensions the GNU Compiler Collection supports. Among the ones that are particularly interesting, as far as performance is concerned, are:

- Built-in functions

- Vector instructions

> **NOTE:** Visit `http://gcc.gnu.org/onlinedocs/gcc/C-Extensions.html` for an exhaustive list of the GCC C extensions.

Built-in Functions

Built-in functions, sometimes referred to as intrinsics, are functions handled in a special manner by the compiler. Built-in functions are often used to allow for some constructs the language does not support, and are often inlined, that is, the compiler replaces the call with a series of instructions specific to the target and typically optimized. For example, a call to the `__builtin_clz()` function would result in a CLZ instruction being generated (if the code is compiled for ARM and the CLZ instruction is available). When no optimized version of the built-in function exists, or when optimizations are turned off, the compiler simply makes a call to a function containing a generic implementation.

For example, GCC supports the following built-in functions:

- __builtin_return_address
- __builtin_frame_address
- __builtin_expect
- __builtin_assume_aligned
- __builtin_prefetch
- __builtin_ffs
- __builtin_clz
- __builtin_ctz
- __builtin_clrsb
- __builtin_popcount
- __builtin_parity
- __builtin_bswap32
- __builtin_bswap64

Using built-in functions allows you to keep your code more generic while still taking advantage of optimizations available on some platforms.

Vector Instructions

Vector instructions are not really common in C code. However, with more and more CPUs supporting SIMD instructions, using vectors in your algorithms can accelerate your code quite significantly.

Listing 3–31 shows how you can define your own vector type using the vector_size variable attribute and how you can add two vectors.

Listing 3–31. *Vectors*

```
typedef int v4int __attribute__ ((vector_size (16))); // vector of four 4 integers (16
bytes)

void add_buffers_vectorized (int* dst, const int* src, int size)
{
    v4int* dstv4int = (v4int*) dst;
    const v4int* srcv4int = (v4int*) src;
    int i;

    for (i = 0; i < size/4; i++) {
        *dstv4int++ += *srcv4int++;
    }

    // leftovers
    if (size & 0x3) {
        dst = (int*) dstv4int;
        src = (int*) srcv4int;

        switch (size & 0x3) {
            case 3: *dst++ += *src++;
            case 2: *dst++ += *src++;
            case 1:
            default:  *dst += *src;
        }
    }
}

// simple implementation
void add_buffers (int* dst, const int* src, int size)
{
    while (size--) {
        *dst++ += *src++;
    }
}
```

How this code will be compiled depends on whether the target supports SIMD instructions and whether the compiler is told to use these instructions. To tell the compiler to use NEON instructions, simply add the .neon suffix to the file name in Android.mk's LOCAL_SRC_FILES. Alternatively, you can define LOCAL_ARM_NEON to true if all files need to be compiled with NEON support.

Listing 3–32 shows the resulting assembly code when the compiler does not use ARM SIMD instructions (NEON) whereas Listing 3–33 shows the use of the NEON instructions. (The add_buffers function is compiled the same way and is not shown in the second listing.) The loop is shown in bold in both listings.

Listing 3–32. *Without NEON Instructions*

```
00000000 <add_buffers_vectorized>:
   0:   e92d 0ff0       stmdb   sp!, {r4, r5, r6, r7, r8, r9, sl, fp}
   4:   f102 0803       add.w   r8, r2, #3     ; 0x3
   8:   ea18 0822       ands.w  r8, r8, r2, asr #32
```

```
   c:    bf38            it    cc
   e:    4690            movcc   r8, r2
  10:    b08e            sub   sp, #56
  12:    4607            mov   r7, r0
  14:    468c            mov   ip, r1
  16:    ea4f 08a8       mov.w   r8, r8, asr #2
  1a:    9201            str   r2, [sp, #4]
  1c:    f1b8 0f00       cmp.w   r8, #0      ; 0x0
  20:    4603            mov   r3, r0
  22:    460e            mov   r6, r1
  24:    dd2c            ble.n   80 <add_buffers_vectorized+0x80>
  26:    2500            movs   r5, #0
  28:    f10d 0928       add.w   r9, sp, #40      ; 0x28
  2c:    462e            mov   r6, r5
  2e:    f10d 0a18       add.w   sl, sp, #24      ; 0x18
  32:    f10d 0b08       add.w   fp, sp, #8      ; 0x8
  36:    197c            adds   r4, r7, r5
  38:    3601            adds   r6, #1
  3a:    e894 000f       ldmia.w   r4, {r0, r1, r2, r3}
  3e:    e889 000f       stmia.w   r9, {r0, r1, r2, r3}
  42:    eb0c 0305       add.w   r3, ip, r5
  46:    3510            adds   r5, #16
  48:    4546            cmp   r6, r8
  4a:    cb0f            ldmia   r3!, {r0, r1, r2, r3}
  4c:    e88a 000f       stmia.w   sl, {r0, r1, r2, r3}
  50:    9b0a            ldr   r3, [sp, #40]
  52:    9a06            ldr   r2, [sp, #24]
  54:    4413            add   r3, r2
  56:    9a07            ldr   r2, [sp, #28]
  58:    9302            str   r3, [sp, #8]
  5a:    9b0b            ldr   r3, [sp, #44]
  5c:    4413            add   r3, r2
  5e:    9a08            ldr   r2, [sp, #32]
  60:    9303            str   r3, [sp, #12]
  62:    9b0c            ldr   r3, [sp, #48]
  64:    4413            add   r3, r2
  66:    9a09            ldr   r2, [sp, #36]
  68:    9304            str   r3, [sp, #16]
  6a:    9b0d            ldr   r3, [sp, #52]
  6c:    4413            add   r3, r2
  6e:    9305            str   r3, [sp, #20]
  70:    e89b 000f       ldmia.w   fp, {r0, r1, r2, r3}
  74:    e884 000f       stmia.w   r4, {r0, r1, r2, r3}
  78:    d1dd            bne.n   36 <add_buffers_vectorized+0x36>
  7a:    0136            lsls   r6, r6, #4
  7c:    19bb            adds   r3, r7, r6
  7e:    4466            add   r6, ip
  80:    9901            ldr   r1, [sp, #4]
  82:    f011 0203       ands.w   r2, r1, #3      ; 0x3
  86:    d007            beq.n   98 <add_buffers_vectorized+0x98>
  88:    2a02            cmp   r2, #2
  8a:    d00f            beq.n   ac <add_buffers_vectorized+0xac>
  8c:    2a03            cmp   r2, #3
  8e:    d007            beq.n   a0 <add_buffers_vectorized+0xa0>
  90:    6819            ldr   r1, [r3, #0]
  92:    6832            ldr   r2, [r6, #0]
```

```
94:     188a            adds    r2, r1, r2
96:     601a            str     r2, [r3, #0]
98:     b00e            add     sp, #56
9a:     e8bd 0ff0       ldmia.w    sp!, {r4, r5, r6, r7, r8, r9, sl, fp}
9e:     4770            bx      lr
a0:     6819            ldr     r1, [r3, #0]
a2:     f856 2b04       ldr.w   r2, [r6], #4
a6:     188a            adds    r2, r1, r2
a8:     f843 2b04       str.w   r2, [r3], #4
ac:     6819            ldr     r1, [r3, #0]
ae:     f856 2b04       ldr.w   r2, [r6], #4
b2:     188a            adds    r2, r1, r2
b4:     f843 2b04       str.w   r2, [r3], #4
b8:     e7ea            b.n     90 <add_buffers_vectorized+0x90>
ba:     bf00            nop

00000000 <add_buffers>:
   0:   b470            push    {r4, r5, r6}
   2:   b14a            cbz     r2, 18 <add_buffers+0x18>
   4:   2300            movs    r3, #0
   6:   461c            mov     r4, r3
   8:   58c6            ldr     r6, [r0, r3]
   a:   3401            adds    r4, #1
   c:   58cd            ldr     r5, [r1, r3]
   e:   1975            adds    r5, r6, r5
  10:   50c5            str     r5, [r0, r3]
  12:   3304            adds    r3, #4
  14:   4294            cmp     r4, r2
  16:   d1f7            bne.n   8 <add_buffers+0x8>
  18:   bc70            pop     {r4, r5, r6}
  1a:   4770            bx      lr
```

Listing 3–33. *With NEON Instructions*

```
00000000 <add_buffers_vectorized>:
   0:   b470            push    {r4, r5, r6}
   2:   1cd6            adds    r6, r2, #3
   4:   ea16 0622       ands.w  r6, r6, r2, asr #32
   8:   bf38            it      cc
   a:   4616            movcc   r6, r2
   c:   4604            mov     r4, r0
   e:   460b            mov     r3, r1
  10:   10b6            asrs    r6, r6, #2
  12:   2e00            cmp     r6, #0
  14:   dd0f            ble.n   36 <add_buffers_vectorized+0x36>
  16:   460d            mov     r5, r1
  18:   2300            movs    r3, #0
  1a:   3301            adds    r3, #1
  1c:   ecd4 2b04       vldmia  r4, {d18-d19}
  20:   ecf5 0b04       vldmia  r5!, {d16-d17}
  24:   42b3            cmp     r3, r6
  26:   ef62 08e0       vadd.i32   q8, q9, q8
  2a:   ece4 0b04       vstmia  r4!, {d16-d17}
  2e:   d1f4            bne.n   1a <add_buffers_vectorized+0x1a>
  30:   011b            lsls    r3, r3, #4
  32:   18c4            adds    r4, r0, r3
  34:   18cb            adds    r3, r1, r3
  36:   f012 0203       ands.w  r2, r2, #3      ; 0x3
```

```
3a:    d008            beq.n    4e <add_buffers_vectorized+0x4e>
3c:    2a02            cmp      r2, #2
3e:    4621            mov      r1, r4
40:    d00d            beq.n    5e <add_buffers_vectorized+0x5e>
42:    2a03            cmp      r2, #3
44:    d005            beq.n    52 <add_buffers_vectorized+0x52>
46:    680a            ldr      r2, [r1, #0]
48:    681b            ldr      r3, [r3, #0]
4a:    18d3            adds     r3, r2, r3
4c:    600b            str      r3, [r1, #0]
4e:    bc70            pop      {r4, r5, r6}
50:    4770            bx       lr
52:    6820            ldr      r0, [r4, #0]
54:    f853 2b04       ldr.w    r2, [r3], #4
58:    1882            adds     r2, r0, r2
5a:    f841 2b04       str.w    r2, [r1], #4
5e:    6808            ldr      r0, [r1, #0]
60:    f853 2b04       ldr.w    r2, [r3], #4
64:    1882            adds     r2, r0, r2
66:    f841 2b04       str.w    r2, [r1], #4
6a:    e7ec            b.n      46 <add_buffers_vectorized+0x46>
```

You can quickly see that the loop was compiled in far fewer instructions when NEON instructions are used. As a matter of fact, the vldmia instruction loads four integers from memory, the vadd.i32 instruction performs four additions, and the vstmia instruction stores four integers in memory. This results in more compact and more efficient code.

Using vectors is a double-edged sword though:

- They allow you to use SIMD instructions when available while still maintaining a generic code that can compile for any ABI, regardless of its support for SIMD instructions. (The code in Listing 3–31 compiles just fine for the x86 ABI as it is not NEON-specific.)

- They can result in low-performing code when the target does not support SIMD instructions. (The add_buffers function is far simpler than its "vectorized" equivalent and results in simpler assembly code: see how many times data is read from and written to the stack in add_buffers_vectorized when SIMD instructions are not used.)

> **NOTE:** Visit http://gcc.gnu.org/onlinedocs/gcc/Vector-Extensions.html for more information about vectors.

Tips

The following are a few things you can do in your code relatively easily to achieve better performance.

Inlining Functions

Because function calls can be expensive operations, inlining functions (that is, the process of replacing the function call with the body of the function itself) can make your code run faster. Making a function inlined is simply a matter of adding the "inline" keyword as part of its definition. An example of inline function is showed in Listing 3–30.

You should use this feature carefully though as it can result in bloated code, negating the advantages of the instruction cache. Typically, inlining works better for small functions, where the overhead of the call itself is significant.

> **NOTE:** Alternatively, use macros.

Unrolling Loops

A classic way to optimize loops is to unroll them, sometimes partially. Results will vary and you should experiment in order to measure gains, if any. Make sure the body of the loop does not become too big though as this could have a negative impact on the instruction cache.

Listing 3–34 shows a trivial example of loop unrolling.

Listing 3–34. *Unrolling*

```
void add_buffers_unrolled (int* dst, const int* src, int size)
{
    int i;

    for (i = 0; i < size/4; i++) {
        *dst++ += *src++;
        *dst++ += *src++;
        *dst++ += *src++;
        *dst++ += *src++;
        // GCC not really good at that though... No LDM/STM generated
    }

    // leftovers
    if (size & 0x3) {
        switch (size & 0x3) {
            case 3: *dst++ += *src++;
            case 2: *dst++ += *src++;
            case 1:
            default:  *dst += *src;
        }
    }
}
```

Preloading Memory

When you know with a certain degree of confidence that specific data will be accessed or specific instructions will be executed, you can preload (or prefetch) this data or these instructions before they are used.

Because moving data from external memory to the cache takes time, giving enough time to transfer the data from external memory to the cache can result in better performance as this may cause a cache hit when the instructions (or data) are finally accessed.

To preload data, you can use:

- GCC's `__builtin_prefetch()`
- PLD and PLDW ARM instructions in assembly code

You can also use the PLI ARM instruction (ARMv7 and above) to preload instructions.

Some CPUs automatically preload memory, so you may not always observe any gain. However, since you have a better knowledge of how your code accesses data, preloading data can still yield great results.

> **TIP:** You can use the PLI ARM instruction (ARMv7 and above) to preload instructions.

Listing 3–35 shows how you can take advantage of the preloading built-in function.

Listing 3–35. *Preloading Memory*

```
void add_buffers_unrolled_prefetch (int* dst, const int* src, int size)
{
    int i;

    for (i = 0; i < size/8; i++) {
        __builtin_prefetch(dst + 8, 1, 0); // prepare to write
        __builtin_prefetch(src + 8, 0, 0); // prepare to read

        *dst++ += *src++;
        *dst++ += *src++;
        *dst++ += *src++;
        *dst++ += *src++;
        *dst++ += *src++;
        *dst++ += *src++;
        *dst++ += *src++;
        *dst++ += *src++;
    }

    // leftovers
    for (i = 0; i < (size & 0x7); i++) {
        *dst++ += *src++;
    }
}
```

You should be careful about preloading memory though as it may in some cases degrade the performance. Anything you decide to move into the cache will cause other things to be removed from the cache, possibly impacting performance negatively. Make sure that what you preload is very likely to be needed by your code or else you will simply pollute the cache with useless data.

> **NOTE:** While ARM supports the PLD, PLDW, and PLI instructions, x86 supports the PREFETCHT0, PREFETCHT1, PREFETCHT2, and PREFETCHNTA instructions. Refer to the ARM and x86 documentations for more information. Change the last parameter of `__builtin_prefetch()` and compile for x86 to see which instructions will be used.

LDM/STM Instead Of LDR/STD

Loading multiple registers with a single LDM instruction is faster than loading registers using multiple LDR instructions. Similarly, storing multiple registers with a single STM instruction is faster than using multiple STR instructions.

While the compiler is often capable of generating such instructions (even when memory accesses are somewhat scattered in your code), you should try to help the compiler as much as possible by writing code that can more easily be optimized by the compiler. For example, the code in Listing 3–36 shows a pattern the compiler should quite easily recognize and generate LDM and STM instructions for (assuming an ARM ABI). Ideally, access to memory should be grouped together whenever possible so that the compiler can generate better code.

Listing 3–36. *Pattern to Generate LDM And STM*

```
unsigned int a, b, c, d;

// assuming src and dst are pointers to int

// read source values
a = *src++;
b = *src++;
c = *src++;
d = *src++;

// do something here with a, b, c and d

// write values to dst buffer
*dst++ = a;
*dst++ = b;
*dst++ = c;
*dst++ = d;
```

> **NOTE:** Unrolling loops and inlining functions can also help the compiler generate LDM or STM instructions more easily.

Unfortunately, the GCC compiler does not always do a great job at generating LDM and STM instructions. Review the generated assembly code and write the assembly code yourself if you think performance would improve significantly with the use of the LDM and STM instructions.

Summary

Dennis Ritchie, the father of the C language, said C has the power of assembly language and the convenience of… assembly language. In this chapter you saw that in some cases you may have to use assembly language to achieve the desired results. Although assembly is a very powerful language that provides an unobfuscated view of the machine capabilities, it can make maintenance significantly more difficult as by definition assembly language targets a specific architecture. However, assembly code or built-in functions would typically be found in very small portions of your application, where performance is critical, and therefore maintenance should remain relatively easy. If you carefully select which part of your application should be written in Java, which part should be written in C, and which part should be written in assembly, you can make sure your application's performance is astonishing and impresses your users.

Chapter 4

Using Memory Efficiently

Applications spend a significant part of their time dealing with data in memory. While many developers are aware of the need to try to use as little memory as possible on devices like phones or tablets, not all realize the impact of memory usage on performance. In this chapter, you will learn how choosing the right data type and how arranging your data in memory can boost your application's performance. Also, we will review a basic yet often overlooked feature of Java: memory management using garbage collection and references.

A Word On Memory

No matter how much an application is given, it could always ask for more.

There are two big differences between an Android device, like a phone or tablet, and a traditional computer:

- The amount of physical memory
- The ability to do virtual memory swapping

Typically, today's computers come installed with several gigabytes of RAM (few come installed with only 1GB or less), however Android devices often have a maximum of 512MB of RAM. To add insult to injury, computers use swapping, which Android devices don't have, to give the system and applications the illusion of more memory. For example, an application could still address up to 4GB of memory even with a system that has only 256MB of RAM. Your Android application simply does not have this luxury, and therefore you have to be more careful about how much memory your application uses.

> **NOTE:** You can find applications on Android Market that enable swapping, but they require root access and a different Linux kernel. Assume the Android devices your applications will be running on do not have swapping capabilities.

The Java language defines the size of most primitive types, as shown in Table 4–1, together with their matching native types. If you are primarily familiar with C/C++ code, then you need to pay extra attention to two things:

- Java's char is 16-bit (UTF-16).

- Java's long is 64–bit (while C long is usually 32-bit and C long long is usually 64–bit).

Table 4–1. *Java Primitive Types*

Java primitive type	Native type	Size
boolean	jboolean	8 bits (VM dependent)
byte	jbyte	8 bits
char	jchar	16 bits
short	jshort	16 bits
int	jint	32 bits
long	jlong	64 bits
float	jfloat	32 bits
double	jdouble	64 bits

A good rule of thumb is to use as little memory as possible, which is just common sense as your Android device and applications have a limited amount of memory. But in addition to reducing the risk of an OutOfMemoryError exception, using less memory can also increase performance.

Performance depends mostly on three things:

- How the CPU can manipulate a certain data type

- How much space is needed to store data and instructions

- How data is laid out in memory

We will cover each one of these items, looking at both native code and Java code, measuring execution times, and comparing several implementations of simple algorithms to improve performance.

Data Types

You already got an aperçu of the first point, how the CPU can manipulate a certain data type, in Chapter 2 with the native code version of `computeIterativelyFaster()`, which used two add instructions to add two 64–bit integers, as shown in Listing 4–1.

Listing 4–1. *Adding Two 64–bit Integers*

```
448:    e0944002        adds    r4, r4, r2
44c:    e0a55003        adc     r5, r5, r3
```

Because the ARM registers are 32-bit wide, two instructions are needed to add two 64–bit integers; the lowest 32-bit integers are stored in one register (r4), and the highest 32-bit are stored in another register (r5). Adding two 32-bit values would require a single instruction.

Let's now consider the trivial C function, shown in Listing 4–2, which simply returns the sum of two 32-bit values passed as parameters.

Listing 4–2. *Sum of Two Values*

```
int32_t add_32_32 (int32_t value1, int32_t value2)
{
    return value1 + value2;
}
```

The assembly code for this function is shown in Listing 4–3.

Listing 4–3. Assembly Code

```
000016c8 <add_32_32>:
    16c8:       e0810000        add     r0, r1, r0
    16cc:       e12fff1e        bx      lr
```

As expected, only one instruction is needed to add the two values (and `bx lr` is the equivalent of `return`). We can now create new functions that are very much like `add_32_32`, but with different types for `value1` and `value2`. For example, `add_16_16` adds two `int16_t` values, as shown in Listing 4–4, and `add_16_32` adds an `int16_t` value and an `int32_t` value, as shown in Listing 4–5.

Listing 4–4. *add_16_16's C and Assembly*

```
int16_t add_16_16 (int16_t value1, int16_t value2)
{
    return value1 + value2;
}

000016d0 <add_16_16>:
    16d0:       e0810000        add     r0, r1, r0
    16d4:       e6bf0070        sxth    r0, r0
    16d8:       e12fff1e        bx      lr
```

Listing 4–5. *add_16_32's C And Assembly*

```
int32_t add_16_32 (int16_t value1, int32_t value2)
{
    return value1 + value2;
```

```
}

000016dc <add_16_32>:
    16dc:       e0810000            add     r0, r1, r0
    16e0:       e12fff1e            bx      lr
```

You can see that adding two 16- values required an additional instruction in order to convert the result from 16-bit to 32-bit.

Listing 4–6 shows five more functions, repeating basically the same algorithm but for different data types.

Listing 4–6. *More Assembly Code*

```
000016e4 <add_32_64>:
    16e4:       e0922000            adds    r2, r2, r0
    16e8:       e0a33fc0            adc     r3, r3, r0, asr #31
    16ec:       e1a00002            mov     r0, r2
    16f0:       e1a01003            mov     r1, r3
    16f4:       e12fff1e            bx      lr

000016f8 <add_32_float>:
    16f8:       ee070a10            fmsr    s14, r0
    16fc:       eef87ac7            fsitos  s15, s14
    1700:       ee071a10            fmsr    s14, r1
    1704:       ee777a87            fadds   s15, s15, s14
    1708:       eefd7ae7            ftosizs s15, s15
    170c:       ee170a90            fmrs    r0, s15
    1710:       e12fff1e            bx      lr

00001714 <add_float_float>:
    1714:       ee070a10            fmsr    s14, r0
    1718:       ee071a90            fmsr    s15, r1
    171c:       ee377a27            fadds   s14, s14, s15
    1720:       ee170a10            fmrs    r0, s14
    1724:       e12fff1e            bx      lr

00001728 <add_double_double>:
    1728:       ec410b16            vmov    d6, r0, r1
    172c:       ec432b17            vmov    d7, r2, r3
    1730:       ee366b07            faddd   d6, d6, d7
    1734:       ec510b16            vmov    r0, r1, d6
    1738:       e12fff1e            bx      lr

0000173c <add_float_double>:
    173c:       ee060a10            fmsr    s12, r0
    1740:       eeb77ac6            fcvtds  d7, s12
    1744:       ec432b16            vmov    d6, r2, r3
    1748:       ee376b06            faddd   d6, d7, d6
    174c:       ec510b16            vmov    r0, r1, d6
    1750:       e12fff1e            bx      lr
```

> **NOTE:** The generated native code may differ from what is shown here as a lot depends on the context of the addition. (Code that is inline may look different as the compiler may reorder instructions or change the register allocation.)

As you can see, using a smaller type is not always beneficial to performance as it may actually require more instructions, as demonstrated in Listing 4–4. Besides, if add_16_16 were called with two 32-bit values as parameters, these two values would first have to be converted to 16-bit values before the actual call, as shown in Listing 4–7. Once again, the sxth instruction is used to convert the 32-bit values into 16-bit values by performing a "sign extend" operation.

Listing 4–7. *Calling add_16_16 With Two 32-Bit Values*

```
00001754 <add_16_16_from_32_32>:
    1754:       e6bf0070       sxth     r0, r0
    1758:       e6bf1071       sxth     r1, r1
    175c:       eaffffdb       b        16d0 <add_16_16>
```

Comparing Values

Let's now consider another basic function, which takes two parameters and returns 0 or 1 depending on whether the first parameter is greater than the second one, as shown in Listing 4–8.

Listing 4–8. *Comparing Two Values*

```
int32_t cmp_32_32 (int32_t value1, int32_t value2)
{
    return (value1 > value2) ? 1 : 0;
}
```

Again, we can see the assembly code for this function and its variants in Listing 4–9.

Listing 4–9. *Comparing Two Values In Assembly*

```
00001760 <cmp_32_32>:
    1760:       e1500001       cmp      r0, r1
    1764:       d3a00000       movle    r0, #0   ; 0x0
    1768:       c3a00001       movgt    r0, #1   ; 0x1
    176c:       e12fff1e       bx       lr

00001770 <cmp_16_16>:
    1770:       e1500001       cmp      r0, r1
    1774:       d3a00000       movle    r0, #0   ; 0x0
    1778:       c3a00001       movgt    r0, #1   ; 0x1
    177c:       e12fff1e       bx       lr

00001780 <cmp_16_32>:
    1780:       e1500001       cmp      r0, r1
    1784:       d3a00000       movle    r0, #0   ; 0x0
    1788:       c3a00001       movgt    r0, #1   ; 0x1
    178c:       e12fff1e       bx       lr
```

```
00001790 <cmp_32_64>:
    1790:       e92d0030        push    {r4, r5}
    1794:       e1a04000        mov     r4, r0
    1798:       e1a05fc4        asr     r5, r4, #31
    179c:       e1550003        cmp     r5, r3
    17a0:       e3a00000        mov     r0, #0   ; 0x0
    17a4:       ca000004        bgt     17bc <cmp_32_64+0x2c>
    17a8:       0a000001        beq     17b4 <cmp_32_64+0x24>
    17ac:       e8bd0030        pop     {r4, r5}
    17b0:       e12fff1e        bx      lr
    17b4:       e1540002        cmp     r4, r2
    17b8:       9afffffb        bls     17ac <cmp_32_64+0x1c>
    17bc:       e3a00001        mov     r0, #1   ; 0x1
    17c0:       eafffff9        b       17ac <cmp_32_64+0x1c>

000017c4 <cmp_32_float>:
    17c4:       ee070a10        fmsr    s14, r0
    17c8:       eef87ac7        fsitos  s15, s14
    17cc:       ee071a10        fmsr    s14, r1
    17d0:       eef47ac7        fcmpes  s15, s14
    17d4:       eef1fa10        fmstat
    17d8:       d3a00000        movle   r0, #0   ; 0x0
    17dc:       c3a00001        movgt   r0, #1   ; 0x1
    17e0:       e12fff1e        bx      lr

000017e4 <cmp_float_float>:
    17e4:       ee070a10        fmsr    s14, r0
    17e8:       ee071a90        fmsr    s15, r1
    17ec:       eeb47ae7        fcmpes  s14, s15
    17f0:       eef1fa10        fmstat
    17f4:       d3a00000        movle   r0, #0   ; 0x0
    17f8:       c3a00001        movgt   r0, #1   ; 0x1
    17fc:       e12fff1e        bx      lr

00001800 <cmp_double_double>:
    1800:       ee060a10        fmsr    s12, r0
    1804:       eeb77ac6        fcvtds  d7, s12
    1808:       ec432b16        vmov    d6, r2, r3
    180c:       eeb47bc6        fcmped  d7, d6
    1810:       eef1fa10        fmstat
    1814:       d3a00000        movle   r0, #0   ; 0x0
    1818:       c3a00001        movgt   r0, #1   ; 0x1
    181c:       e12fff1e        bx      lr

00001820 <cmp_float_double>:
    1820:       ee060a10        fmsr    s12, r0
    1824:       eeb77ac6        fcvtds  d7, s12
    1828:       ec432b16        vmov    d6, r2, r3
    182c:       eeb47bc6        fcmped  d7, d6
    1830:       eef1fa10        fmstat
    1834:       d3a00000        movle   r0, #0   ; 0x0
    1838:       c3a00001        movgt   r0, #1   ; 0x1
    183c:       e12fff1e        bx      lr
    1840:       e3a00001        mov     r0, #1   ; 0x1
    1844:       e12fff1e        bx      lr
```

Using the long type appears to be slower than using the short and int types because of the higher number of instructions having to be executed. Similarly, using the double type and mixing float and double seems to be slower than using the float type alone.

> **NOTE:** The number of instructions alone is not enough to determine whether code will be slower or not. Because not all instructions take the same amount of time to complete, and because of the complex nature of today's CPUs, one cannot simply count the number of instructions to know how much time a certain operation will take.

Other Algorithms

Now that we have seen what difference data types can make on the generated code, it is time to see how slightly more sophisticated algorithms perform when dealing with more significant amounts of data.

Listing 4–10 shows three simple methods: one that sorts an array by simply calling the static Arrays.sort() method, one that finds the minimum value in an array, and one that adds all the elements in an array.

Listing 4–10. *Sorting, Finding, and Summing in Java*

```java
private static void sort (int array[]) {
    Arrays.sort(array);
}

private static int findMin (int array[]) {
    int min = Integer.MAX_VALUE;
    for (int e : array) {
        if (e < min) min = e;
    }
    return min;
}

private static int addAll (int array[]) {
    int sum = 0;
    for (int e : array) {
        sum += e; // this could overflow but we'll ignore that
    }
    return sum;
}
```

Table 4–2 shows how many milliseconds each of these functions took to complete when given an array of one million random elements. In addition to these, the results for the variants of these methods (using short, long, float, and double types) are also shown. Refer to Chapter 6 for more information on how to measure execution times.

Table 4–2. *Execution Times With 1,000,000-Element Array*

Java primitive type	sort	findMin	addAll
short	93	27	25
int	753	31	30
long	1,240	57	54
float	1,080	41	33
double	1,358	58	55

We can make a couple of comments on these results:

- Sorting the short array is much faster than sorting any of the other arrays.

- Working with 64–bit types (long or double) is slower than working with 32-bit types.

Sorting Arrays

Sorting an array of 16-bit values can be much faster than sorting an array of 32- or 64–bit values simply because it is using a different algorithm. While the int and long arrays are sorted using some version of Quicksort algorithm, the short array was sorted using counting sort, which sorts in linear time. Using the short type in that case is killing two birds with one stone: less memory is consumed (2 megabytes instead of 4 for the array of int values, and 8 megabytes for the array of long values) and performance is improved.

> **NOTE:** Many wrongly believe Quicksort is always the most efficient sorting algorithm. You can refer to Arrays.java in the Android source code to see how each type of array is sorted.

A less common solution is to use multiple arrays to store your data. For example, if your application needs to store many integers all in the range 0 to 100,000, then you may be tempted to allocate an array of 32-bit values for storage as the short type can be used only to store values from -32,768 to 32,767. Depending on how values are distributed, you may end up with many values equal to or less than 32,767. In such an event, it may be beneficial to use two arrays: one for all the values between 0 and 32,767 (that is, an array of short values), and one for all values greater than 32,767 (an array of int values). While this most likely would result in a greater complexity, the memory savings and potential performance increase may make that solution worthwhile, and perhaps even allow you to optimize the implementation of certain methods. For example, a method that finds the maximum element may only have to go through the array of int values. (Only if the array of int values is empty would it go through the array of short values.)

One of the types that was not shown in Listing 4–9 and Table 4–2 is the boolean type. In fact, sorting an array of boolean values makes little sense. However, there may be occasions where you need to store a rather large number of boolean values and refer to them by index. For that purpose, you could simply create an array. While this would work, this would result in many bits being wasted as 8 bits would be allocated for each entry in the array when actually a boolean value can only be true or false. In other words, only one bit is needed to represent a boolean value. For that purpose, the BitSet class was defined: it allows you to store boolean values in an array (and allows you to refer to them by index) while at the same time using the minimum amount of memory for that array (one bit per entry). If you look at the public methods of the BitSet class and its implementation in BitSet.java, you may notice a few things that deserve your attention:

- BitSet's backend is an array of long values. You may achieve better performance using an array of int values. (Tests showed a gain of about 10% when switching to an int array.)

- Some notes in the code indicate some things should be changed for better performance (for example, see the comment starting with FIXME).

- You may not need all the features from that class.

For all these reasons, it would be acceptable for you to implement your own class, possibly based on BitSet.java to improve performance.

Defining Your Own Classes

Listing 4–11 shows a very simple implementation that would be acceptable if the array does not need to grow after the creation of the object, and if the only operations you need to perform are to set and get the value of a certain bit in the array, for example as you implement your own Bloom filter. When using this simple implementation versus BitSet, tests showed performance improved by about 50%. We achieved even better performance by using a simple array instead of the SimpleBitSet class: using an array alone was about 50% faster than using a SimpleBitSet object (that is, using an array was 4 times faster than using a BitSet object). This practice actually goes against the encapsulation principle of object-oriented design and languages, so you should do this with care.

Listing 4–11. *Defining Your Own BitSet-like Class*

```
public class SimpleBitSet {
    private static final int SIZEOF_INT = 32;
    private static final int OFFSET_MASK = SIZEOF_INT - 1; // 0x1F

    private int[] bits;

    SimpleBitSet(int nBits) {
        bits = new int[(nBits + SIZEOF_INT - 1) / SIZEOF_INT];
    }

    void set(int index, boolean value) {
```

```
            int i = index / SIZEOF_INT;
            int o = index & OFFSET_MASK;
            if (value) {
                bits[i] |= 1 << o; // set bit to 1
            } else {
                bits[i] &= ~(1 << o); // set bit to 0
            }
        }
    }

    boolean get(int index) {
        int i = index / SIZEOF_INT;
        int o = index & OFFSET_MASK;
        return 0 != (bits[i] & (1 << o));
    }
}
```

Alternatively, if most bits are set to the same value, you may want to use a
SparseBooleanArray to save memory (possibly at the cost of performance). Once again,
you could use the Strategy pattern discussed in Chapter 2 to easily select one
implementation or the other.

All in all, these examples and techniques can be summarized as follows:

- When dealing with large amounts of data, use the smallest type
  possible that meets your requirements. For example, choose an
  array of short values over an array of int values, for both
  performance and memory consumption reasons. Use float instead
  of double if you don't need the extra precision (and use FloatMath
  class if needed).

- Avoid conversions from one type to another. Try to be consistent
  and use a single type in your computations, if possible.

- Reinvent the wheel if necessary to achieve better performance, but
  do it with care.

Of course, these rules are not set in stone. For example, you may find yourself in a
situation where converting from one type to another could actually give better
performance, despite the conversion overhead. Be pragmatic and fix a problem only
when you determine there is a one.

More often than not, using less memory is a good rule to follow. In addition to simply
leaving more memory available for other tasks, using less memory can improve
performance as CPUs use caches to quickly access data or instructions.

Accessing Memory

As we saw earlier, manipulating larger types can be more costly because of the higher
number of instructions involved. Intuitively, more instructions often result in lower
performance simply because of the extra work the CPU has to perform to execute them.
In addition to that, code and data both reside in memory, and accessing memory itself
has a cost.

Because accessing memory is a costly operation, a CPU caches the memory that was recently accessed, whether it was memory that was read from or memory that was written to. In fact, a CPU typically uses two caches organized in a hierarchy:

- Level 1 cache (L1)

- Level 2 cache (L2)

The L1 cache is the faster but also the smaller of the two. For example, the L1 cache could be 64 kilobytes (32 kilobytes for data cache, and 32 kilobytes for instruction cache) whereas an L2 cache could be 512 kilobytes.

> **NOTE:** Some processors may also have a Level 3 cache, typically several megabytes in size, but you won't find that on embedded devices yet.

When data or instructions cannot be found in a cache, a cache miss occurs. This is when data or instructions need to be fetched from main memory. There are several kinds of cache misses:

- Read miss in instruction cache

- Read miss in data cache

- Write miss

The first type of cache miss is the most critical, as the CPU has to wait until the instruction is read from memory before it can be executed. The second type of cache miss can be as critical as the first type, although the CPU may still be able to execute other instructions that do not depend on the data being fetched. This effectively results in an out-of-order execution of the instructions. The last type of cache miss is much less critical, as the CPU can typically continue executing instructions. You will have little control over write misses, but you should not worry about it much. Your focus should be on the first two types, which are the kinds of cache misses you want to avoid.

The Cache's Line Size

Besides its total size, another important property of a cache is its line size. Each entry in the cache is a line, which contains several bytes. For example, a cache line on a Cortex A8 L1 cache is 64 bytes (16 words). The idea behind the cache and cache line is the principle of locality: if your application reads from or writes to a certain address, it is likely to read from or write to the same address, or a close-enough address in the near future. For example, this behavior was obvious in the implementation of the findMin() and addAll() methods in Listing 4–9.

There is no easy way for your application to know the size of a cache and the size of a cache line. However, knowing the caches exist and having some knowledge about how caches work can help you write better code and achieve better performance. The following tips can help you take advantage of the cache without having to recourse to low-level optimization, as shown in Chapter 3 with the `PLD` and `PLI` assembly instructions. To reduce the number of cache read misses from the instruction cache:

- Compile your native libraries in Thumb mode. There is no guarantee this will make your code faster though as Thumb code can be slower than ARM code (because more instructions may have to be executed). Refer to Chapter 2 for more information on how to compile libraries in Thumb mode.

- Keep your code relatively dense. While there is no guarantee dense Java code will ultimately result in dense native code, this is still quite often a true assumption.

To reduce the number of cache read misses from the data cache:

- Again, use the smallest type possible when storing a large amount of data in arrays.

- Choose sequential access over random access. This maximizes the reuse of data already in the cache, and can prevent data from being removed from the cache only to be loaded in the cache again later.

> **NOTE:** Modern CPUs are capable of prefetching memory automatically to avoid, or at least limit, cache misses.

As usual, apply these tips on performance-critical sections of your application, which usually is only a small part of your code. On the one hand, compiling in Thumb mode is an easy optimization that does not really increase your maintenance effort. On the other hand, writing dense code may make things more complicated in the long run. There is no one-size-fits-all optimization, and you will have the responsibility of balancing the multiple options you have.

While you don't necessarily have control over what goes into the cache, how you structure and use your data can have an impact on what ends up being in the cache, and therefore can impact performance. In some cases, you may be able to arrange your data in a specific manner to maximize cache hits, albeit possibly creating greater complexity and maintenance cost.

Laying Out Your Data

Once again, the principle of encapsulation will be broken. Let's assume your application needs to store records of some sort, and each record contains two fields: an id and a value. A very object-oriented approach is to define a `Record` class, as shown in Listing 4–12.

Listing 4–12. *Record Class*

```java
public class Record {
    private final short id;
    private final short value;
    // and possibly more

    public Record(short id, short value) {
        this.id = id;
        this.value = value;
    }

    public final short getId() {
        return id;
    }

    public final short getValue() {
        return value;
    }

    public void doSomething() {
        // do something here
    }
}
```

Now that the Record class is defined, your application could simply allocate an array, save the records in that array, and provide additional methods, as shown in Listing 4–13.

Listing 4–13. *Saving Records*

```java
public class MyRecords {
    private Record[] records;
    int nbRecords;

    public MyRecords (int size) {
        records = new Record[size];
    }

    public int addRecord (short id, short value) {
        int index;
        if (nbRecords < records.length) {
            index = nbRecords;
            records[nbRecords] = new Record(id, value);
            nbRecords++;
        } else {
            index = -1;
        }
        return index;
    }

    public void deleteRecord (int index) {
        if (index < 0) {
            // throw exception here - invalid argument
        }
        if (index < nbRecords) {
            nbRecords--;
            records[index] = records[nbRecords];
            records[nbRecords] = null; // don't forget to delete reference
```

```
        }
    }

    public int sumValues (int id) {
        int sum = 0;
        for (int i = 0; i < nbRecords; i++) {
            Record r = records[i];
            if (r.getId() == id) {
                sum += r.getValue();
            }
        }
        return sum;
    }

    public void doSomethingWithAllRecords () {
        for (int i = 0; i < nbRecords; i++) {
            records[i].doSomething();
        }
    }
}
```

All of this would work and would result in a pretty clean design. However, there are drawbacks that may not be visible until you actually run the code:

- A new object is created every single time a record is added to the array. While each object is lightweight, memory allocations are still somewhat costly and could be avoided.

- Calls to getId() and getValue() could be avoided if id and value were public.

If you are allowed to modify the Record class, making id and value public is obviously trivial. The implementation of sumValues() would then be slightly modified, as shown in Listing 4–14.

Listing 4–14. *Modified sumValues()*

```
    public int sumValues (int id) {
        int sum = 0;
        for (Record r : records) {
            if (r.id == id) {
                sum += r.value;
            }
        }
        return sum;
    }
```

However, this alone does not reduce the number of allocations at all; record objects still need to be created as records are added to the array.

NOTE: You could avoid allocations easily in C/C++, but in Java all objects are actually references and have to be created with the new operator.

Since all objects are allocated in the heap, and you can only store references to objects in the array, you can modify the MyRecords class to use an array of short values to remove the allocations. The modified class is shown in Listing 4–15.

Listing 4–15. *Modified MyRecords Class Using a Short Array*

```java
public class MyRecords {
    private short[] records;
    int nbRecords;

    public MyRecords (int size) {
        records = new short[size * 2];
    }

    public int addRecord (short id, short value) {
        int index;
        if (nbRecords < records.length) {
            index = nbRecords;
            records[nbRecords * 2] = id;
            records[nbRecords * 2 + 1] = value;
            nbRecords++;
        } else {
            index = -1;
        }
        return index;
    }

    public void deleteRecord (int index) {
        if (index < 0) {
            // throw exception here - invalid argument
        }
        if (index < nbRecords) {
            nbRecords--;
            records[index * 2] = records[nbRecords * 2];
            records[index * 2 + 1] = records[nbRecords * 2 + 1];
        }
    }

    public int sumValues (int id) {
        int sum = 0;
        for (int i = 0; i < nbRecords; i++) {
            if (records[i * 2] == id) {
                sum += records[i * 2 + 1];
            }
        }
        return sum;
    }

    public void doSomethingWithAllRecords () {
        Record r = new Record(0, 0);
        for (int i = 0; i < nbRecords; i++) {
            r.id = records[i * 2];
            r.value = records[i * 2 + 1];
            r.doSomething();
        }
    }
}
```

Let's imagine that, later on, you find out these things about how the MyRecords class is used:

- sumValues() is called much more often than doSomethingWillAllRecords().

- Only a few records in the array share the same id.

In other words, that would tell you the id field is read much more often than the value field. Given this additional piece of information, you could come up with the following solution to improve performance: using two arrays instead of one, to keep all the ids close together, maximizes cache hits when sequentially going through the array of ids in sumValues(). The first array contains only record ids, while the second array contains only record values. Consequently, more record ids are found in the cache when sumValues() runs as twice as many record ids would be stored in a single cache line.

The new implementation of MyRecords is shown in Listing 4–16.

Listing 4–16. *Modified MyRecords Class Using Two Arrays*

```java
public class MyRecords {
    private short[] recordIds; // first array only for ids
    private short[] recordValues; // second array only for values
    int nbRecords;

    public MyRecords (int size) {
        recordIds = new short[size];
        recordValues = new short[size];
    }

    public int addRecord (short id, short value) {
        int index;
        if (nbRecords < recordIds.length) {
            index = nbRecords;
            recordIds[nbRecords] = id;
            recordValues[nbRecords] = value;
            nbRecords++;
        } else {
            index = -1;
        }
        return index;
    }

    public void deleteRecord (int index) {
        if (index < 0) {
            // throw exception here - invalid argument
        }
        if (index < nbRecords) {
            nbRecords--;
            recordIds[index] = recordIds[nbRecords];
            recordValues[index] = recordValues[nbRecords];
        }
    }

    public int sumValues (int id) {
        int sum = 0;
        for (int i = 0; i < nbRecords; i++) {
```

```
            if (recordIds[i] == id) {
                sum += recordValues[i]; // we only read the value if the id matches
            }
        }
        return sum;
    }

    public void doSomethingWithAllRecords () {
        Record r = new Record(0, 0);
        for (int i = 0; i < nbRecords; i++) {
            r.id = recordIds[i];
            r.value = recordValues[i];
            r.doSomething();
        }
    }
}
```

You may not always be able to apply this kind of optimization though. For example, the listing above assumes doSomething() does not modify the Record object and assumes MyRecords does not provide any method to retrieve Record objects from the array. If these assumptions ever become false, then the implementations in Listings 4–15 and 4–16 would no longer be equivalent to the one in Listing 4–13.

Keep in mind that you may not be able to optimize your code properly until you find out how your code is used. Again, follow a pragmatic approach: don't start optimizing until you know what problem you are trying to solve, as optimizing one usage pattern may negatively impact other patterns.

Garbage Collection

One of the great benefits of Java is garbage collection. The garbage collector frees (or reclaims) memory as objects are no longer in use. For example, the Record object allocated in doSomethingWithAllRecords() in Listing 4–15 is made eligible for garbage collection when the method returns, as a reference to that object no longer exists. There are two very important things to note:

- Memory leaks can still exist.

- Use the garbage collector to help you manage memory as it does more than just freeing memory not in used anymore.

Memory Leaks

As memory can be reclaimed only when an object is no longer referenced, a memory leak can occur when a reference to an object is kept around. A typical example from the Android documentation is when the whole Activity object is leaked as the screen turns (for example, from portrait to landscape orientation). This particular example is easy to reproduce and is quite serious as an Activity object uses quite a bit of memory (and often contains references to even more objects). There is no easy solution to avoiding memory leaks, however Android provides you with tools and APIs to help you.

The DDMS perspective in Eclipse lets you track memory usage and memory allocation with the Heap and Allocation Tracker, respectively. Once again, these tools are not going to tell you where the memory leak is (if there is any), but you can use them to analyze your application's memory usage and hopefully find out if your application has leaks.

> **TIP:** Use the Eclipse Memory Analyzer to even better analyze your memory usage. You can download it from `http://www.eclipse.org/mat`.

Android 2.3 defines the `StrictMode` class, which can be of great help to detect potential memory leaks. While `StrictMode`'s virtual machine policy in Android 2.3 lets you detect only when SQLite objects (such as cursors) are not closed, `StrictMode`'s VM policy in Android 3.0 and above also lets you detect these potential leaks:

- Activity leaks
- Leaks of other objects
- Leaks when objects are not closed (see Android documentation for complete list of classes implementing the Closeable interface)

> **NOTE:** The `StrictMode` class was introduced in Android 2.3 (API level 9), but additional functionalities were added in Android 3.0 (API level 11) in both the VM policy and thread policy. For example, Honeycomb's `StrictMode`'s thread policy supports flashing the screen when a violation is detected.

Listing 4–17 shows how to use the `StrictMode` class to detect memory leaks in your application. You should enable this feature only during development and testing, and disable it as you release your application into the wild.

Listing 4–17. *Using* `StrictMode`

```
public class MyApplication extends Application {

    @Override
    public void onCreate() {
        super.onCreate();

        StrictMode.VmPolicy.Builder builder = new StrictMode.VmPolicy.Builder();
        builder.detectLeakedSqlLiteObjects();
        if (VERSION.SDK_INT >= Build.VERSION_CODES.HONEYCOMB) {
            builder.detectActivityLeaks().detectLeakedClosableObjects();
        }
        // or you could simply call builder.detectAll()

        // penalty
        builder.penaltyLog(); // other penalties exist (e.g. penaltyDeath()) and can be
combined

        StrictMode.VmPolicy vmp = builder.build();
```

```
        StrictMode.setVmPolicy(vmp);
    }
}
```

In that particular instance, StrictMode detects a violation when a closeable object (SQLite object or other) is not closed, and will only log the violation. To verify the behavior, you can simply query a database and purposely forget to close the returned cursor, for example by modifying the code shown in Listing 1-25 in Chapter 1.

As the StrictMode class evolves, it is recommended you simply use detectAll(), which allows you to test your application with future Android releases while taking advantage of the new functionalities the StrictMode class supports.

References

While freeing memory is an important feature of the garbage collector, it does more than that as it is a complete memory management system. Everybody writing Java code has heard about references and how an object can be referenced or not. However, too few seem to know about the multiple types of references. In fact, Java defines four types of references:

- Strong

- Soft

- Weak

- Phantom

Strong References

Strong references are the references Java developers are the most familiar with. Creating such a reference is trivial and is done all the time in Java, as shown in Listing 4–18. In fact, they are the references your application should use most of the time. Two strong references are created, one to an Integer object and one to a BigInteger object.

Listing 4–18. *Strong References*

```
    public void printTwoStrings (int n) {
        BigInteger bi = BigInteger.valueOf(n); // strong reference
        Integer i = new Integer(n); // strong reference

        System.out.println(i.toString());
        i = null; // Integer object freshly created is now eligible for garbage
collection

        System.out.println(bi.toString());
        bi = null; // BigInteger object may not be eligible for garbage collection here!
    }
```

The important thing to notice here is that while setting i to null does make the Integer object eligible for garbage collection, setting bi to null may not. Because the BigInteger.valueOf() method may return a preallocated object (for example,

`BigInteger.ZERO`), setting `bi` to `null` merely removes one strong reference to the `BigInteger` object, but more strong references to that same object may still exist. Two more strong references are created in that method, and they may not be as obvious as the other ones: the calls to `i.toString()` and `bi.toString()` each create a strong reference to a `String` object.

> **NOTE:** Strictly speaking, you would have to know the implementation of the Integer constructor to make sure no strong reference to the new `Integer` object is created anywhere else and therefore make sure that setting `i` to `null` does indeed make the object eligible for garbage collection.

As discussed earlier, keeping strong references to objects around can cause memory leaks. We've probably used the term "strong reference" too many times, so it is time to say that Java does not really define such a term or class. Strong references are "normal" references, simply referred to (pun intended) as references.

Soft, Weak, and Phantom References

Soft and weak references are similar in nature, as they are references that are not strong enough to keep an object from being deleted (or reclaimed). They differ in how aggressively the garbage collector will try to reclaim the object they have a reference to.

An object that is softly reachable, that is, for which there exists a soft reference but no strong reference, is likely to be left alone by the garbage collector when the collection occurs but there is still enough memory to hold the object. However, if the garbage collector determines it needs to reclaim more memory, then it is free to reclaim the softly reachable object's memory. This type of reference is the perfect candidate for a cache that can automatically remove its entries.

> **TIP:** When using a cache, make sure you understand what type of reference it uses. For example, Android's LruCache uses strong references.

Weakly reachable objects, that is, objects for which there exists a weak reference but no strong or soft reference, may be reclaimed as soon as the next collection happens. In other words, the garbage collector will more aggressively reclaim the memory of weakly reachable objects. This type of reference is the perfect candidate for mappings that can be removed automatically as keys are no longer referenced. Use the `WeakHashMap` class for this purpose.

> **NOTE:** How aggressive the garbage collector is depends on the actual implementation.

Phantom references are the weakest of the references and are rarely used. They can be useful if your application needs to know when an object is being garbage collected and you need to perform some clean-up at that time. To be truly useful, phantom references should be registered with a reference queue.

Soft, weak, and phantom references are actually objects themselves and offer a level of indirection to any other object. For example, you could create a phantom reference to a soft reference to a weak reference. In practice though, you will almost always create soft, weak, or phantom references to "strong" references. Listing 4–19 shows an example of soft and weak references being created, each associated with a different reference queue.

Listing 4–19. *References and Reference Queues*

```java
    private Integer strongRef;
    private SoftReference<Integer> softRef;
    private WeakReference<Integer> weakRef;
    private ReferenceQueue<Integer> softRefQueue = new ReferenceQueue<Integer>();
    private ReferenceQueue<Integer> weakRefQueue = new ReferenceQueue<Integer>();

    public void reset () {
        strongRef = new Integer(1);
        softRef = new SoftReference<Integer>(strongRef, softRefQueue);
        weakRef = new WeakReference<Integer>(strongRef, weakRefQueue);
    }

    public void clearStrong () {
        strongRef = null; // no more strong reference, but weak and soft references may
still exist
    }

    public void clearSoft () {
        softRef = null; // no more soft reference, but strong and weak references may
still exist
    }

    public void clearWeak () {
        weakRef = null; // no more weak reference, but strong and soft references may
still exist
    }

    public void pollAndPrint () {
        Reference<? extends Integer> r;
        if ((r = softRefQueue.poll()) != null) {
            do {
                Log.i(TAG, "Soft reference: " + r);
            } while ((r = softRefQueue.poll()) != null);
        } else {
            Log.i(TAG, "Soft reference queue empty");
        }
        if ((r = weakRefQueue.poll()) != null) {
            do {
                Log.i(TAG, "Weak reference: " + r);
            } while ((r = weakRefQueue.poll()) != null);
        } else {
            Log.i(TAG, "Weak reference queue empty");
        }
    }
```

```
public void gc() {
    System.gc();
}
```

Experiment with this code to see when references are enqueued and how this can affect your application. To take full advantage of the garbage collector's memory management abilities, it is important to understand references. You should not try to implement a similar memory management system when working with caches or maps. Most of the things you would want to achieve may be left to the garbage collector with a careful use of references.

Garbage Collection

Garbage collection can occur at various times, and you have little control over when it is happening. You may be able to give some hint to Android by calling System.gc(), but ultimately the Dalvik virtual machine gets to decide when garbage collection actually occurs. There are five situations that prompt garbage collection to occur, and I'll refer to them by their log messages, which you can see when using logcat.

- GC_FOR_MALLOC: Occurs when the heap is too full to allocate memory, and memory must be reclaimed before the allocation can proceed

- GC_CONCURRENT: Occurs when a (possibly partial) collection kicks in, usually as there are enough objects to reclaim

- GC_EXPLICIT: Can occur when you call System.gc() to explicitly request a garbage collection

- GC_EXTERNAL_ALLOC: Does not occur anymore on Honeycomb or later (as everything is allocated in the heap)

- GC_HPROF_DUMP_HEAP: Occurs when you create an HPROF file

Listing 4–20 shows some log messages from the garbage collector.

Listing 4–20. *Garbage Collection Messages*

```
GC_CONCURRENT freed 103K, 69% free 320K/1024K, external 0K/0K, paused 1ms+1ms
GC_EXPLICIT freed 2K, 55% free 2532K/5511K, external 1625K/2137K, paused 55ms
```

As garbage collection takes time, reducing the number of objects you allocate and then release can improve performance. This is especially true in Android 2.2 and earlier versions because garbage collection occurred in the application's main thread and could cause pretty serious issues with responsiveness and performance. For example, some frames in a real-time game could be dropped because too much time was spent doing garbage collection. Things got better with Android 2.3, with most of the garbage collection work relocated to a separate thread. As garbage collection occurs, the main thread is still affected a little bit (a pause of 5 milliseconds or less), but much less than in previous versions of Android. It is not uncommon for a complete garbage collection to take over 50 milliseconds. For reference, a 30 frames-per-second game would need about 33 milliseconds to render and display each frame, so it is easy to see why garbage collection on pre-Android 2.3 systems could cause problems.

APIs

Android defines several APIs you can use to learn about how much memory is available on the system and how much is being used:

- ActivityManager's getMemoryInfo()
- ActivityManager's getMemoryClass()
- ActivityManager's getLargeMemoryClass()
- Debug's dumpHprofData()
- Debug's getMemoryInfo()
- Debug's getNativeHeapAllocatedSize()
- Debug's getNativeHeapSize()

> **TIP:** Set android:largeHeap to true in your application's manifest file to use a large heap. This attribute was introduced in Android 3.0. Note that there is no guarantee the large heap is any larger than the regular heap. You should try hard to prevent your application from having to depend on this setting.

Listing 4–21 shows how to use the two getMemoryInfo() methods.

Listing 4–21. *Calling getMemoryInfo()*

```
ActivityManager am = (ActivityManager) getSystemService(Context.ACTIVITY_SERVICE);

ActivityManager.MemoryInfo memInfo = new ActivityManager.MemoryInfo();
am.getMemoryInfo(memInfo);
// use information from memInfo here...

Debug.MemoryInfo debugMemInfo = new Debug.MemoryInfo();
Debug.getMemoryInfo(debugMemInfo);
// use information from debugMemInfo here...
```

Low Memory

Your application is not alone. It has to share resources with many other applications and also the system as a whole. Consequently, there may be times when there is not enough memory for everyone and in this case, Android will ask applications and applications' components (such as activities or fragments) to tighten their belts.

The ComponentCallbacks interface defines the onLowMemory() API, which is common to all application components. When it is called, a component is basically asked to release objects it does not really need. Typically, your implementation of onLowMemory() would release:

- Caches or cache entries (for example, LruCache as it uses strong references)
- Bitmap objects that can be generated again on demand
- Layout objects that are not visible
- Database objects

You should be careful about deleting objects that are costly to recreate. However, not releasing enough memory may cause Android to be more aggressive and start killing processes, possibly even your own application. If your application is killed, then it will have to start from scratch again the next time the user wants to use it. Consequently, your application should play nice and release as many resources as it can, because it should benefit not only other applications but also your own. Using lazy initializations in your code is a good habit; it allows you to implement onLowMemory() later without having to modify the rest of your code significantly.

Summary

On embedded devices, memory is a scarce resource. Even though today's cellular phones and tablets have more and more memory, these devices also run more and more complex systems and applications. Using memory effectively not only allows your application to run on older devices with less memory but also to run faster. Remember, if you give your application memory, it will ask for more.

Chapter 5

Multithreading and Synchronization

Chapter 1 introduced the concept of the main thread, or UI thread, in which most events are handled. Even though you are not prevented from executing all your code from within the main thread, your application typically uses more than one thread. As a matter of fact, several threads are created and run as part of your application even if you don't create new threads yourself. For example, Eclipse's DDMS perspective shows these threads when an application runs on an Android 3.1-based Galaxy Tab 10.1:

- main

- HeapWorker

- GC (Garbage Collector)

- Signal Catcher

- JDWP (Java Debug Wire Protocol)

- Compiler

- Binder Thread #1

- Binder Thread #2

So far, we've discussed only the first one in the list, the main thread, so you probably were not expecting these extra seven. The good news is that you don't have to worry about these other threads, which exist mostly for housekeeping; besides, you don't have much control over what they actually do. Your focus should be on the main thread and on not performing any long operation within that thread, to keep your application responsive.

The particular housekeeping threads Android spawns depends on which Android version an application is running on. For example, Android 2.1 generates six threads (as opposed to the eight listed above) because garbage collection takes place in a separate thread only in Android 2.3 and above, and the Just-In-Time compiler was not introduced until Android 2.2.

In this chapter you learn how to create your own threads, how to communicate between them, how objects can safely be shared between threads, and how, in general, you can tailor your code to take full advantage of your device's multithreading capabilities. We also review common pitfalls to avoid when working with threads in an Android application.

Threads

A Thread object, that is, an instance of the Thread class defined by Java, is a unit of execution with its own call stack. Applications can create additional threads easily, as shown in Listing 5–1. Of course, your application is free to create additional threads to perform some operations outside of the main thread; very often you will have to do exactly that to keep your application responsive.

Listing 5–1. *Creating Two Threads*

```
// the run() method can simply be overridden…
Thread thread1 = new Thread("cheese1") {
    @Override
    public void run() {
        Log.i("thread1", "I like Munster");
    }
};

// …or a Runnable object can be passed to the Thread constructor
Thread thread2 = new Thread(new Runnable() {
    public void run() {
        Log.i("thread2", "I like Roquefort");
    }
}, "cheese2");

// remember to call start() or else the threads won't be spawned and nothing will
happen
    thread1.start();
    thread2.start();
```

Executing that code may actually give different results. Because each thread is a separate unit of execution, and both threads have the same default priority, there is no guarantee "I like Munster" will be displayed before "I like Roquefort," even though thread1 is started first. The actual result depends on the scheduling, which is implementation-dependent.

> **NOTE:** A typical mistake is to call the run() method instead of start(). This causes the run() method from the Thread object (and the Runnable object if applicable) to be called from the current thread. In other words, no new thread would be generated.

The two threads above were simply started, with no expectation of a result transmitted back to the thread that spawned them. While this is sometimes the desired effect, often you want to get some sort of result from what is being executed in different threads. For example, your application may want to compute a Fibonacci number in a separate thread, to keep the application responsive, but would want to update the user interface with the result of the computation. This scenario is shown in Listing 5–2, where mTextView is a reference to a TextView widget in your layout and onClick is the method called when the user clicks on a button, or a view in general (see the android:onClick attribute in XML layout).

Listing 5–2. *Worker Thread to Compute Fibonacci Number*

```
public void onClick (View v) {
    new Thread(new Runnable() {
        public void run() {
            // note the 'final' keyword here (try removing it and see what happens)
            final BigInteger f =
Fibonacci.recursiveFasterPrimitiveAndBigInteger(100000);
            mTextView.post(new Runnable() {
                public void run() {
                    mTextView.setText(f.toString());
                }
            });
        }
    }, "fibonacci").start();
}
```

While this would work just fine, it is also quite convoluted and makes your code harder to read and maintain. You may be tempted to simplify the code from Listing 5–2 and replace it with the code shown in Listing 5–3. Unfortunately, this would be a bad idea as this would simply throw a CalledFromWrongThreadException exception, the reason being that the Android UI toolkit can be called only from the UI thread. The exception's description says "only the original thread that created a view hierarchy can touch its views." It is therefore mandatory for the application to make sure TextView.setText() is called from the UI thread, for example by posting a Runnable object to the UI thread.

Listing 5–3. *Invalid Call From Non-UI Thread*

```
public void onClick (View v) {
    new Thread(new Runnable() {
        public void run() {
            BigInteger f = Fibonacci.recursiveFasterPrimitiveAndBigInteger(100000);
            mTextView.setText(f.toString()); // will throw an exception
        }
    }, "fibonacci").start();
}
```

> **TIP:** To facilitate debugging, it is good practice to name the threads you spawn. If no name is specified, a new name will be generated. You can get the name of a thread by calling Thread.getName().

Each thread, regardless of how it was created, has a priority. The scheduler uses the priority to decide which thread to schedule for execution, that is, which thread gets to use the CPU. You can change the priority of a thread by calling `Thread.setPriority()`, as shown in Listing 5–4.

Listing 5–4. *Setting a Thread's Priority*

```
Thread thread = new Thread("thread name") {
    @Override
    public void run() {
        // do something here
    }
};
thread.setPriority(Thread.MAX_PRIORITY); // highest priority (higher than UI thread)
thread.start();
```

If the priority is not specified, the default priority is used. The `Thread` class defines three constants:

- MIN_PRIORITY (1)

- NORM_PRIORITY (5) – the default priority

- MAX_PRIORITY (10)

If your application attempts to set a thread's priority to some out-of-range value, that is, less than 1 or greater than 10, then an `IllegalArgumentException` exception will be thrown.

Android provides another way to set a thread's priority, based on Linux priorities, with the `Process.setThreadPriority` APIs in the android.os package. The following eight priorities are defined:

- THREAD_PRIORITY_AUDIO (-16)

- THREAD_PRIORITY_BACKGROUND (10)

- THREAD_PRIORITY_DEFAULT (0)

- THREAD_PRIORITY_DISPLAY (-4)

- THREAD_PRIORITY_FOREGROUND (-2)

- THREAD_PRIORITY_LOWEST (19)

- THREAD_PRIORITY_URGENT_AUDIO (-19)

- THREAD_PRIORITY_URGENT_DISPLAY (-8)

You can also use the `Process.THREAD_PRIORITY_LESS_FAVORABLE` (+1) and `Process.THREAD_PRIORITY_MORE_FAVORABLE` as increments (-1). For example to set a thread's priority to a slightly higher priority than default, you could set the priority to (`THREAD_PRIORITY_DEFAULT` + `THREAD_PRIORITY_MORE_FAVORABLE`).

> **TIP:** Use THREAD_PRIORITY_LESS_FAVORABLE and THREAD_PRIORITY_MORE_FAVORABLE instead of +1 and -1 so you won't have to remember whether a higher number means lower of higher priority. Also, avoid mixing calls to Thread.setPriority and Process.setThreadPriority as this could make your code confusing. Note that Linux priorities go from -20 (highest) to 19 (lowest) whereas Thread priorities go from 1 (lowest) to 10 (highest).

Be very careful when you decide to change the priority of your threads. Increasing the priority of one thread may result in a faster execution of this particular thread but may negatively impact the other threads, which may not get access to the CPU resource as quickly as they should, therefore disrupting the user experience as a whole. Consider implementing a priority aging algorithm if it makes sense for your application.

Even though creating a thread to perform a background task is trivial in Android, as demonstrated in Listing 5–1, updating the user interface can be quite tedious: it requires posting the result back to the main thread because calling any View method must be done from the UI thread.

AsyncTask

Very often, your application has to deal with the sequence that was shown in Listing 5–2:

- Event is received in UI thread
- Operation is to be executed in non-UI thread in response to event
- UI needs to be updated with result of operation

To simplify this common pattern, Android defines the AsyncTask class in Android 1.5 and above. The AsyncTask class allows your application to easily perform a background operation and publish the result in the UI thread. Threads, Runnables, and other related objects are hidden from you for simplicity. Listing 5–5 shows how you would implement the sequence from Listing 5–2 using the AsyncTask class.

Listing 5–5. *Using AsyncTask*

```
public void onClick (View v) {
    // AsyncTask<Params, Progress, Result> anonymous class
    new AsyncTask<Integer, Void, BigInteger>() {
        @Override
        protected BigInteger doInBackground(Integer... params) {
            return Fibonacci.recursiveFasterPrimitiveAndBigInteger(params[0]);
        }

        @Override
        protected void onPostExecute(BigInteger result) {
            mTextView.setText(result.toString());
        }
    }.execute(100000);
}
```

Since doInBackground() is an abstract method, it has to be implemented. While you don't have to override onPostExecute(), it is likely you will since one of the main purposes of AsyncTask is to let you publish the result to the UI thread. The following AsyncTask protected methods are all called from the UI thread:

- onPreExecute()

- onProgressUpdate(Progress… values)

- onPostExecute(Result result)

- onCancelled()

- onCancelled(Result result) (API introduced in Android 3.0)

The onProgressUpdate() method is called when publishProgress() is called from within doInBackground(). This method allows you to do things like update the UI as the background operations are progressing. A typical example would be to update a progress bar as a file is being downloaded in the background. Listing 5–6 shows how multiple files can be downloaded.

Listing 5–6. *Downloading Multiple Files*

```
AsyncTask<String, Object, Void> task = new AsyncTask<String, Object, Void>() {

    private ByteArrayBuffer downloadFile(String urlString, byte[] buffer) {
        try {
            URL url = new URL(urlString);
            URLConnection connection = url.openConnection();
            InputStream is = connection.getInputStream();
            //Log.i(TAG, "InputStream: " + is.getClass().getName()); // if you are
curious
            //is = new BufferedInputStream(is); // optional line, try with and without
            ByteArrayBuffer baf = new ByteArrayBuffer(640 * 1024);
            int len;
            while ((len = is.read(buffer)) != -1) {
                baf.append(buffer, 0, len);
            }
            return baf;
        } catch (MalformedURLException e) {
            return null;
        } catch (IOException e) {
            return null;
        }
    }

    @Override
    protected Void doInBackground(String... params) {
        if (params != null && params.length > 0) {
            byte[] buffer = new byte[4 * 1024]; // try different sizes (1 for example
will give lower performance)
            for (String url : params) {
                long time = System.currentTimeMillis();
                ByteArrayBuffer baf = downloadFile(url, buffer);
                time = System.currentTimeMillis() - time;
                publishProgress(url, baf, time);
            }
```

```
        } else {
            publishProgress(null, null);
        }
        return null; // we don't care about any result but we still have to return
something
    }

    @Override
    protected void onProgressUpdate(Object... values) {
        // values[0] is the URL (String), values[1] is the buffer (ByteArrayBuffer),
values[2] is the duration
        String url = (String) values[0];
        ByteArrayBuffer buffer = (ByteArrayBuffer) values[1];
        if (buffer != null) {
            long time = (Long) values[2];
            Log.i(TAG, "Downloaded " + url + " (" + buffer.length() + " bytes) in " +
time + " milliseconds");
        } else {
            Log.w(TAG, "Could not download " + url);
        }

        // update UI accordingly, etc
    }
};

String url1 = "http://www.google.com/index.html";
String url2 = "http://d.android.com/reference/android/os/AsyncTask.html";
task.execute(url1, url2);
//task.execute("http://d.android.com/resources/articles/painless-threading.html"); //
try that to get exception
```

The example in Listing 5–6 simply downloads the files in memory (a ByteArrayBuffer object). If you want to save the file to permanent storage, you should also perform that operation in a thread other than the UI thread. In addition, the example showed files downloaded one after the other. Depending on your application's needs, it may be better to download several files in parallel.

NOTE: An AsyncTask object must be created in the UI thread and can be executed only once.

When the doInBackground() task is actually scheduled depends on the Android version. Before Android 1.6, tasks were executed serially, so only one background thread was needed. Starting with Android 1.6, the single background thread was replaced by a pool of threads allowing multiple tasks to be executed in parallel to allow for better performance. However, executing several tasks in parallel can cause serious problems when synchronization is not implemented properly or when tasks are executed or completed in a certain order (which may not be the order the developer anticipated). Consequently, the Android team plans to revert back to a single background thread model by default after Honeycomb. To continue to allow applications to execute tasks in parallel, a new executeOnExecutor() API was added in Honeycomb, providing time for application developers to update their applications accordingly. This new API can be used together with AsyncTask.SERIAL_EXECUTOR for serial execution or AsyncTask.THREAD_POOL_EXECUTOR for parallel execution.

The planned future change shows that parallel execution requires a careful design and thorough tests. The Android team may have underestimated the potential problems or overestimated the applications' abilities to deal with them when switching to a pool of threads in Android 1.6, triggering the decision to revert back to a single thread model after Honeycomb. Applications' overall quality will improve while more experienced developers will still have the flexibility to execute tasks in parallel for better performance.

The AsyncTask class can simplify your code when dealing with background tasks and user-interface updates, however it is not meant to fully replace the more basic classes Android defines to communicate between threads.

Handlers and Loopers

Android defines two classes in the android.os package that will often be the cornerstones of the interthread communication in your multithreaded applications:

- Handler
- Looper

While creating an AsyncTask object hides the Handler and Looper details from you, in some cases you need to use handlers and loopers explicitly, for example when you need to post a Runnable to a thread other than the main thread.

Handlers

Listing 5–2 gave you a glimpse of how the Handler and Looper work together: you use a Handler object to post a Runnable in a Looper's message queue. Your application's main thread already has a message queue, so you don't have to create one explicitly. However, the threads you create do not come automatically with a message queue and message loop, so you would have to create one yourself if needed. Listing 5–7 shows how you can create a thread with a Looper.

Listing 5–7. *Thread Class With Message Queue*

```
public class MyThread extends Thread {
    private static final String TAG = "MyThread";
    private Handler mHandler;

    public MyThread(String name) {
        super(name);
    }

    public Handler getHandler() {
        return mHandler;
    }

    @Override
```

```
    public void run() {
        Looper.prepare(); // binds a looper to this thread

        mHandler = new Handler() {
            @Override
            public void handleMessage(Message msg) {
                switch (msg.what) {
                    // process messages here
                }
            }
        };
        // the handler is bound to this thread's looper

        Looper.loop(); // don't forget to call loop() to start the message loop

        // loop() won't return until the loop is stopped (e.g., when Looper.quit() is
called)
    }
}
```

> **NOTE:** The handler object is created in the run() method as it needs to be bound to a specific
> looper, which is also created in run() when Looper.prepare() is called. Consequently,
> calling getHandler() before the thread is spawned will return null.

Once the thread is running, you can post Runnable objects or send messages to its
message queue, as shown in Listing 5–8.

Listing 5–8. *Posting Runnables and Sending Messages*

```
MyThread thread = new MyThread("looper thread");
thread.start();

// later...
Handler handler = thread.getHandler();
// careful: this could return null if the handler is not initialized yet!

// to post a runnable
handler.post(new Runnable() {
    public void run() {
        Log.i(TAG, "Where am I? " + Thread.currentThread().getName());
    }
});

// to send a message
int what = 0; // define your own values
int arg1 = 1;
int arg2 = 2;
Message msg = Message.obtain(handler, what, arg1, arg2);
handler.sendMessage(msg);

// another message...
what = 1;
msg = Message.obtain(handler, what, new Long(Thread.currentThread().getId()));
handler.sendMessageAtFrontOfQueue(msg);
```

> **TIP:** Use one of the `Message.obtain()` or `Handler.obtainMessage()` APIs to get a `Message` object, as they return a `Message` object from the global message pool, which is more efficient than allocating a new instance every single time a message is needed. These APIs also make it simpler to set the various fields of the message.

Loopers

Android provides an easier way to work with looper threads with the `HandlerThread` class, which also makes it easier to avoid the potential race condition mentioned in Listing 5–8, where `getHandler()` may still return null even after the thread has been started. Listing 5–9 shows how to use the `HandlerThread` class.

Listing 5–9. *Using the `HandlerThread` Class*

```java
public class MyHandlerThread extends HandlerThread {
    private static final String TAG = "MyHandlerThread";
    private Handler mHandler;

    public MyHandlerThread(String name) {
        super(name);
    }

    public Handler getHandler() {
        return mHandler;
    }

    @Override
    public void start() {
        super.start();
        Looper looper = getLooper(); // will block until thread's Looper object is
initialized
        mHandler = new Handler(looper) {
            @Override
            public void handleMessage(Message msg) {
                switch (msg.what) {
                    // process messages here
                }
            }
        };
    }
}
```

Since the handler is created in the `start()` method instead of in the `run()` method, it will be available (via a call to `getHandler()`) after the `start()` method returns without any race condition.

Data Types

We have seen two ways to spawn a thread, using the `Thread` and `AsyncTask` classes. When two or more threads access the same data, you need to make sure the data types support concurrent access. The Java language defines many classes in the `java.util.concurrent` package for that purpose:

- ArrayBlockingQueue
- ConcurrentHashMap
- ConcurrentLinkedQueue
- ConcurrentSkipListMap
- ConcurrentSkipListSet
- CopyOnWriteArrayList
- CopyOnWriteArraySet
- DelayQueue
- LinkedBlockingDeque
- LinkedBlockingQueue
- PriorityBlockingQueue
- SynchronousQueue

You will have to carefully select your data types based on your application's requirements. Also, the fact that they are concurrent implementations does not necessarily imply that operations are atomic. In fact, many operations are not atomic and by design are not meant to be. For example, the `putAll()` method in the `ConcurrentSkipListMap` class is not atomic. A concurrent implementation merely means that the data structure will not be corrupted when accessed by multiple threads.

Synchronized, Volatile, Memory Model

If you want to share objects between multiple threads but have not implemented any fine-grained locking mechanism, you can use the `synchronized` keyword to make sure your access is thread-safe, as shown in Listing 5–10.

Listing 5–10. *Using the `Synchronized` Keyword*

```
public class MyClass {
    private int mValue;

    public MyClass(int n) {
        mValue = n;
    }

    public synchronized void add (int a) {
```

```
        mValue += a;
    }

    public synchronized void multiplyAndAdd (int m, int a) {
        mValue = mValue * m + a;
    }
}
```

The two methods add and multiplyAndAdd in Listing 5–7 are synchronized methods. This means two things:

- If one thread is executing a synchronized method, other threads trying to call any synchronized method for the same object have to wait until the first thread is done.

- When a synchronized method exits, the updated state of the object is visible to all other threads.

The first item is quite intuitive. The second one should be as well although it still requires an explanation. As a matter of fact, the Java memory model is such that a modification to a variable in one thread may not immediately be visible to other threads. Actually, it may never be visible. Consider the code in Listing 5–11: if one thread calls MyClass.loop(), and at some point in the future another thread calls Myclass.setValue(100), the first thread may still not terminate; may carry on looping forever and always print out a value other than 100, simply because of the Java language's memory model.

Listing 5–11. *Java Memory Model Impact*

```
public class MyClass {
    private static final String TAG = "MyClass";
    private static int mValue = 0;

    public static void setValue(int n) {
        mValue = n;
    }

    public static void loop () {
        while (mValue != 100) {
            try {
                Log.i(TAG, "Value is " + mValue);
                Thread.sleep(1000);
            } catch (Exception e) {
                // ignored
            }
        }
    }
}
```

You have two options to fix that:

- Use the synchronized keyword, as shown in Listing 5–12.

- Use the volatile keyword, as shown in Listing 5–13.

Listing 5–12. *Adding the* Synchronized *Keyword*

```
public class MyClass {
    private static final String TAG = "MyClass";
    private static int mValue = 0;

    public static synchronized void setValue(int n) {
        mValue = n;
    }

    public static synchronized int getValue() {
        return mValue;
    }

    public static void loop () {
        int value;
        while ((value = getValue()) != 100) {
            try {
                Log.i(TAG, "Value is " + value);
                Thread.sleep(1000);
            } catch (Exception e) {
                // ignored
            }
        }
    }
}
```

Listing 5–13. *Adding the* Volatile *Keyword*

```
public class MyClass {
    private static final String TAG = "MyClass";
    private static volatile int mValue = 0; // we add the volatile keyword and remove
the synchronize keyword

    public static void setValue(int n) {
        mValue = n; // you'd still have to use synchronized if that statement were
mValue += n (not atomic)
    }

    public static void loop () {
        while (mValue != 100) {
            try {
                Log.i(TAG, "Value is " + mValue);
                Thread.sleep(1000);
            } catch (Exception e) {
                // ignored
            }
        }
    }
}
```

> **NOTE:** Make sure you understand which statements are atomic. For example, value++ is not atomic while value = 1 is. This is important as the volatile keyword can only fix concurrency issues if the statements using the variable are atomic. If they are not, then you have to use the synchronized keyword instead.

You can improve concurrency and throughput by using synchronized statements, as shown in Listing 5–14, as opposed to making whole methods synchronized. In these cases, you want to protect only the part that needs to be protected (that is, where mValue is being modified), but leave the log message outside of the synchronized block. You can also use objects other than this as a lock.

Listing 5–14. *Synchronized Statements*

```
public class MyOtherClass {
    private static final String TAG = "MyOtherClass";
    private int mValue;
    private Object myLock = new Object(); // more than this… there is

    public MyClass(int n) {
        mValue = n;
    }

    public void add (int a) {
        synchronized (myLock) {
            mValue += a;
        }
        Log.i(TAG, "add: a=" + a); // no need to block
    }

    public void multiplyAndAdd (int m, int a) {
        synchronized (myLock) {
            mValue = mValue * m + a;
        }
        Log.i(TAG, " multiplyAndAdd: m=" + m + ", a=" + a); // no need to block
    }
}
```

Making methods or statements synchronized is the easiest way to guarantee your class supports concurrent access. However, it may reduce the throughput when not everything needs to be protected, and even worse, it can cause deadlocks. Indeed, deadlocks can occur when you call another object's method from within a synchronized block, which may attempt to acquire a lock on an object that is already locked and waiting for your own object's lock.

> **TIP:** Don't call another object's method within a synchronized block unless you can guarantee no deadlock will occur. Usually, you can guarantee that only when you are the author of the code of the other object's class.

In general, it is best to avoid accessing the same object from different threads if you have any doubt about whether it will work or not. The classes defined by Java are a good reference, and since the Android code is available, you can refer to the implementation of these classes to understand the various techniques you can take advantage of. In addition, to simplify your development, Java defines many classes that already support thread-safe or concurrent programming, which can be used as the basis for some of your own algorithms.

Concurrency

More classes are defined in the java.util.concurrent.atomic and java.util.concurrent.locks packages. The java.util.concurrent.atomic package contains the following classes:

- AtomicBoolean
- AtomicInteger
- AtomicIntegerArray
- AtomicIntegerFieldUpdater (abstract)
- AtomicLong
- AtomicLongArray
- AtomicLongFieldUpdater (abstract)
- AtomicMarkableReference
- AtomicReference
- AtomicReferenceArray
- AtomicReferenceFieldUpdater (abstract)
- AtomicStampedReference

Most of these classes require little explanation as they simply define methods to update values atomically. For example, the AtomicInteger class defines the addAndGet() method, which adds a given value to the current value of the AtomicInteger object while returning the updated value. The abstract classes defined in this package are used internally but would very rarely be used directly in your applications' code.

In addition to the CountDownLatch, CyclicBarrier, and Semaphore classes from the java.util.concurrent package, more synchronization aids are defined in the java.util.concurrent.locks package:

- AbstractOwnableSynchronizer (abstract, since API level 5)
- AbstractQueuedLongSynchronizer (abstract, since API level 9)
- AbstractQueuedLongSynchronizer (since API level 9)
- AbstractQueuedSynchronizer (abstract)
- AbstractQueuedSynchronizer.ConditionObject
- LockSupport
- ReentrantLock
- ReentrantReadWriteLock
- ReentrantReadWriteLock.ReadLock
- ReentrantReadWriteLock.WriteLock

These classes are not commonly used in typical Android applications. Perhaps the most common one you would still use is the ReentrantReadWriteLock class, together with its ReentrantReadWriteLock.ReadLock and ReentrantReadWriteLock.WriteLock companions, as they allow for multiple reader threads to have access to the data (as long as there is no writer thread modifying the data) while there can only be one writer thread at a time. This is a common object when multiple threads access the same data for reading only, and you want to maximize throughput.

As a general rule, sharing data between threads creates problems (throughput, concurrency issues). Synchronization can become quite complex, and you need to have a solid understanding of the subject and of your code to enable shared data successfully. Debugging issues related to synchronization can also be quite an endeavor, so you should aim for simplicity before you try to optimize things like throughput. Focus on your application's quality first before any optimization.

Multicore

Recently, a number of Android devices came out based on multicore architecture. For example, the Samsung Galaxy Tab 10.1 and Motorola Xoom tablets both use a dual-core processor (Cortex A9 cores). A multicore processor, unlike a single-core processor, can execute multiple threads simultaneously. That being said, it is easy to see how this could improve performance as a dual-core processor can theoretically do twice as much as a single-core one (everything else being equal, for example, clock frequency). Although optimizing for multiple cores is not as easy as it sounds, and some caveats exist, your application can definitely leverage the additional power that today's multicore processors bring. Devices with dual-core CPUs include:

- Samsung Galaxy Tab 10.1
- Motorola Xoom
- Motorola Phonton 4G
- Motorola Droid 3
- HTC EVO 3D
- LG Optimus 2X
- Samsung Galaxy Nexus

In many cases, you won't have to worry about how many cores a device has. Delegating certain operations to a separate thread using a Thread object or AsyncTask is usually enough as you can still create multiple threads even on a single-core processor. If the processor has several cores, then threads will simply run on different processor units, which will be transparent to your application.

That being said, there may be times when you really need to get the most out of the CPU to achieve an acceptable level of performance and design algorithms especially tailored for multiple cores.

To achieve the best performance, your application may first need to find out how many cores are available, simply by calling the RunTime.availableProcessors() method, as shown in Listing 5–15.

Listing 5–15. *Getting the Number Of Processors*

```
    // will return 2 on a Galaxy Tab 10.1 or BeBox Dual603, but only 1 on a Nexus S or
Logitech Revue
    final int proc = Runtime.getRuntime().availableProcessors();
```

Typically, the number of "available processors" is 1 or 2 although future products will be using quad-core CPUs. Current Android notebooks may already be using quad-core architecture. Depending on when you plan on making your application available, you may want to focus on only 1- and 2-core CPUs and only later publish an update to take advantage of more cores.

> **NOTE:** Assume the number of cores may not always be a power of 2.

Modifying Algorithm For Multicore

Some of the Fibonacci algorithms presented in Chapter 1 are good candidates to take advantage of multiple cores. Let's start with the divide-and-conquer algorithm whose implementation is shown in Listing 5–16 (which is the same implementation shown in Listing 1-7 in Chapter 1).

Listing 5–16. *Fibonacci Divide-and-Conquer Algorithm*

```
public class Fibonacci
{
    public static BigInteger recursiveFasterBigInteger (int n)
    {
        if (n > 1) {
            int m = (n / 2) + (n & 1);

            // two simpler sub-problems
            BigInteger fM = recursiveFasterBigInteger(m);
            BigInteger fM_1 = recursiveFasterBigInteger(m - 1);

            // results are combined to compute the solution to the original problem
            if ((n & 1) == 1) {
                // F(m)^2 + F(m-1)^2
                return fM.pow(2).add(fM_1.pow(2));
            } else {
                // (2*F(m-1) + F(m)) * F(m)
                return fM_1.shiftLeft(1).add(fM).multiply(fM);
            }
        }
        return (n == 0) ? BigInteger.ZERO : BigInteger.ONE;
    }
}
```

This algorithm does what divide-and-conquer algorithms do:

- The original problem is divided into simpler sub-problems.

- The results are then combined to compute the solution to the original problem.

Since the two sub-problems are independent, it is possible to execute them in parallel without much synchronization. The Java language defines the ExecutorService interface, which is implemented by several classes you can use to schedule work to be done. An example is shown in Listing 5–17, which uses the factory method from the Executors class to create a thread pool.

Listing 5–17. *Using ExecutorService*

```
public class Fibonacci {
    private static final int proc = Runtime.getRuntime().availableProcessors();
    private static final ExecutorService executorService =
Executors.newFixedThreadPool(proc + 2);

    public static BigInteger recursiveFasterBigInteger (int n) {
        // see Listing 5-16 for implementation
    }

    public static BigInteger recursiveFasterBigIntegerAndThreading (int n) {
        int proc = Runtime.getRuntime().availableProcessors();
        if (n < 128 || proc <= 1) {
            return recursiveFasterBigInteger(n);
        }

        final int m = (n / 2) + (n & 1);
        Callable<BigInteger> callable = new Callable<BigInteger>() {
            public BigInteger call() throws Exception {
                return recursiveFasterBigInteger(m);
            }
        };
        Future<BigInteger> ffM = executorService.submit(callable); // submit first job
as early as possible

        callable = new Callable<BigInteger>() {
            public BigInteger call() throws Exception {
                return recursiveFasterBigInteger(m-1);
            }
        };
        Future<BigInteger> ffM_1 = executorService.submit(callable); // submit second
job

        // getting partial results and combining them
        BigInteger fM, fM_1, fN;

        try {
            fM = ffM.get(); // get result of first sub-problem (blocking call)
        } catch (Exception e) {
            // if exception, compute fM in current thread
            fM = recursiveFasterBigInteger(m);
        }
        try {
```

```
            fM_1 = ffM_1.get(); // get result of second sub-problem (blocking call)
        } catch (Exception e) {
            // if exception, compute fM in current thread
            fM_1 = recursiveFasterBigInteger(m-1);
        }

        if ((n & 1) != 0) {
            fN = fM.pow(2).add(fM_1.pow(2));
        } else {
            fN = fM_1.shiftLeft(1).add(fM).multiply(fM);
        }

        return fN;
    }
}
```

As you can clearly see, the code is harder to read. Moreover, this implementation is still based on a low-performance code: as we saw in Chapter 1, the two sub-problems would end up computing many of the same Fibonacci numbers. Better implementations were using a cache to remember the Fibonacci numbers already computed, saving significant time. Listing 5–18 shows a very similar implementation, but using a cache.

Listing 5–18. *Using* ExecutorService *and Caches*

```
public class Fibonacci {
    private static final int proc = Runtime.getRuntime().availableProcessors();
    private static final ExecutorService executorService =
Executors.newFixedThreadPool(proc + 2);

    private static BigInteger recursiveFasterWithCache (int n, Map<Integer, BigInteger>
cache)
    {
        // see Listing 1-11 for implementation (slightly different though as it was
using SparseArray)
    }

    public static BigInteger recursiveFasterWithCache (int n)
    {
        HashMap<Integer , BigInteger> cache = new HashMap<Integer , BigInteger>();
        return recursiveFasterWithCache(n, cache);
    }

    public static BigInteger recursiveFasterWithCacheAndThreading (int n) {
        int proc = Runtime.getRuntime().availableProcessors();
        if (n < 128 || proc <= 1) {
            return recursiveFasterWithCache (n);
        }

        final int m = (n / 2) + (n & 1);
        Callable<BigInteger> callable = new Callable<BigInteger>() {
            public BigInteger call() throws Exception {
                return recursiveFasterWithCache (m);
            }
        };
        Future<BigInteger> ffM = executorService.submit(callable);

        callable = new Callable<BigInteger>() {
```

```
              public BigInteger call() throws Exception {
                  return recursiveFasterWithCache (m-1);
              }
          };
          Future<BigInteger> ffM_1 = executorService.submit(callable);

          // getting partial results and combining them
          BigInteger fM, fM_1, fN;

          try {
              fM = ffM.get(); // get result of first sub-problem (blocking call)
          } catch (Exception e) {
              // if exception, compute fM in current thread
              fM = recursiveFasterBigInteger(m);
          }
          try {
              fM_1 = ffM_1.get(); // get result of second sub-problem (blocking call)
          } catch (Exception e) {
              // if exception, compute fM in current thread
              fM_1 = recursiveFasterBigInteger(m-1);
          }

          if ((n & 1) != 0) {
              fN = fM.pow(2).add(fM_1.pow(2));
          } else {
              fN = fM_1.shiftLeft(1).add(fM).multiply(fM);
          }


          return fN;
      }
  }
```

Using Concurrent Cache

One thing to notice in this implementation is the fact that each sub-problem will use its own cache object and therefore duplicate values will still be computed. For the two sub-problems to share a cache, we need to change the cache from a SparseArray object to an object that allows concurrent access from different threads. Listing 5–19 shows such an implementation, using a ConcurrentHashMap object as the cache.

Listing 5–19. *Using ExecutorService and a Single Cache*

```
public class Fibonacci {
    private static final int proc = Runtime.getRuntime().availableProcessors();
    private static final ExecutorService executorService =
Executors.newFixedThreadPool(proc + 2);

    private static BigInteger recursiveFasterWithCache (int n, Map<Integer, BigInteger>
cache)
    {
        // see Listing 1-11 for implementation (slightly different though as it was
using SparseArray)
    }

    public static BigInteger recursiveFasterWithCache (int n)
```

```java
    {
        HashMap<Integer , BigInteger> cache = new HashMap<Integer , BigInteger>();
        return recursiveFasterWithCache(n, cache);
    }

    public static BigInteger recursiveFasterWithCacheAndThreading (int n) {
        int proc = Runtime.getRuntime().availableProcessors();
        if (n < 128 || proc <= 1) {
            return recursiveFasterWithCache (n);
        }

        final ConcurrentHashMap<Integer, BigInteger> cache =
            new ConcurrentHashMap<Integer, BigInteger>(); // concurrent access ok

        final int m = (n / 2) + (n & 1);

        Callable<BigInteger> callable = new Callable<BigInteger>() {
            public BigInteger call() throws Exception {
                return recursiveFasterWithCache (m, cache); // first and second jobs
share the same cache
            }
        };
        Future<BigInteger> ffM = executorService.submit(callable);

        callable = new Callable<BigInteger>() {
            public BigInteger call() throws Exception {
                return recursiveFasterWithCache (m-1, cache); // first and second jobs
share the same cache
            }
        };
        Future<BigInteger> ffM_1 = executorService.submit(callable);

        // getting partial results and combining them
        BigInteger fM, fM_1, fN;

        try {
            fM = ffM.get(); // get result of first sub-problem (blocking call)
        } catch (Exception e) {
            // if exception, compute fM in current thread
            fM = recursiveFasterBigInteger(m);
        }
        try {
            fM_1 = ffM_1.get(); // get result of second sub-problem (blocking call)
        } catch (Exception e) {
            // if exception, compute fM in current thread
            fM_1 = recursiveFasterBigInteger(m-1);
        }

        if ((n & 1) != 0) {
            fN = fM.pow(2).add(fM_1.pow(2));
        } else {
            fN = fM_1.shiftLeft(1).add(fM).multiply(fM);
        }

        return fN;
    }
}
```

> **NOTE:** The second parameter of `recursiveFasterWithCache` is a map so that it can be called with any cache that implements the Map interface, for example a `ConcurrentHashMap` or `HashMap` object. A `SparseArray` object is not a map.

You may not always observe performance gains when dividing a problem into sub-problems and assigning each sub-problem to a different thread. Since there could still be dependency between data, and synchronization would have to occur, threads may spend some or most of their time waiting for the access to data to be possible. Also, performance gains may not be as significant as you would hope for. Even though theoretically you would expect to double the performance on a dual-core processor and quadruple the performance on a quad-core processor, reality can show you otherwise.

In practice, it is easier to use multiple threads to perform unrelated tasks (therefore avoiding the need for synchronization), or tasks that need to be synchronized only either sporadically or regularly if the frequency is "low enough." For example, a video game would typically use one thread for the game logic and another thread to do the rendering. The rendering thread would therefore need to read the data manipulated by the logic thread 30 or 60 times per second (for every frame being rendered), and could relatively quickly make a copy of the data needed to start rendering a frame, therefore blocking the access for only a very short moment.

Activity Lifecycle

The threads you create are not automatically aware of the changes in your activity's lifecycle. For example, a thread you spawned would not automatically be notified that your activity's `onStop()` method has been called, and the activity is not visible anymore, or that your activity's `onDestroy()` method has been called. This means you may need to do additional work to synchronize your threads with your application's lifecycle. Listing 5–20 shows a simply example of an `AsyncTask` still running even after the activity has been destroyed.

Listing 5–20. *Computing a Fibonacci Number In the Background Thread and Updating the User Interface Accordingly*

```
public class MyActivity extends Activity {
    private TextView mResultTextView;
    private Button mRunButton;

    @Override
    protected void onCreate(Bundle savedInstanceState) {
        super.onCreate(savedInstanceState);
        setContentView(R.layout.main);

        // layout contains TextView and Button
        mResultTextView = (TextView) findViewById(R.id.resultTextView); // where result
will be displayed
        mRunButton = (Button) findViewById(R.id.runButton); // button to start
computation
    }
```

```
    public void onClick (View v) {
        new AsyncTask<Integer, Void, BigInteger>() {
            @Override
            protected void onPreExecute() {
                // button is disabled so the user can only start one computation at a
time
                mRunButton.setEnabled(false);
            }

            @Override
            protected void onCancelled() {
                // button is enabled again to let the user start another computation
                mRunButton.setEnabled(true);
            }

            @Override
            protected BigInteger doInBackground(Integer... params) {
                return Fibonacci.recursiveFasterPrimitiveAndBigInteger(params[0]);
            }

            @Override
            protected void onPostExecute(BigInteger result) {
                mResultTextView.setText(result.toString());
                // button is enabled again to let the user start another computation
                mRunButton.setEnabled(true);
            }
        }.execute(100000); // for simplicity here, we hard-code the parameter
    }
}
```

This example does two simple things when the user presses the button:

- It computes a Fibonacci number in a separate thread.

- The button is disabled while the computation is ongoing and enabled once the computation is completed so that the user can start only one computation at a time.

On the surface, it looks correct. However, if the user turns the device while the computation is being executed, the activity will be destroyed and created again. (We assume here that the manifest file does not specify that this activity will handle the orientation change by itself.) The current instance of MyActivity goes through the usual sequence of onPause(), onStop(), and onDestroy() calls, while the new instance goes through the usual sequence of onCreate(), onStart(), and onResume() calls. While all of this is happening, the AsyncTask's thread still runs as if nothing had happened, unaware of the orientation change, and the computation eventually completes. Again, it looks correct so far, and this would seem to be the behavior one would expect.

However, one thing happened that you may not have been expecting: the button became enabled again after the change of orientation was completed. This is easily explained since the Button you see after the change of orientation is actually a new button, which was created in onCreate() and is enabled by default. As a consequence, the user could start a second computation while the first one is still going. While relatively harmless, this breaks the user-interface paradigm you had established when deciding to disable the button while a computation is ongoing.

Passing Information

If you want to fix this bug, you may want the new instance of the activity to know whether a computation is already in progress so that is can disable the button after it is created in onCreate(). Listing 2-21 shows the modifications you could make to communicate information to the new instance of MyActivity.

Listing 5–21. *Passing Information From One Activity Instance to Another*

```
public class MyActivity extends Activity {
    private static final String TAG = "MyActivity";

    private TextView mResultTextView;
    private Button mRunButton;
    private AsyncTask<Integer, Void, BigInteger> mTask; // we'll pass that object to the
other instance

    @Override
    protected void onCreate(Bundle savedInstanceState) {
        super.onCreate(savedInstanceState);
        setContentView(R.layout.main);

        // we add a log message here to know what instance of MyActivity is now created
        Log.i(TAG, "MyActivity instance is " + MyActivity.this.toString());
        Log.i(TAG, "onCreate() called in thread " + Thread.currentThread().getId());

        // layout contains TextView and Button
        mResultTextView = (TextView) findViewById(R.id.resultTextView); // where result
will be displayed
        mRunButton = (Button) findViewById(R.id.runButton); // button to start
computation

        // we get the object returned in onRetainNonConfigurationInstance() below
        mTask = (AsyncTask<Integer, Void, BigInteger>)
getLastNonConfigurationInstance();
        if (mTask != null) {
            mRunButton.setEnabled(false); // computation still in progress so we disable
the button
        }
    }

    @Override
    public Object onRetainNonConfigurationInstance() {
        return mTask; // will be non-null if computation is in progress
    }

    public void onClick (View v) {
        // we keep a reference to the AsyncTask object
        mTask = new AsyncTask<Integer, Void, BigInteger>() {
            @Override
            protected void onPreExecute() {
```

```
                    // button is disabled so the user can start only one computation at a
time
                    mRunButton.setEnabled(false);
            }

            @Override
            protected void onCancelled() {
                // button is enabled again to let the user start another computation
                mRunButton.setEnabled(true);
                mTask = null;
            }

            @Override
            protected BigInteger doInBackground(Integer... params) {
                return Fibonacci.recursiveFasterPrimitiveAndBigInteger(params[0]);
            }

            @Override
            protected void onPostExecute(BigInteger result) {
                mResultTextView.setText(result.toString());
                // button is enabled again to let the user start another computation
                mRunButton.setEnabled(true);
                mTask = null;

                // we add a log message to know when the computation is done
                Log.i(TAG, "Computation completed in " + MyActivity.this.toString());
                Log.i(TAG, "onPostExecute () called in thread " +
Thread.currentThread().getId());
            }
        }.execute(100000); // for simplicity here, we hard-code the parameter
    }
}
```

> **NOTE:** onRetainNonConfigurationInstance() is now deprecated in favor of the Fragment
> APIs available in API level 11 or on older platforms through the Android compatibility package.
> This deprecated method is used here for simplicity; you will find more sample code using this
> method. However, you should write new applications using the Fragment APIs.

If you execute that code, you'll then find that the button remains disabled when you rotate your device and a computation is in progress. This would seem to fix the problem we encountered in Listing 5–20. However, you may notice a new problem: if you rotate the device while a computation is in progress and wait until the computation is done, the button is not enabled again even though onPostExecute() was called. This is a much more significant problem since the button can never be enabled again! Moreover, the result of the computation is not propagated on the user interface. (This problem is also in Listing 5–20, so probably you would have noticed that issue before the fact that the button was enabled again after the orientation change.)

Once again this can easily be explained (but may not be obvious if you are relatively new to Java): while onPostExecute was called in the same thread as onCreate (the first activity was destroyed but the main thread is still the same), the mResultTextView and mRunButton objects used in onPostExecute actually belong to the first instance of MyActivity, not to the new instance. The anonymous inner class declared when the new AsyncTask object was created is associated with the instance of its enclosing class (this is why the AsyncTask object we created can reference the fields declared in MyActivity such as mResultTextView and mTask), and therefore it won't have access to the fields of the new instance of MyActivity. Basically, the code in Listing 5–21 has two major flaws when the user rotates the device while a computation is in progress:

- The button is never enabled again, and the result is never showed.

- The previous activity is leaked since mTask keeps a reference to an instance of its enclosing class (so two instances of MyActivity exist when the device is rotated).

Remembering State

One way to solve this problem is to simply let the new instance of MyActivity know that a computation was in progress and to start this computation again. The previous computation can be canceled in onStop() or onDestroy() using the AsyncTask.cancel() API. Listing 5–22 shows a possible implementation.

Listing 5–22. *Remembering a Computation In Progress*

```
public class MyActivity extends Activity {
    private static final String TAG = "MyActivity";

    private static final String STATE_COMPUTE = "myactivity.compute";

    private TextView mResultTextView;
    private Button mRunButton;
    private AsyncTask<Integer, Void, BigInteger> mTask;

    @Override
    protected void onStop() {
        super.onStop();
        if (mTask != null) {
            mTask.cancel(true); // although it is canceled now, the thread may still be
running for a while
        }
    }

    @Override
    protected void onSaveInstanceState(Bundle outState) {
        // if called, it is guaranteed to be called before onStop()
        super.onSaveInstanceState(outState);
        if (mTask != null) {
            outState.putInt(STATE_COMPUTE, 100000); // for simplicity, hard-coded value
        }
    }

    @Override
    protected void onCreate(Bundle savedInstanceState) {
        super.onCreate(savedInstanceState);
        setContentView(R.layout.main);
```

```java
        // we add a log message here to know what instance of MyActivity is now created
        Log.i(TAG, "MyActivity instance is " + MyActivity.this.toString());
        Log.i(TAG, "onCreate() called in thread " + Thread.currentThread().getId());

        // layout contains TextView and Button
        mResultTextView = (TextView) findViewById(R.id.resultTextView); // where result
will be displayed
        mRunButton = (Button) findViewById(R.id.runButton); // button to start
computation

        // make sure you check whether savedInstanceState is null
        if (savedInstanceState != null && savedInstanceState.containsKey(STATE_COMPUTE))
{
            int value = savedInstanceState.getInt(STATE_COMPUTE);
            mTask = createMyTask().execute(value); // button will be disabled in
onPreExecute()
        }
    }

    // creation of AsyncTask moved to private method as it can now be created from 2
places
    private AsyncTask<Integer, Void, BigInteger> createMyTask() {
        return new AsyncTask<Integer, Void, BigInteger>() {
            @Override
            protected void onPreExecute() {
                // button is disabled so the user can start only one computation at a
time
                mRunButton.setEnabled(false);
            }

            @Override
            protected void onCancelled() {
                // button is enabled again to let the user start another computation
                mRunButton.setEnabled(true);
                mTask = null;
            }

            @Override
            protected BigInteger doInBackground(Integer... params) {
                return Fibonacci.recursiveFasterPrimitiveAndBigInteger(params[0]);
            }

            @Override
            protected void onPostExecute(BigInteger result) {
                mResultTextView.setText(result.toString());
                // button is enabled again to let the user start another computation
                mRunButton.setEnabled(true);
                mTask = null;

                // we add a log message to know when the computation is done
                Log.i(TAG, "Computation completed in " + MyActivity.this.toString());
                Log.i(TAG, "onPostExecute () called in thread " +
Thread.currentThread().getId());
            }
        };
    }
```

```
    public void onClick (View v) {
        // we keep a reference to the AsyncTask object
        mTask = createMyTask.execute(100000); // for simplicity here, we hard-code the
parameter
    }
}
```

With this implementation, we basically tell the new instance that the previous instance was computing a certain value when it was destroyed. The new instance will then start the computation again, and the user interface will be updated accordingly.

A device does not have to be rotated to generate a change of configuration as other events are also considered a configuration change. For example, these include a change of locale or an external keyboard being connected. While a Google TV device may not be rotated (at least for now), you should still take the configuration change scenario into account when you target Google TV devices specifically as other events are still likely to occur. Besides, new events may be added in the future, which could also result in a configuration change.

NOTE: onSaveInstanceState() is not always called. It will basically be called only when Android has a good reason to call it. Refer to the Android documentation for more information.

Canceling an AsyncTask object does not necessarily mean the thread will stop immediately though. The actual behavior depends on several things:

- Whether the task has been started already

- Which parameter (true or false) was passed to cancel()

Calling AsyncTask.cancel() triggers a call to onCancelled() after doInBackground() returns, instead of a call to onPostExecute(). Because doInBackground() may still have to complete before onCancelled() is called, you may want to call AsyncTask.isCancelled() periodically in doInBackground() to return as early as possible. While this was not relevant in our example, this may make your code a little bit harder to maintain since you would have to interleave AsyncTask-related calls (isCancelled()) and code doing the actual work (which should ideally be AsyncTask-agnostic).

NOTE: Threads don't always have to be interrupted when the activity is destroyed. You can use the Activity.isChangingConfiguration() and Activity.isFinishing() APIs to learn more about what is happening and plan accordingly. For example, in Listing 5–22 we could decide to cancel the task in onStop() only when isFinishing() returns true.

In general, you should at least try to pause the background threads when your activity is paused or stopped. This prevents your application from using resources (CPU, memory, internal storage) other activities could be in dire need of.

> **TIP:** Have a look at the source code of Shelves on `http://code.google.com/p/shelves` and PhotoStream on `http://code.google.com/p/apps-for-android` for more examples on saving a state between instantiations of activities.

Summary

Using threads can make your code more efficient and easier to maintain even on single-threaded devices. However, multithreading can also add complexity to your application, especially when synchronization is involved and the state of the application needs to be preserved for a better user experience. Make sure you understand the ramifications of using multiple threads in your application as this can easily get out of control, and debugging can become quite difficult. Although sometimes not trivial, using multithreading can dramatically boost your application's performance. Because multicore architectures are quickly becoming ubiquitous, adding multithreading support in your application is definitely something most of your users will benefit from.

Benchmarking And Profiling

Being able to measure performance is required in order to determine whether optimizations are needed, and whether the optimizations actually improved anything.

Performance in most cases will be measured as a function of the time it takes to complete an operation. For example, the performance of a game will very often be measured in how many frames per second can be rendered, which directly depends on how much time it takes to render frames: to achieve a constant frame rate of 60 frames per second, each frame should take less than 16.67 milliseconds to render and display. Also, as we discussed in Chapter 1, a response time of 100 milliseconds is often desired in order for results to appear instantaneous.

In this chapter you learn the various ways of measuring time in your application. You also learn how to use a profiling tool, Traceview, to trace Java code and native code and easily identify bottlenecks in your application. Finally, you learn about the logging mechanism in Android and how to take advantage of the filtering capabilities.

Measuring Time

How much time an operation or sequence of operations takes to complete is a critical piece of information when it is time to optimize code. Without knowing how much time is spent doing something, your optimizations are impossible to measure. Java and Android provide the following simple APIs your application can use to measure time and therefore performance:

- System.currentTimeMillis
- System.nanoTime
- Debug.threadCpuTimeNanos
- SystemClock.currentThreadTimeMillis

■   SystemClock.elapsedRealtime

■   SystemClock.uptimeMillis

Typically, your application needs to make two calls to these methods as a single call is hardly meaningful. To measure time, your application needs a start time and an end time, and performance is measured as the difference between these two values. At the risk of sounding overly patronizing, now is a good time to state that there are 1,000,000,000 nanoseconds in one second, or in other words, a nanosecond is one billionth of a second.

> **NOTE:** Even though some methods return a time expressed in nanoseconds, it does not imply nanosecond accuracy. The actual accuracy depends on the platform and may differ between devices. Similarly, System.currentTimeMillis() returns a number of milliseconds but does not guarantee millisecond accuracy.

A typical usage is shown in Listing 6–1.

Listing 6–1. *Measuring Time*

```
long startTime = System.nanoTime();

// perform operation you want to measure here

long duration = System.nanoTime() - startTime;

System.out.println("Duration: " + duration);
```

An important detail is the fact that Listing 6–1 does not use anything Android-specific. As a matter of fact, this measurement code is only using the java.lang.System, java.lang.String and java.io.PrintStream packages. Consequently, you could use similar code in another Java application that is not meant to run on an Android device. The Debug and SystemClock classes are, on the other hand, Android-specific.

While System.currentTimeMillis() was listed as a method to measure time, it is actually not recommended to use this method, for two reasons:

■   Its precision and accuracy may not be good enough.

■   Changing the system time can affect the results.

Instead, your application should use System.nanoTime() as it offers better precision and accuracy.

System.nanoTime()

Because the reference time is not defined, you should only use System.nanoTime() to measure time intervals, as shown in Listing 6–1. To get the time (as a clock), use System.currentTimeMillis() as it defines the return value as the number of milliseconds since January 1, 1970 00:00:00 UTC.

Listing 6–2 shows you how to measure, roughly, the time it takes for System.nanoTime()
to complete.

Listing 6–2. *Measuring* System.nanoTime()

```
private void measureNanoTime() {
    final int ITERATIONS = 100000;
    long total = 0;
    long min = Long.MAX_VALUE;
    long max = Long.MIN_VALUE;

    for (int i = 0; i < ITERATIONS; i++) {
        long startTime = System.nanoTime();
        long time = System.nanoTime() - startTime;
        total += time;
        if (time < min) {
            min = time;
        }
        if (time > max) {
            max = time;
        }
    }

    Log.i(TAG, "Average time: " + ((float)total / ITERATIONS) + " nanoseconds");
    Log.i(TAG, " Minimum: " + min);
    Log.i(TAG, " Maximum: " + max);
}
```

On a Samsung Galaxy Tab 10.1, the average time is about 750 nanoseconds.

> **NOTE:** How much time a call to System.nanoTime() takes depends on the implementation
> and the device.

Because the scheduler is ultimately responsible for scheduling threads to run on the
processing units, the operation you want to measure may sometimes be interrupted,
possibly several times, to make room for another thread. Therefore, your measurement
may include time spent on executing some other code, which can make your
measurement incorrect, and therefore misleading.

To have a better idea of how much time your own code needs to complete, you can use
the Android-specific Debug.threadCpuTimeNanos() method.

Debug.threadCpuTimeNanos()

Because it measures only the time spent in the current thread,
Debug.threadCpuTimeNanos() should give you a better idea of how much time your own
code takes to complete. However, if what you are measuring is executed in multiple
threads, a single call to Debug.threadCpuTimeNanos() won't give you an accurate
estimate, and you would have to call this method from all the threads of interest and
sum the results.

Listing 6–3 shows a simple example of how `Debug.threadCpuTimeNanos()` can be used. The usage is no different from `System.nanoTime()`'s, and it should only be used to measure a time interval.

Listing 6–3. *Using* `Debug.threadCpuTimeNanos()`

```
long startTime = Debug.threadCpuTimeNanos();
// warning: this may return -1 if the system does not support this operation

// simply sleep for one second (other threads will be scheduled to run during that
time)
try {
    TimeUnit.SECONDS.sleep(1);
    // same as Thread.sleep(1000);
} catch (InterruptedException e) {
    e.printStackTrace();
}

long duration = Debug.threadCpuTimeNanos() - startTime;

Log.i(TAG, "Duration: " + duration + " nanoseconds");
```

While the code will take about one second to complete because of the call to `TimeUnit.SECONDS.sleep()`, the actual time spent executing code is much less. In fact, running that code on a Galaxy Tab 10.1 shows that the duration is only about 74 microseconds. This is expected as nothing much is done in between the two calls to `Debug.threadCpuTimeNanos()` other than putting the thread to sleep for one second.

> **NOTE:** Refer to the `TimeUnit` class documentation. `TimeUnit` offers convenient methods for converting time between different units and also performing thread-related operations such as `Thread.join()` and `Object.wait()`.

Of course, you can also measure time in your application's C code using "standard" C time functions, as shown in Listing 6–4.

Listing 6–4. *Using C Time Function*

```
#include <time.h>

void foo() {
    double duration;
    time_t time = time(NULL);

    // do something here you want to measure

    duration = difftime(time(NULL), time); // duration in seconds
}
```

Tracing

Once you identify what is taking too much time, you probably want to be able to know in more detail which methods are the culprits. You can do this by creating trace files with the help of a tracing-specific method, and then analyze them with the Traceview tool.

Debug.startMethodTracing()

Android provides the Debug.startMethodTracing() method to create trace files that can then be used with the Traceview tool to debug and profile your application. There are actually four variants of the Debug.startMethodTracing() method:

- startMethodTracing()

- startMethodTracing(String traceName)

- startMethodTracing(String traceName, int bufferSize)

- startMethodTracing(String traceName, int bufferSize, int flags)

The traceName parameter specifies the name of the file to write the trace information into. (If the file already exists it will be truncated.) You need to make sure your application has write access to this file. (By default, the file will be created in the sdcard directory unless an absolute path is given.) The bufferSize parameter specifies the maximum size of the trace file. Trace information can use a fair amount of space and your storage capacity may be limited so try to use a sensible value (default is 8MB). Android currently defines only one flag, Debug.TRACE_COUNT_ALLOCS, so the flags parameter should be set to either 0 or Debug.TRACE_COUNT_ALLOCS (to add the results from Debug.startAllocCounting() to the trace, that is, the number and aggregate size of memory allocations). Android also provides the Debug.stopMethodTracing() method, which, you would have guessed, stops the method tracing. The usage is very similar to time measurements seen earlier, as shown in Listing 6–5.

Listing 6–5. *Enabling Tracing*

```
Debug.startMethodTracing("/sdcard/awesometrace.trace");

// perform operation you want to trace here
BigInteger fN = Fibonacci.computeRecursivelyWithCache(100000);

Debug.stopMethodTracing();

    // now there should be a file named awesometrace.trace in /mnt/sdcard, get it in
Eclipse DDMS
```

The trace file will be saved onto your Android device (or the emulator), so you will need to copy the file from the device to your host machine, for example in Eclipse (using DDMS) or with the "adb pull" command.

Using the Traceview Tool

The Android SDK comes with a tool named Traceview, which can use these trace files and give you a graphical representation of the trace, as shown in Figure 6–1. You can find the Traceview tool in the SDK's tools directory and simply type **traceview awesometrace.trace** on a command line to start Traceview.

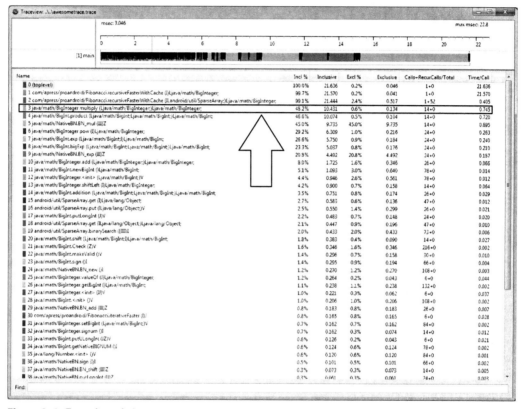

Figure 6–1. *Traceview window*

The trace basically contains the list of all the function calls together with how much time these calls took and how many were made. Seven columns are displayed:

- Name: the name of the method

- Incl %: the percentage of time spent in that method (including children methods)

- Inclusive: the time in milliseconds spent in that method (including children methods)

- Excl %: the percentage of time spent in that method (excluding children methods)

- Exclusive: the time in milliseconds spent in that method (excluding children methods)
- Calls+RecurCalls/Total: the number of calls and recursive calls
- Time/Call: the average time per call in milliseconds

For example, a total of 14 calls to `BigInteger.multiply()` were made for a total of 10.431 milliseconds, or 745 microseconds per call. Because the VM will run more slowly when tracing is enabled, you should not consider the time values as definitive numbers. Instead, use these time values simply to determine which method or run is faster.

If you click on a method name, Traceview will show you more detailed information for that specific method, as shown in Figure 6–2. This includes:

- Parents (the methods calling this method)
- Children (the methods called by this method)
- Parents while recursive (if method is recursive)
- Children while recursive (if method is recursive)

As you can see in Figure 6–2, most of the time is spent on four methods:

- BigInteger.multiply()
- BigInteger.pow()
- BigInteger.add()
- BigInteger.shiftLeft()

Even though we established where the bottlenecks were in Chapter 1 already, Traceview allows you to very quickly determine where they can be without having to perform any expansive research. In this particular case, you can quickly see that `BigInteger.multiply()` is where most of the time is spent, followed by `BigInteger.pow()`. This is not surprising as multiplications are intuitively more complicated than additions and shifts done by `BigInteger.add()` and `BigInteger.shiftLeft()`.

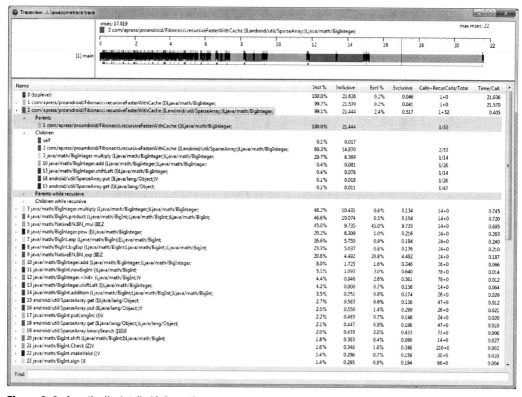

Figure 6–2. *A method's detailed information*

At the top of the window, you can see the timeline for the main thread. You can zoom in by selecting a certain region in this timeline, and zoom out by double-clicking on the time scale. Familiarize yourself with the Traceview tool and learn how to navigate from one method to another. Hint: it's easy. Just click on a method's name!

Because the Just-In-Time compiler is disabled when tracing is enabled, the results you get can be somewhat misleading. In fact, you may think a method takes a certain time when in reality it can be much faster since it can be compiled into native code by the Dalvik Just-In-Time compiler. Also, the trace won't show you how much time is spent in native functions. For example, Figure 6–1 shows calls to `NativeBN.BN_mul()` and `NativeBN.BN_exp()`, but if you click on these methods, you won't see what other methods they may call.

Traceview in DDMS

Another way to trace calls and use Traceview is to generate a trace file directly from the Eclipse DDMS perspective. After you select a specific process, you can click on the Start Method Profiling icon, and then click again to stop profiling. Once you stop profiling, the trace will be visible in the Debug perspective in Eclipse and it will be like using Traceview. Figure 6–3 shows how to start method profiling from the DDMS perspective, and Figure 6–4 shows you the method profiling view in the Debug perspective.

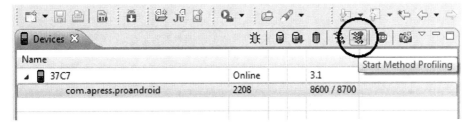

Figure 6–3. *Starting method profiling from the DDMS perspective*

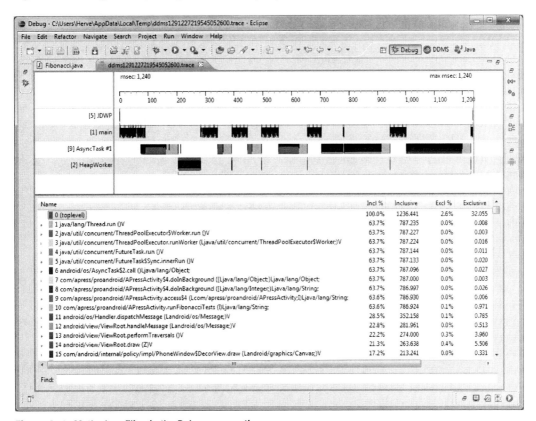

Figure 6–4. *Method profiling in the Debug perspective*

As you can see in Figure 6–4, timelines for multiple threads can be shown.

Traceview is not perfect, however it can give you great insight into what code is actually executed and where the bottlenecks may be. When it is time to achieve better performance, this should be one of your preferred tools to detect where you should focus your attention.

> **TIP:** Remember to delete the trace files when you are done with your debugging and profiling. You can use the Eclipse DDMS perspective to delete files from your device.

Native Tracing

In addition to profiling Java methods with the `startMethodTracing()` APIs, Android also supports native tracing (including kernel code). Native tracing is also referred to as QEMU tracing. In this section you learn how to generate the QEMU trace files and how to convert them into a file Traceview can interpret..

To generate QEMU traces, you have to do two things:

- Start the emulator using the `-trace` option (for example, "emulator –trace mytrace –avd myavd").

- Start and then stop native tracing, either by calling `Debug.startNativeTracing()` and `Debug.stopNativeTracing()`, or by pressing the F9 key (the first time will start tracing, the second time will stop tracing).

In the AVD's traces directory on your host machine, you will then find a `mytrace` directory containing several QEMU emulator trace files:

- qtrace.bb

- qtrace.exc

- qtrace.insn

- qtrace.method

- qtrace.pid

- qtrace.static

> **NOTE:** QEMU is an open-source emulator. Refer to `http://wiki.qemu.org` for more information.

Generating Trace File For Traceview

To use the traces in Traceview like we did for Java methods, you need to generate a trace file that Traceview can understand. To do this, you will use the `tracedmdump` command (not to be confused with the dmtracedump SDK tool, which is a tool used to create the call stack as a tree diagram). The `tracedmdump` command is defined in the Android source code, in `build/envsetup.sh`. For access to this command, you have to download the Android source code and compile Android.

CHAPTER 6: Benchmarking And Profiling   173

To download the full Android code, follow the instructions on:

`http://source.android.com/source/downloading.html`.

To compile Android, follow the instructions on

`http://source.android.com/source/building.html`

You can also compile your own emulator from the Android source code instead of relying on the one from the SDK. Once Android is compiled, you should have all the tools you need to create the trace file Traceview needs.

In the AVD's traces directory, you can now simply run `tracedmdump mytrace`, which will create a trace file you can open with Traceview, as shown in Figure 6–5. Make sure your path is set so that all the commands executed by `tracedmdump` can succeed. If `tracedmdump` fails with a "command not found" error message, it is likely your path is not set properly. For example, `tracedmdump` will call `post_trace`, which is located in the `out/host/linux-x86/bin` directory.

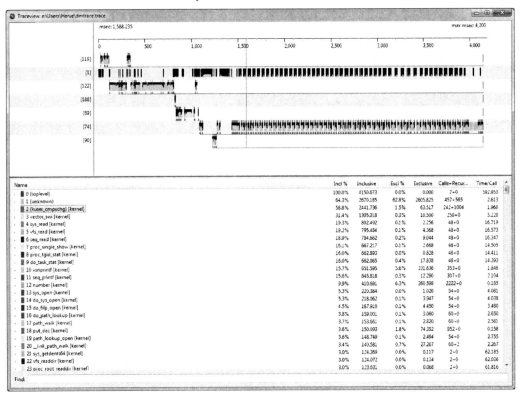

Figure 6–5. *Native tracing with Traceview*

While the user interface stays the same, what you actually see in Figure 6–5 is the list of native functions being called, such as `vsnprintf()` and `sys_open()`, respectively #10 and #13.

Two files representing the same data are actually created by `tracedmdump`:

- dmtrace
- dmtrace.html

The first file is to be used with Traceview while the second can be opened with any web browser, including Lynx.

> **NOTE:** Many users report problems when using `tracedmdump`, and error messages are not always very clear. If you encounter an error, search for a solution on the Internet as it is very likely someone had the same problem and published a solution.

Sometimes simply having a real-time, human-readable description of what is happening in your application can help you tremendously. Logging messages have been used for a very long time before sophisticated debugging tools were invented, and many developers will heavily rely on logs to debug or profile applications.

Logging

As we have seen in many listings already, you can use the `Log` class to print out messages to LogCat. In addition to the Java traditional logging mechanism such as `System.out.println()`, Android defines six log levels, each having its own methods:

- verbose (Log.v)
- debug (Log.d)
- info (Log.i)
- warning (Log.w)
- error (Log.e)
- assert (Log.wtf)

For example, a call to `Log.v(TAG, "my message")` is equivalent to a call to `Log.println(Log.VERBOSE, TAG, "my message")`.

> **NOTE:** The `Log.wtf()` methods were introduced in API level 8, but `Log.ASSERT` exists since API level 1. If you want to use the ASSERT log level but want to guarantee compatibility with older Android devices, use `Log.println(Log.ASSERT, …)` instead of `Log.wtf(…)`.

You can then use LogCat in Eclipse (**Window ➤ Show View ➤ LogCat**) and/or in a terminal (adb `logcat`, or simply `logcat` from an adb shell) and see the messages generated while your application runs.

Since many messages may be displayed, many of them not coming from your application, you may want to create filters so you can focus on the output that is relevant to you. You can filter messages based on their tags, priority levels, and PIDs. In Eclipse, you can use the Create Filter feature, as shown in Figure 6–6.

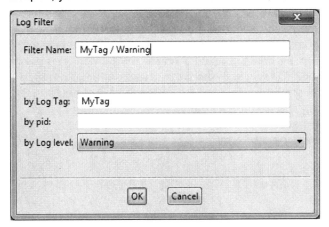

Figure 6–6. *Creating LogCat filter with Eclipse*

Eclipse currently does not support creating a filter on multiple tags, so you will have to use adb logcat instead if you want to do that. For example, to show only log messages with the tag "MyTag" at priority "Debug" or above (that is, Debug, Info, Warning, Error, and Assert), and log messages with the tag "MyOtherTag" at priority "Warning" or above, you can type:

```
adb logcat MyTag:D MyOtherTag:W *:S
```

Make sure you don't forget the *:S part since it means all other log messages will be filtered out. (S is for Silent.)

Logging functions are also available in the NDK, so you can use LogCat as well to log messages from your C/C++ code. Functions are defined in the NDK's android/log.h:

- __android_log_write
- __android_log_print
- __android_log_vprint
- __android_log_assert

For example, the equivalent of Log.i("MyTag", "Hello") would be __android_log_write(ANDROID_LOG_INFO, "MyTag", "Hello").

Because these are Android-specific routines and because their use makes your code a little too wordy, it is recommended you create a wrapper around these functions. As a matter of fact, this is exactly what the Android source code does in the cutils/log.h file by creating macros such as LOGI and LOGE, the equivalent of Log.i and Log.e, respectively. You should design your wrapper so you can easily use it in non-Android code as well.

Summary

Being able to measure performance is a simple yet critical feature in optimizations, and Android provides simple yet powerful tools to assist you. Traceview, whether it is used for Java or native tracing, is one of the most useful tools you will use, but remember that only actual measurements on a real device give you a definitive answer as Traceview disables the Dalvik Just-In-Time compiler. While considered quite trivial, these topics are important, and you should become comfortable with the various tools Android offers. You should also always check for new tools in new versions of the SDK that could improve your profiling, benchmarking, and debugging capabilities. Remember to first find where bottlenecks are before you start optimizing code as you want to focus your effort on the things that actually need to be optimized.

Chapter 7

Maximizing Battery Life

With little power comes great responsibility. Android portable devices run on batteries, and everything your application does draws a certain amount of power from the device's battery. Since most devices are charged at home during the night and will be used during the day when there is no opportunity to recharge the battery, most device owners expect the battery to last at least about 12 hours. Typical usage may cause the battery to drain more quickly: for example, charging stations were available at Google I/O as many were using their devices for periods of time longer than usual during the event.

Even though applications sometimes do not seem to be doing much, it is actually quite easy to draw so much power from the battery that the device runs out of juice in the middle of the day, leaving the user without a phone or tablet for several hours. An application that empties the battery quickly will most likely become a strong candidate for deletion, poor reviews, and possibly lower revenues. As a consequence, you as a developer should try to use as little power as possible and make sensible use of the device's battery.

In this chapter, you learn how to measure battery usage and how to make sure you can conserve power without negatively impacting the user experience, using some of the very things that make Android applications appealing: networking, access to location information, and sensors. You also learn how to work efficiently with more internal components of Android, such as broadcast receivers, alarms, and wake locks.

Batteries

Different devices have different capacities. Battery capacity for phones and tablets is often measured in mAh—that is, milliampere-hour. Table 7–1 shows the capacities of the devices mentioned in Chapter 2.

> **NOTE:** The ampere, named after André-Marie Ampère, is an SI unit of electric current and is often shortened to "amp." One ampere-hour equals 3,600

coulombs, and therefore one ampere-second equals one coulomb, and one mAh equals 3.6 coulombs. The coulomb, an SI unit named after Charles-Augustin de Coulomb, is rarely used in the descriptions of consumer products.

Table 7–1. *Capacities of Some Android Devices' Batteries*

Device	Manufacturer	Battery capacity
Blade	ZTE	1,250 mAh
LePhone	Lenovo	1,500 mAh
Nexus S	Samsung	1,500 mAh
Xoom	Motorola	6,500 mAh
Galaxy Tab (7")	Samsung	4,000 mAh
Galaxy Tab 10.1	Samsung	7,000 mAh
Revue (set-top box)	Logitech	n/a (not battery-powered)
NSZ-GT1 (Blu-ray player)	Sony	n/a (not battery-powered)

The fact that tablets use batteries with much larger capacities is a strong indicator that the screen alone consumes a lot of power. Android provides a way for the user to know approximately how much power is used by applications and system components. Figure 7–1 shows how much power was used on a Galaxy Tab 10.1 while spending most of the time using a slingshot to throw choleric feathered animals at swine.

Figure 7–1. *Battery usage*

Two items clearly stand out in this screenshot: Screen and Wi-Fi. As these two components use a lot of power, devices provide ways for end-users to configure their usage. For example, users can change the brightness of the screen (manually or automatically based on the image displayed), define after how much time without activity the screen should turn off, and also have Wi-Fi turned off whenever the screen turns off. For instance, the Wi-Fi connection may represent only a few percent of the total battery usage when it is turned off as soon as the screen turns off.

> **NOTE:** The Galaxy Tab 10.1 used here is a Wi-Fi-only version. Other items will show with different devices, for example "Cell standby" or "Voice calls."

Although users themselves can proactively manage the battery usage, this is not without its own limitations. Ultimately, how much power is used on a device is heavily dependent on what all the applications do, and therefore dependent on how you designed and implemented your application.

Typical things your applications do are:

- Executing code (Captain Obvious would not have said it better)
- Transferring data (downloading and uploading, using Wi-Fi, EDGE, 3G, 4G)
- Tracking location (using network or GPS)
- Using sensors (accelerometer, gyroscope)
- Rendering images (using GPU or CPU)
- Waking up to perform various tasks

Before we learn how to minimize the battery usage, we should have a way to measure how much power the application uses.

Measuring Battery Usage

Unfortunately, such accurate measurements require electrical equipment most developers don't have access to. However, Android provides APIs to get information about the battery usage. While there is no API such as getBatteryInfo(), it is possible to retrieve the battery information via a so-called sticky intent, that is, a broadcast intent that is always around, as shown in Listing 7–1.

Listing 7–1. *Activity Showing Battery Information*

```
import static android.os.BatteryManager.*;
// note the static keyword here (don't know what it does? Remove it and see!)

public class BatteryInfoActivity extends Activity {
    private static final String TAG = "BatteryInfo";

    private BroadcastReceiver mBatteryChangedReceiver;
    private TextView mTextView; // layout contains TextView to show battery information

    private static String healthCodeToString(int health) {
        switch (health) {
        //case BATTERY_HEALTH_COLD: return "Cold"; // API level 11 only
        case BATTERY_HEALTH_DEAD: return "Dead";
        case BATTERY_HEALTH_GOOD: return "Good";
        case BATTERY_HEALTH_OVERHEAT: return "Overheat";
        case BATTERY_HEALTH_OVER_VOLTAGE: return "Over voltage";
        case BATTERY_HEALTH_UNSPECIFIED_FAILURE: return "Unspecified failure";
        case BATTERY_HEALTH_UNKNOWN:
        default: return "Unknown";
        }
    }

    private static String pluggedCodeToString(int plugged) {
        switch (plugged) {
        case 0: return "Battery";
        case BATTERY_PLUGGED_AC: return "AC";
        case BATTERY_PLUGGED_USB: return "USB";
        default: return "Unknown";
        }
    }

    private static String statusCodeToString(int status) {
        switch (status) {
        case BATTERY_STATUS_CHARGING: return "Charging";
        case BATTERY_STATUS_DISCHARGING: return "Discharging";
        case BATTERY_STATUS_FULL: return "Full";
        case BATTERY_STATUS_NOT_CHARGING: return "Not charging";
        case BATTERY_STATUS_UNKNOWN:
        default: return "Unknown";
        }
    }
```

```java
    private void showBatteryInfo(Intent intent) {
        if (intent != null) {
            int health = intent.getIntExtra(EXTRA_HEALTH, BATTERY_HEALTH_UNKNOWN);
            String healthString = "Health: " + healthCodeToString(health);
            Log.i(TAG, healthString);

            int level = intent.getIntExtra(EXTRA_LEVEL, 0);
            int scale = intent.getIntExtra(EXTRA_SCALE, 100);
            float percentage = (scale != 0) ? (100.f * (level / (float)scale)) : 0.0f;
            String levelString = String.format("Level: %d/%d (%.2f%%)", level, scale,
percentage);
            Log.i(TAG, levelString);

            int plugged = intent.getIntExtra(EXTRA_PLUGGED, 0);
            String pluggedString = "Power source: " + pluggedCodeToString(plugged);
            Log.i(TAG, pluggedString);

            boolean present = intent.getBooleanExtra(EXTRA_PRESENT, false);
            String presentString = "Present? " + (present ? "Yes" : "No");
            Log.i(TAG, presentString);

            int status = intent.getIntExtra(EXTRA_STATUS, BATTERY_STATUS_UNKNOWN);
            String statusString = "Status: " + statusCodeToString(status);
            Log.i(TAG, statusString);

            String technology = intent.getStringExtra(EXTRA_TECHNOLOGY);
            String technologyString = "Technology: " + technology;
            Log.i(TAG, technologyString);

            int temperature = intent.getIntExtra(EXTRA_STATUS, Integer.MIN_VALUE);
            String temperatureString = "Temperature: " + temperature;
            Log.i(TAG, temperatureString);

            int voltage = intent.getIntExtra(EXTRA_VOLTAGE, Integer.MIN_VALUE);
            String voltageString = "Voltage: " + voltage;
            Log.i(TAG, voltageString);

            String s = healthString + "\n";
            s += levelString + "\n";
            s += pluggedString + "\n";
            s += presentString + "\n";
            s += statusString + "\n";
            s += technologyString + "\n";
            s += temperatureString + "\n";
            s += voltageString;
            mTextView.setText(s);

            // Note: using a StringBuilder object would have been more efficient

            int id = intent.getIntExtra(EXTRA_ICON_SMALL, 0);
            setFeatureDrawableResource(Window.FEATURE_LEFT_ICON, id);
        } else {
            String s = "No battery information";
            Log.i(TAG, s);
            mTextView.setText(s);

            setFeatureDrawable(Window.FEATURE_LEFT_ICON, null);
```

```java
        }
    }

    private void showBatteryInfo() {
        // no receiver needed
        Intent intent = registerReceiver(null, new
IntentFilter(Intent.ACTION_BATTERY_CHANGED));
        showBatteryInfo(intent);
    }

    private void createBatteryReceiver() {
        mBatteryChangedReceiver = new BroadcastReceiver() {

            @Override
            public void onReceive(Context context, Intent intent) {
                showBatteryInfo(intent);
            }
        };
    }

    /** Called when the activity is first created. */
    @Override
    public void onCreate(Bundle savedInstanceState) {
        super.onCreate(savedInstanceState);
        requestWindowFeature(Window.FEATURE_LEFT_ICON);
        setContentView(R.layout.main);

        mTextView = (TextView) findViewById(R.id.battery);

        showBatteryInfo(); // no receiver needed
    }

    @Override
    protected void onPause() {
        super.onPause();

        // unregistering the receiver when the application is not in the foreground
saves power
        unregisterReceiver(mBatteryChangedReceiver);
    }

    @Override
    protected void onResume() {
        super.onResume();
        if (mBatteryChangedReceiver == null) {
            createBatteryReceiver();
        }
        registerReceiver(mBatteryChangedReceiver,
            new IntentFilter(Intent.ACTION_BATTERY_CHANGED));
    }

    @Override
    public void onLowMemory() {
        super.onLowMemory();
        unregisterReceiver(mBatteryChangedReceiver);
        mBatteryChangedReceiver = null;
    }
}
```

As you can see, the battery information is part of the intent's extra information. This activity wants to be notified of changes therefore it registers a broadcast receiver in onResume(). However, since the sole purpose of the notification is to update the user interface with the new battery information, the activity needs to be notified only when it is in the foreground and when the user is directly interacting with the application, and consequently it unregisters the broadcast receiver in onPause().

> **NOTE:** Another possible implementation is to move the registration and un-registration of the receiver to onStart() and onStop() respectively. To achieve greater power savings, it is usually better to register and unregister broadcast receivers in onResume() and onPause() though.

If you need to know the current battery information but do not need to be notified of changes, you can simply get the sticky intent containing the battery information without registering any broadcast receiver by calling registerReceiver() and passing null as the broadcast receiver.

To measure the battery usage, it is recommended you get the battery level when your application starts, use your application for a while, and then when the application exits once again get the battery level. While the difference between the two levels won't tell you exactly how much power your own application uses (as other applications can still be running at the same time), it should give you a good idea of your application's power usage. For example, you could determine how much time one could use your application before the battery is empty.

Disabling Broadcast Receivers

To preserve the battery, applications should avoid executing code that serves no purpose. In the example above, updating the TextView's text when the user interface is not in the foreground is of little value and will only draw power from the battery unnecessarily.

In addition to the ACTION_BATTERY_CHANGED sticky intent containing the battery information shown above, Android defines four more broadcast intents your application can use:

- ACTION_BATTERY_LOW
- ACTION_BATTERY_OKAY
- ACTION_POWER_CONNECTED
- ACTION_POWER_DISCONNECTED

While you could not receive the ACTION_BATTERY_CHANGED broadcast intent by simply declaring a receiver in your application's manifest (this receiver has to be registered explicitly with a call to registerReceiver()), these other intents allow you to register the receivers in your application's manifest file, as shown in Listing 7–2.

Listing 7–2. *Declaring Broadcast Receiver In Manifest*

```xml
<?xml version="1.0" encoding="utf-8"?>
<manifest xmlns:android="http://schemas.android.com/apk/res/android"
      package="com.apress.proandroid.ch07" android:versionCode="1"
android:versionName="1.0">
    <uses-sdk android:minSdkVersion="8" />

    <application android:icon="@drawable/icon" android:label="@string/app_name">
        <activity android:name=".BatteryInfoActivity"
                  android:label="@string/app_name">
            <intent-filter>
                <action android:name="android.intent.action.MAIN" />
                <category android:name="android.intent.category.LAUNCHER" />
            </intent-filter>
        </activity>
        <receiver android:name=".BatteryReceiver">
            <intent-filter>
                <action android:name="android.intent.action.BATTERY_LOW" />
            </intent-filter>
            <intent-filter>
                <action android:name="android.intent.action.BATTERY_OKAY" />
            </intent-filter>
            <intent-filter>
                <action android:name="android.intent.action.ACTION_POWER_CONNECTED" />
            </intent-filter>
            <intent-filter>
                <action android:name="android.intent.action.ACTION_POWER_DISCONNECTED"
/>
            </intent-filter>
        </receiver>

    </application>
</manifest>
```

A simple implementation of the broadcast receiver is shown in Listing 7–3. Here we define a single `BatteryReceiver` broadcast receiver that is responsible for handling all four actions.

Listing 7–3. `BatteryReceiver` *Implementation*

```java
public class BatteryReceiver extends BroadcastReceiver {
    private static final String TAG = "BatteryReceiver";

    @Override
    public void onReceive(Context context, Intent intent) {
        String action = intent.getAction();
        String text;

        // the four actions are processed here

        if (Intent.ACTION_BATTERY_LOW.equals(action)) {
            text = "Low power";
        } else if (Intent.ACTION_BATTERY_OKAY.equals(action)) {
            text = "Power okay (not low anymore)";
        } else if (Intent.ACTION_POWER_CONNECTED.equals(action)) {
            text = "Power now connected";
        } else if (Intent.ACTION_POWER_DISCONNECTED.equals(action)) {
```

```
        text = "Power now disconnected";
    } else {
        return;
    }

    Log.i(TAG, text);
    Toast.makeText(context, text, Toast.LENGTH_SHORT).show();
    }
}
```

As it is now, the application can be considered to have a serious flaw. As a matter of fact, the application will start (if it is not started already) whenever one of these four actions occurs. While this may be the desired behavior, in many cases you may want your application to behave differently. In this case for example, we can argue it only makes sense to show the Toast messages when the application is the foreground application, as the Toast messages would actually interfere with other applications should we always show them, therefore worsening the user experience.

When the application is not running or is in the background, let's say we want to disable these Toast messages. There are basically two ways to do this:

- We can add a flag in the application that is set to true in the activity's onResume() and set to false in onPause(), and modify the receiver's onReceive() method to check that flag.

- We can enable the broadcast receiver only when the application is the foreground application.

While the first approach would work fine, it would not prevent the application from being started whenever one of the four actions triggers. This would ultimately result in unnecessary instructions being executed, which would still draw power from the battery for what is essentially a no-op. Besides, you may have to modify that flag in multiple files should your application define several activities.

The second approach is much better as we can guarantee instructions are executed only when they serve an actual purpose, and therefore power will be drawn from the battery only for a good reason. To achieve this, there are two things we need to do in the application:

- The broadcast receiver needs to be disabled by default.

- The broadcast receiver needs to be enabled in onResume() and disabled again in onPause().

Disabling and Enabling the Broadcast Receiver

Listing 7–4 shows how to disable the broadcast receiver in the application's manifest file.

Listing 7–4. *Disabling Broadcast Receiver In Manifest*

```
...
<receiver android:name=".BatteryReceiver" android:enabled="false" >
...
```

> **NOTE:** The `<application>` element has its own enabled attribute. The broadcast receiver will be enabled when both the application and receiver attributes are set to `true`, and will be disabled when either one of them is set to `false`.

Listing 7–5 shows how to enable and disable the broadcast receiver in onResume() and onPause().

Listing 7–5. *Enabling and Disabling Broadcast Receiver*

```
public class BatteryInfoActivity extends Activity {

    ...

    private void enableBatteryReceiver(boolean enabled) {
        PackageManager pm = getPackageManager();
        ComponentName receiverName = new ComponentName(this, BatteryReceiver.class);
        int newState;

        if (enabled) {
            newState = PackageManager.COMPONENT_ENABLED_STATE_ENABLED;
        } else {
            newState = PackageManager.COMPONENT_ENABLED_STATE_DISABLED;
        }

        pm.setComponentEnabledSetting(receiverName, newState,
PackageManager.DONT_KILL_APP);
    }

    ...

    @Override
    protected void onPause() {
        super.onPause();
        unregisterReceiver(mBatteryChangedReceiver);

        enableBatteryReceiver(false); // battery receiver now disabled

        // unregistering the receivers when the application is not in the foreground
saves power
    }

    @Override
```

```
protected void onResume() {
    super.onResume();
    if (mBatteryChangedReceiver == null) {
        createBatteryReceiver();
    }
    registerReceiver(mBatteryChangedReceiver, new
        IntentFilter(Intent.ACTION_BATTERY_CHANGED));

    enableBatteryReceiver(true); // battery receiver now enabled
}

…

}
```

Enabling broadcast receivers only when they are really needed can make a big difference in power consumption. While this is an aspect that can be easily overlooked when developing an application, special attention should be given to receivers so that they are enabled only when required.

Networking

Many Android applications transfer data between the device and a server, or between devices. Like the battery state, applications may need to retrieve information about the network connections on the device. The ConnectivityManager class provides APIs applications can call to have access to the network information. Android devices often have multiple data connections available:

- Bluetooth
- Ethernet
- Wi-Fi
- WiMAX
- Mobile (EDGE, UMTS, LTE)

Listing 7–6 shows how to retrieve information about the active connection as well as all the connections.

Listing 7–6. *Network Information*

```
private void showNetworkInfoToast() {
    ConnectivityManager cm = (ConnectivityManager)
        getSystemService(Context.CONNECTIVITY_SERVICE);

    // to show only the active connection
    NetworkInfo info = cm.getActiveNetworkInfo();
    if (info != null) {
        Toast.makeText(this, "Active: " + info.toString(),
Toast.LENGTH_LONG).show();
    }

    // to show all connections
    NetworkInfo[] array = cm.getAllNetworkInfo();
```

```
            if (array != null) {
                String s = "All: ";
                for (NetworkInfo i: array) {
                    s += i.toString() + "\n";
                }
                Toast.makeText(this, s, Toast.LENGTH_LONG).show();
            }
        }
```

> **NOTE:** Your application needs the ACCESS_NETWORK_STATE permission to be able to retrieve the network information.

Since the focus is on maximizing the battery life, we need to be aware of certain things:

- Background data setting
- Data transfer rates

Background Data

Users have the ability to specify whether background data transfer is allowed or not in the settings, presumably to preserve battery life. If your application needs to perform data transfers when it is not the foreground application, it should check that flag, as shown in Listing 7–7. Services typically have to check that setting before initiating any transfer.

Listing 7–7. *Checking Background Data Setting*

```
private void transferData(byte[] array) {
    ConnectivityManager cm = (ConnectivityManager)
        getSystemService(Context.CONNECTIVITY_SERVICE);
    boolean backgroundDataSetting = cm.getBackgroundDataSetting();
    if (backgroundDataSetting) {
        // transfer data
    } else {
        // honor setting and do not transfer data
    }
}
```

Because this is a voluntary check, your application could actually ignore that setting and transfer data anyway. However, since it would go against the wish of the user, potentially slow down foreground data transfers, and impact battery life, such behavior would likely cause your application to be uninstalled by the user eventually.

To be notified when the background data setting changes, your application can register a broadcast receiver explicitly in the Java code using the ConnectivityManager.ACTION_BACKGROUND_DATA_SETTING_CHANGED string to build the intent filter or android.net.conn.BACKGROUND_DATA_SETTING_CHANGED in the application's manifest file. Because this setting is to control background data transfer, it actually makes more sense to disable this broadcast receiver in onResume() and enable it again in onPause().

> **NOTE:** The getBackgroundDataSetting() method is deprecated in Android 4.0 and will always return true. Instead, the network will appear disconnected when background data transfer is not available.

Data Transfer

Transfer rates can vary wildly, typically from less than 100 kilobits per second on a GPRS data connection to several megabits per second on an LTE or Wi-Fi connection. In addition to the connection type, the NetworkInfo class specifies the subtype of a connection. This is particularly important when the connection type is TYPE_MOBILE. Android defines the following connection subtypes (in the TelephonyManager class):

- NETWORK_TYPE_GPRS   (API level 1)
- NETWORK_TYPE_EDGE   (API level 1)
- NETWORK_TYPE_UMTS   (API level 1)
- NETWORK_TYPE_CDMA   (API level 4)
- NETWORK_TYPE_EVDO_0   (API level 4)
- NETWORK_TYPE_EVDO_A   (API level 4)
- NETWORK_TYPE_1xRTT   (API level 4)
- NETWORK_TYPE_HSDPA   (API level 5)
- NETWORK_TYPE_HSUPA   (API level 5)
- NETWORK_TYPE_HSPA   (API level 5)
- NETWORK_TYPE_IDEN   (API level 8)
- NETWORK_TYPE_EVDO_B   (API level 9)
- NETWORK_TYPE_LTE   (API level 11)
- NETWORK_TYPE_EHRPD   (API level 11)
- NETWORK_TYPE_HSPAP   (API level 13)

Subtypes are added as new technologies are created and deployed. For example, the LTE subtype was added in API level 11, whereas the HSPAP subtype was added in API level 13. If your code depends on these values, make sure you handle the case where your application is presented with a new value it does not know about; otherwise it could result in your application not being able to transfer data. You should update your code when new subtypes are defined, so pay attention to each release of the Android SDK. A list of differences is available on http://d.android.com/sdk/api_diff/13/changes.html, for example.

Intuitively, your application should prefer faster connections. Even if the 3G radio chip consumes less power than the Wi-Fi radio chip, the Wi-Fi transfer rate may ultimately mean the Wi-Fi transfer reduces power consumption as the transfer can be completed in a shorter time.

> **NOTE:** Since data plans now typically allow for a limited amount of data to be transferred (for example, $30 for 2GB a month), Wi-Fi connections are usually preferred. Also, your application can use NetworkInfo.isRoaming() to know if the device is currently roaming on the given network. Since this can incur additional cost, you should avoid transferring data when isRoaming() returns true.

Table 7–2 shows the memory consumption of various components on the T-Mobile G1 phone (also known as the HTC Dream, or Era G1). While the phone is somewhat old now (it was released in late 2008), the numbers still give a pretty good overview of how much power each component draws.

Table 7–2. *Android G1Phone Power Consumption (source: Google I/O 2009)*

Component	Power consumption
Idle, airplane mode (radios turned off)	2 mA
Idle, 3G radio on	5 mA
Idle, EDGE radio on	5 mA
Idle, Wi-Fi radio on	12 mA
Display (LCD)	90 mA (min brightness: 70 mA; max brightness: 110 mA)
CPU (100% load)	110 mA
Sensors	80 mA
GPS	85 mA
3G (max transfer)	150 mA
EDGE (max transfer)	250 mA
Wi-Fi (max transfer)	275 mA

While the exact numbers vary between devices, it is important to know roughly how much power your application would use. Since the G1 had a 1,150 mAh battery, an application that downloads and plays videos (for example, YouTube) would empty the battery in about three hours assuming it uses a 3G connection: 150mA for 3G, 90 mA for

CPU, and 90mA for LCD would total 330 mA, or three and a half hours of usage (assuming nothing else runs on the phone).

If you have control over what kind of data gets transferred, then you should consider compressing the data before it is sent to the device. While the CPU will have to decompress the data before it can be used (and therefore more power will be needed for that purpose), the transfer will be faster and the radios (for example, 3G, Wi-Fi) can be turned off again faster, preserving battery life. The things to consider are:

- Compress text data using GZIP and use the GZIPInputStream to access the data.
- Use JPEG instead of PNG if possible.
- Use assets that match the resolution of the device (for example, there is no need to download a 1920x1080 picture if it is going to be resized to 96x54).

The slower the connection (for example, EDGE) the more important compression is, as you want to reduce the time the radios are turned on.

Since Android is running on more and more devices, from cell phones to tablets, from set-top boxes to netbooks, generating assets for all these devices can become tedious. However, using the right assets can greatly improve the battery life and therefore make your application more desirable. In addition to saving power, faster downloads and uploads will make your application more responsive.

Location

Any real estate agent will tell you the three most important things are location, location, location. Android understands that and lets your application know where the device is. (It won't tell you if the device is in a good school district, although I am pretty sure there is an application for that.) Listing 7–8 shows how to request location updates using the system location services.

Listing 7–8. *Receiving Location Updates*

```
private void requestLocationUpdates() {
    LocationManager lm = (LocationManager)
getSystemService(Context.LOCATION_SERVICE);

    List<String> providers = lm.getAllProviders();

    if (providers != null && ! providers.isEmpty()) {
        LocationListener listener = new LocationListener() {

            @Override
            public void onLocationChanged(Location location) {
                Log.i(TAG, location.toString());
            }

            @Override
            public void onProviderDisabled(String provider) {
```

```
                       Log.i(TAG, provider + " location provider disabled");
                   }

                   @Override
                   public void onProviderEnabled(String provider) {
                       Log.i(TAG, provider + " location provider enabled");
                   }

                   @Override
                   public void onStatusChanged(String provider, int status, Bundle extras)
{
                       Log.i(TAG, provider + " location provider status changed to " +
status);
                   }
               };

               for (String name : providers) {
                   Log.i(TAG, "Requesting location updates on " + name);
                   lm.requestLocationUpdates(name, 0, 0, listener);
               }
           }
       }
```

> **NOTE:** Your application needs either the ACCESS_COARSE_LOCATION permission or the
> ACCESS_FINE_LOCATION permission to be able to retrieve the location information. The GPS
> location provider requires the ACCESS_FINE_LOCATION permission while the network provider
> requires either ACCESS_COARSE_LOCATION or ACCESS_FINE_LOCATION.

This piece of code has serious flaws, but you should still run it, for example in your application's onCreate() method, in order to see the impact this code has on the battery life.

On a Galaxy Tab 10.1, one can observe the following:

- Three location providers are available (network, gps, and passive).

- GPS location updates are very frequent (one update per second).

- Network location updates are not as frequent (one update every 45 seconds).

If you let your application with this piece of code run for a while, you should see the battery level going down faster than usual. This code's three main flaws are:

- Location listeners are not unregistered.

- Location updates are most likely too frequent.

- Location updates are requested on multiple providers.

Luckily, all these flaws can easily be fixed. Ultimately though, how you need to use the location services depends on what your application needs to do so there is no one single solution for all applications, so what is considered a flaw in one application may be a feature in another. Also note that there is typically not one single solution for all users: you should consider the needs of your users as well and offer different settings in your application to cater for your end-users. For example, some users may be willing to sacrifice battery life to get more frequent location updates while others would rather limit the number of updates to make sure their device does not need to be charged during their lunch break.

Unregistering a Listener

In order to unregister a listener, you can simply call removeUpdates() as showed in Listing 7–9. It is usually good to do that in onPause() like for broadcast receivers but your application many need to do that elsewhere. Listening for location updates for a long period of time will consume a lot of power so your application should try to get the information it needs and then stop listening for updates. In some cases it can be a good idea to offer a way for the user to force a location fix.

Listing 7–9. *Disabling Location Listener*

```
private void disableLocationListener(LocationListener listener) {
    LocationManager lm = (LocationManager)
getSystemService(Context.LOCATION_SERVICE);
    lm.removeUpdates(listener);
}
```

The frequency of the updates can be adjusted when calling requestLocationUpdates().

Frequency of Updates

Even though the LocationManager class defines five requestLocationUpdates() methods, all have two parameters in common: minTime and minDistance. The first one, minTime, specifies the time interval for notifications in milliseconds. This is used only as a hint for the system to save power and the actual time between updates may be greater (or less) than specified. Obviously, greater values will result in greater power savings. The second one, minDistance, specifies the minimum distance interval for notifications. Greater values can still result in power savings as fewer instructions would be executed if your application is not notified of all location updates. Listing 7–10 shows how to register for updates with one hour between updates and a 100-meter threshold.

Listing 7–10. *Receiving Location Updates Not As Frequently*

```
private void requestLocationUpdates() {
    LocationManager lm = (LocationManager)
getSystemService(Context.LOCATION_SERVICE);

    List<String> providers = lm.getAllProviders();

    if (providers != null) {
        for (String name : providers) {
            LocationListener listener = new LocationListener() {
                ...
            };
```

```
                    Log.i(TAG, "Requesting location updates on " + name);
                    lm.requestLocationUpdates(name, DateUtils.HOUR_IN_MILLIS * 1, 100,
listener);
            }
        }
    }
```

Choosing the right interval is more art than science and once again depends on your application. A navigation application would typically require frequent updates, but if the same navigation application can be used by hikers, for example, updates could be less frequent. Moreover, you may have to trade accuracy for power in some cases. Give your users the choice and offer settings that can be adjusted to let them choose the best behavior for themselves.

Multiple Providers

As mentioned earlier, Android defines multiple location providers:

- GPS (Global Positioning System using satellites)
- Network (using Cell-ID and Wi-Fi locations)
- Passive (since API level 8)

The GPS location provider (LocationManager.GPS_PROVIDER) is typically the most accurate one, with a horizontal accuracy of about 10 meters (11 yards). The network location provider is not as accurate as the GPS, and the accuracy will depend on how many locations the system can use to compute the device's location. For example, my own logs show an accuracy of 48 meters for locations coming from the network location provider, or the width of a football field.

While more accurate, GPS locations are expensive in terms of time and battery usage. Getting a "fix" from the GPS location provider requires locking the signals from multiple satellites, which can take from a few seconds in an open field to an infinite amount of time if the device is indoors and signal cannot be locked (like in a parking garage when your car's GPS tries to acquire satellites). For example, it took about 35 seconds to get the first location update after GPS was enabled while inside the house, but only 5 seconds when the same test was repeated outside. When using the network location provider, it took 5 seconds to get the first location update, inside and outside. An Assisted GPS (AGPS) would typically provide faster locations fixes, but actual times would depend on information already cached by the device and the network access.

> **NOTE:** The Galaxy Tab 10.1 used for these measurements is Wi-Fi only. Faster location fixes would be achieved by the network provider if cell ids were also used.

Even though receiving updates from multiple providers was listed as a flow earlier, it may not always be one. As a matter of fact, you may want to receive updates from several providers for a while in order to get a more accurate location fix.

The passive location provider is the one that can preserve the battery the most. When your application uses the passive location provider, it says it is interested in location updates but won't be proactively requesting location fixes. In other words, your application will simply wait for other applications, services, or system components to request location updates and will be notified together with these other listeners. Listing 7–11 shows how to receive passive location updates. To test whether your application receives updates, open another application that makes use of the location services, such as Maps.

Listing 7–11. *Receiving Passive Location Updates*

```java
    private void requestPassiveLocationUpdates() {
        LocationManager lm = (LocationManager)
getSystemService(Context.LOCATION_SERVICE);
        LocationListener listener = new LocationListener() {

            @Override
            public void onLocationChanged(Location location) {
                Log.i(TAG, "[PASSIVE] " + location.toString());

                // let's say you only care about GPS location updates

                if (LocationManager.GPS_PROVIDER.equals(location.getProvider())) {

                    // if you care about accuracy, make sure you call hasAccuracy()
                    // (same comment for altitude and bearing)

                    if (location.hasAccuracy() && (location.getAccuracy() < 10.0f)) {
                        // do something here
                    }
                }
            }

            @Override
            public void onProviderDisabled(String provider) {
                Log.i(TAG, "[PASSIVE] " + provider + " location provider disabled");
            }

            @Override
            public void onProviderEnabled(String provider) {
                Log.i(TAG, "[PASSIVE] " + provider + " location provider enabled");
            }

            @Override
            public void onStatusChanged(String provider, int status, Bundle extras) {
                Log.i(TAG, "[PASSIVE] " + provider + " location provider status changed
to " + status);
            }
        };

        Log.i(TAG, "Requesting passive location updates");
        lm.requestLocationUpdates(LocationManager.PASSIVE_PROVIDER,
            DateUtils.SECOND_IN_MILLIS * 30, 100, listener);
    }
```

If you use that code and disable or enable Wi-Fi or GPS, you will notice the passive listener does not get notified when a provider is disabled or enabled, or when a provider's status changes. While this is usually not important, this may force your application to use the other location providers should it really care about being notified of these changes.

A good trade-off is to register a listener with the network location provider, which uses less power than the GPS provider, while also registering a listener with the passive location provider in order to get possibly more accurate location information from the GPS.

> **NOTE:** Your application will need the `ACCESS_FINE_LOCATION` to use the passive location provider even if it only receives location updates from the network provider. This may end up being a problem if you believe this may raise privacy concerns with your users. There is currently no way to receive passive updates only from the network location provider and only ask for the `ACCESS_COARSE_LOCATION` permission.

Filtering Providers

Since our focus is on battery life, your application may want to filter out location providers with a high power requirement if using a passive location provider is not an option. Listing 7–12 shows how you can get the power requirement of all the location providers.

Listing 7–12. *Location Providers Power Requirement*

```
private static String powerRequirementCodeToString(int powerRequirement) {
    switch (powerRequirement) {
    case Criteria.POWER_LOW: return "Low";
    case Criteria.POWER_MEDIUM: return "Medium";
    case Criteria.POWER_HIGH: return "High";
    default: return String.format("Unknown (%d)", powerRequirement);
    }
}

private void showLocationProvidersPowerRequirement() {
    LocationManager lm = (LocationManager)
getSystemService(Context.LOCATION_SERVICE);

    List<String> providers = lm.getAllProviders();

    if (providers != null) {
        for (String name : providers) {
            LocationProvider provider = lm.getProvider(name);
            if (provider != null) {
                int powerRequirement = provider.getPowerRequirement();
                Log.i(TAG, name + " location provider power requirement: " +
                    powerRequirementCodeToString(powerRequirement));
            }
        }
    }
}
```

> **NOTE:** As one would expect, the power requirement of the passive location provider is unknown.

However, since your application may have very specific needs, it may be easier to first specify as precisely as possible what location provider you are looking for. For example, your application may want to use a location provider that reports speed information in addition to coordinates. Listing 7–13 shows how you can create a Criteria object and find out which location provider you should be using.

Listing 7–13. *Using Criteria to Find Location Provider*

```
    private LocationProvider getMyLocationProvider() {
        LocationManager lm = (LocationManager)
getSystemService(Context.LOCATION_SERVICE);
        Criteria criteria = new Criteria();
        LocationProvider provider = null;

        // define your criteria here
        criteria.setAccuracy(Criteria.ACCURACY_COARSE);
        criteria.setAltitudeRequired(true);
        criteria.setBearingAccuracy(Criteria.NO_REQUIREMENT); // API level 9
        criteria.setBearingRequired(false);
        criteria.setCostAllowed(true); // most likely you want the user to be able to
set that
        criteria.setHorizontalAccuracy(Criteria.ACCURACY_LOW); // API level 9
        criteria.setPowerRequirement(Criteria.POWER_LOW);
        criteria.setSpeedAccuracy(Criteria.ACCURACY_MEDIUM); // API level 9
        criteria.setSpeedRequired(false);
        criteria.setVerticalAccuracy(Criteria.NO_REQUIREMENT); // API level 9

        List<String> names = lm.getProviders(criteria, false); // perfect matches only

        if ((names != null) && ! names.isEmpty()) {
            for (String name : names) {
                provider = lm.getProvider(name);
                Log.d(TAG, "[getMyLocationProvider] " + provider.getName() + " " +
provider);
            }
            provider = lm.getProvider(names.get(0));
        } else {
            Log.d(TAG, "Could not find perfect match for location provider");

            String name = lm.getBestProvider(criteria, false); // not necessarily
perfect match

            if (name != null) {
                provider = lm.getProvider(name);
                Log.d(TAG, "[getMyLocationProvider] " + provider.getName() + " " +
provider);
            }
        }

        return provider;
    }
```

LocationManager.getProviders() and LocationManager.getBestProvider() differ quite significantly. While getProviders() will only return perfect matches, getBestProvider() will first search for a perfect match but may return a location provider that does not meet the criteria if no provider was a perfect match. The criteria are loosened in the following sequence:

- Power requirement
- Accuracy
- Bearing
- Speed
- Altitude

Since this order may not necessarily be the policy you want to adopt to find a location provider, you may have to develop your own algorithm to find the right provider for your needs. Also, the algorithm may depend on the current battery status: your application may not be willing to loosen the power requirement criterion if the battery is low.

Last Known Location

Before you decide to register a location listener with a location provider, you may first want to check if a location is already known (and was cached by the system). The LocationManager class defines the getLastKnownLocation() method, which returns the last known location for a given provider, or null if no known location exists. While this location may be out of date, it is often a good starting point since this location can be retrieved instantly and calling this method won't start the provider. Even applications that register a location listener usually first retrieve the last known location in order to be more responsive as it typically takes a few seconds before any location update is received. Listing 7–14 shows how a last known location can be retrieved.

Listing 7–14. *Last Known Location*

```
    private Location getLastKnownLocation() {
        LocationManager lm = (LocationManager)
getSystemService(Context.LOCATION_SERVICE);
        List<String> names = lm.getAllProviders();
        Location location = null;

        if (names != null) {
            for (String name : names) {
                if (! LocationManager.PASSIVE_PROVIDER.equals(name)) {

                    Location l = lm.getLastKnownLocation(name);

                    if ((l != null) && (location == null || l.getTime() >
location.getTime())) {
                        location = l;

                        /*
                         * Warning: GPS and network providers' clocks may be out of sync
so comparing the times
```

```
                              * may not be such a good idea... We may not get the most recent
location fix after all.
                              */
                      }
                  }
              }
          }

          return location;
      }
```

While a GPS is sensitive to satellite signals, most Android devices come with other types of sensors that can make Android applications more interesting than what you would typically find on a traditional computer.

Sensors

Sensors are fun. Everybody likes them and everybody wants to use them. The way to use sensors is very similar to the way to use location providers: your application registers a sensor listener with a specific sensor and is notified of updates. Listing 7–15 shows how you can register a listener with the device's accelerometer.

Listing 7–15. *Registering Sensor Listener With Accelerometer*

```java
private void registerWithAccelerometer() {
    SensorManager sm = (SensorManager) getSystemService(Context.SENSOR_SERVICE);

    List<Sensor> sensors = sm.getSensorList(Sensor.TYPE_ACCELEROMETER);

    if (sensors != null && ! sensors.isEmpty()) {
        SensorEventListener listener = new SensorEventListener() {

            @Override
            public void onAccuracyChanged(Sensor sensor, int accuracy) {
                Log.i(TAG, "Accuracy changed to " + accuracy);
            }

            @Override
            public void onSensorChanged(SensorEvent event) {
                /*
                 * Accelerometer: array of 3 values
                 *
                 * event.values[0] = acceleration minus Gx on the x-axis
                 * event.values[1] = acceleration minus Gy on the y-axis
                 * event.values[2] = acceleration minus Gz on the z-axis
                 */

                Log.i(TAG, String.format("x:%.2f y:%.2f z:%.2f ",
                    event.values[0], event.values[1], event.values[2]));

                // do something interesting here
            }
        };

        // we simply pick the first one
```

```
        Sensor sensor = sensors.get(0);
        Log.d(TAG, "Using sensor " + sensor.getName() + " from " +
sensor.getVendor());

        sm.registerListener(listener, sensor, SensorManager.SENSOR_DELAY_NORMAL);
    }
}
```

In the same manner we could specify how often we wanted location updates, Android lets applications specify how often they want to receive sensor updates. While we used milliseconds with the location providers, we have to use one of four possible values to specify how often we want to receive sensor updates:

- SENSOR_DELAY_NORMAL

- SENSOR_DELAY_UI

- SENSOR_DELAY_GAME

- SENSOR_DELAY_FASTEST

On a Galaxy Tab 10.1 (using an MPL accelerometer from Invensense), the accelerometer's NORMAL, UI, GAME, and FASTEST delays are about 180, 60, 20, and 10 milliseconds respectively. While these numbers vary depending on devices, faster updates will require more power. For example, on the Android G1 phone, using the NORMAL delay draws 10 mA from the battery while using the FASTEST delay draws 90 mA (15 mA for UI and 80 mA for GAME).

Like for location providers, reducing the frequency of the notification is the best way to preserve battery life. Since every device is different, your application can measure the frequency of the notifications for each of the four delays and choose the one that gives the best user experience while still conserving power. Another strategy, which may not apply to all applications, is to use the NORMAL or UI delay when you detect that the values don't seem to change that much, and switch to a GAME or FASTEST delay when you detect sudden variations. Such strategy may give acceptable results for some applications and would result in a longer battery life.

Like other listeners, the sensor listeners should be disabled whenever notifications are not needed. For this purpose, use the SensorManager's unregisterListener() methods.

Graphics

Applications can spend a lot of time drawing things on the screen. Whether it is a 3D game using the GPU or simply a Calendar application using the CPU for most of its rendering, the idea is to do as little work as possible while still getting the desired results on the screen in order to preserve battery life.

As we saw earlier, the CPU uses less power when it is not running at full speed. Modern CPUs use dynamic frequency scaling and dynamic voltage scaling to conserve power or reduce heat. Such techniques are usually used together and referred to as DVFS

(Dynamic Voltage and Frequency Scaling) and the Linux kernel, Android, and modern processors support such techniques.

Similarly, modern GPUs are able to turn off internal components, from a whole core to an individual pipeline, even between the renderings of two frames.

While you have no direct control over things like voltage, frequency, or what hardware module gets powered off, you do have direct control over what your application renders. While achieving a good frame rate is usually the first priority for most applications, reducing the power consumption should not be forgotten. Even though the frame rate on Android devices is usually capped (for example, at 60 frames per second), optimizing your rendering routines can still be beneficial even if your application has already reached the maximum frame rate. In addition to possibly reducing power consumption, you may also leave more room for other background applications to run, providing a better overall user experience.

For example, a typical pitfall is to ignore the call to onVisibilityChanged() in a live wallpaper. The fact that the wallpaper can be invisible can easily be overlooked, and perpetually drawing the wallpaper can use a lot of power.

For tips on how to optimize rendering, refer to Chapter 8.

Alarms

Your application may for some reason need to wake up every now and then to perform some operation. A typical example would be an RSS reader application that wakes up every 30 minutes to download RSS feeds so that the user always has an updated view of the feed when the application is started, or a stalker application that sends a message to one of your contacts every 5 minutes. Listing 7–16 shows how an alarm can be created to wake up the application and start a service that simply prints out a message and terminates. Listing 7–17 shows the implementation of the service.

Listing 7–16. *Setting Up An Alarm*

```
    private void setupAlarm(boolean cancel) {
        AlarmManager am = (AlarmManager) getSystemService(Context.ALARM_SERVICE);

        Intent intent = new Intent(this, MyService.class);

        PendingIntent pendingIntent = PendingIntent.getService(this, 0, intent, 0);

        if (cancel) {
            am.cancel(pendingIntent); // will cancel all alarms whose intent matches
this one
        } else {
            long interval = DateUtils.HOUR_IN_MILLIS * 1;
            long firstInterval = DateUtils.MINUTE_IN_MILLIS * 30;

            am.setRepeating(AlarmManager.RTC_WAKEUP, firstInterval, interval,
pendingIntent);
            // use am.set(…) to schedule a non-repeating alarm
        }
    }
```

Listing 7–17. *Service Implementation*

```
public class MyService extends Service {
    private static final String TAG = "MyService";

    @Override
    public IBinder onBind(Intent intent) {
        // we return null as client cannot bind to the service
        return null;
    }

    @Override
    public void onStart(Intent intent, int startId) {
        super.onStart(intent, startId);

        Log.i(TAG, "Alarm went off - Service was started");

        stopSelf(); // remember to call stopSelf() when done to free resources
    }
}
```

As seen with the sensor event listeners, a single value can make a big difference as far as power consumption is concerned. Here this value is `AlarmManager.RTC_WAKEUP`. Android defines four types of alarms:

- ELAPSED_TIME
- ELAPSED_TIME_WAKEUP
- RTC
- RTC_WAKEUP

The `RTC` and `ELAPSED_TIME` types differ only in the way the time is represented, in milliseconds since the Unix epoch for both RTC types (`RTC` and `RTC_WAKEUP`) vs. in milliseconds since boot time for both `ELAPSED_TIME` types (`ELAPSED_TIME` and `ELAPSED_TIME_WAKEUP`).

The key here is in the `_WAKEUP` suffix. An `RTC` or `ELAPSED_TIME` alarm that goes off when the device is asleep won't be delivered until the next time the device wakes up, whereas an `RTC_WAKEUP` or `ELAPSED_TIME_WAKEUP` alarm will wake up the device when it goes off. Obviously, waking up the device continuously can have a dramatic impact on power consumption even if the application that is woken up does not do anything:

- The device will wake up to start your own application.
- Other (well-behaved) alarms that were waiting for the device to wake up will be delivered.

As you can see, this can trigger a chain reaction. Even when the other alarms are the ones consuming more power, for example because they end up transferring data over a 3G connection, your application is the one that triggered everything.

Few applications really need to forcibly wake up the device when an alarm goes off. Of course an application such as an alarm clock would need such capability, but it is often preferred to simply wait for the device to wake up (most commonly following a user interaction with the device) before doing any work. As with the location provider, following a passive approach can lead to a longer battery life.

Scheduling Alarms

More often than not, applications need to schedule alarms that go off at some point in the future, without any strict requirement of when exactly they should go off. For that purpose, Android defines the `AlarmManager.setInexactRepeating()`, which takes the same parameters as its sibling `setRepeating()`. The main difference is in the way the system schedules the time the alarm will actually go off: Android can adjust the actual trigger time to fire multiple alarms (possibly from multiple applications) simultaneously. Such alarms are more power-efficient as the system will avoid waking up the device more often than necessary. Android defines five intervals for these alarms:

- INTERVAL_FIFTEEN_MINUTES

- INTERVAL_HALF_HOUR

- INTERVAL_HOUR

- INTERVAL_HALF_DAY

- INTERVAL_DAY

While these values are defined as the number of milliseconds they represent (for example, INTERVAL_HOUR equals 3,600,000), they are the only intervals `setInexactRepeating()` understands to create "inexact alarms." Passing any other value to `setInexactRepeating` will be equivalent to calling setRepeating(). Listing 7–18 shows how to use inexact alarms.

Listing 7–18. *Setting Up An Inexact Alarm*

```
    private void setupInexactAlarm(boolean cancel) {
        AlarmManager am = (AlarmManager) getSystemService(Context.ALARM_SERVICE);

        Intent intent = new Intent(this, MyService.class);

        PendingIntent pendingIntent = PendingIntent.getService(this, 0, intent, 0);

        if (cancel) {
            am.cancel(pendingIntent); // will cancel all alarms whose intent matches
this one
        } else {
            long interval = AlarmManager.INTERVAL_HOUR;
            long firstInterval = DateUtils.MINUTE_IN_MILLIS * 30;

            am.setInexactRepeating(AlarmManager.RTC, firstInterval, interval,
pendingIntent);
        }
    }
```

> **TIP:** There is no `setInexact()` method. If your application needs to schedule an inexact alarm that goes off only once, call `setInexactRepeating()` and cancel the alarm after it goes off the first time.

Clearly, the best results are achieved when all applications use such alarms instead of alarms with exact trigger times. To maximize power savings, your application can also let the user configure how often alarms should go off, as some may find that longer intervals do not negatively impact their user experience.

WakeLocks

Some applications, in some cases, need to prevent the device from going to sleep to maintain a good user experience even if the user is not interacting with the device for an extended period of time. The simplest example, and probably the most relevant, is when a user is watching a video or movie on the device. In such a case, the CPU needs to decode the video while the screen needs to be on for the user to be able to watch it. Also, the screen should not be dimmed while the video is playing.

The WakeLock class allows for such scenarios, as shown in Listing 7–19.

Listing 7–19. *Creating WakeLock*

```
private void runInWakeLock(Runnable runnable, int flags) {
    PowerManager pm = (PowerManager) getSystemService(Context.POWER_SERVICE);

    PowerManager.WakeLock wl = pm.newWakeLock(flags, "My WakeLock");

    wl.acquire();

    runnable.run();

    wl.release();
}
```

> **NOTE:** Your application needs the `WAKE_LOCK` permission to be able to use WakeLock objects.

How the system will behave depends on which flag is used when the WakeLock object is created. Android defines the following flags:

- PARTIAL_WAKE_LOCK (CPU on)
- SCREEN_DIM_WAKE_LOCK (CPU on, display dimmed)
- SCREEN_BRIGHT_WAKE_LOCK (CPU on, bright display)
- FULL_WAKE_LOCK (CPU on, bright display and keyboard)

The flags can be combined with two more flags:

- ACQUIRE_CAUSES_WAKEUP (to turn on screen and/or keyboard)
- ON_AFTER_RELEASE (to keep screen and/or keyboard turned on for a little longer after the WakeLock is released)

While their use is trivial, WakeLocks can cause significant problems if they are not released. A buggy application may simply forget to release a WakeLock, causing, for example, the display to remain on for a very long time, emptying the battery very quickly. In general, WakeLocks should be released as soon as possible. For example, an application acquiring a WakeLock when a video is playing should most likely release it when the video is paused, and acquire it again when the user starts playing the video again. It should also release the WakeLock when the application is paused and acquire it again when the application is resumed (if the video is still playing at that time). As you can see, the number of different cases to handle can grow quickly, making your application prone to have bugs.

Preventing Issues

To prevent possible problems, it is recommended you use the timeout version of WakeLock.acquire(), which will guarantee the WakeLock will be released after the given timeout. For example, an application playing a video could use the duration of the video as the WakeLock timeout.

Alternatively, if keeping the screen on is associated with a view in an activity, you can use the XML attribute android:keepScreenOn in your layout files. A benefit of using that approach is that you don't take the risk of forgetting to release the WakeLock, as it is handled by the system and no additional permission is needed in the application's manifest file. Listing 7–20 shows how to use the attribute with a linear layout element.

Listing 7–20. *keepScreenOn XML Attribute*

```xml
<?xml version="1.0" encoding="utf-8"?>
<LinearLayout xmlns:android="http://schemas.android.com/apk/res/android"
    android:keepScreenOn="true"
    android:orientation="vertical"
    android:layout_width="fill_parent"
    android:layout_height="fill_parent"
    >

...

</LinearLayout>
```

> **TIP:** android:keepScreenOn can be used in any view. As long as one visible view specifies the screen should remain on, the screen will remain on. You can also control whether the screen should remain on with the View.setKeepScreenOn() method.

Despite the problems they may cause, WakeLocks are sometimes necessary. If you have to use them, make sure you carefully think about when they should be acquired and when they should be released. Also make sure you fully understand your application's lifecycle, and make sure the test cases are exhaustive. WakeLocks are only problematic when bugs exist!

Summary

Users typically won't notice if your application preserves battery life. However, they most likely will notice if it does not. All applications need to behave and cooperate as much as possible in order to maximize the battery life, as a single application can ruin all the efforts made by others. As users often uninstall applications that consume too much power, your application needs to make a sensible use of the battery and yet should give the users options to configure certain things as different users will ask for different things. Empower your users.

Chapter 8

Graphics

Quite often you'll have to spend a lot of time defining what your application should look like. Whether it is an e-mail application using standard Android widgets or a game using OpenGL ES, what your applications looks like is one of the first things people will notice when browsing application stores like Android Market or Amazon Appstore.

An application that looks great but has graphics that are slow to appear on the screen or slow to get updated is not likely to become a huge hit. Similarly, a game with high-quality rendering but low frame rate could easily be ignored by users. Reviews will ultimately drive the success of your application and it is therefore important your application is more than just a little eye candy.

In this chapter, you learn the basic methods to optimize your layouts with various techniques and tools as well as some techniques to optimize OpenGL ES rendering to achieve a better frame rate or lower power consumption.

Optimizing Layouts

By now you should already be familiar with XML layouts and the `setContentView()` method. A typical use of this method is shown in Listing 8–1. Even though many consider layouts to be simple to define, especially with the graphical layout interface in Eclipse, it is easy to get carried away and define far from optimal layouts. This section provides several easy ways to simplify layouts and accelerate layout inflation.

Listing 8–1. *Typical `setContentView()` Call*

```
public class MyActivity extends Activity {
    private static final String TAG = "MyActivity";

    /** Called when the activity is first created. */
    @Override
    protected void onCreate(Bundle savedInstanceState) {
        super.onCreate(savedInstanceState);

        // call to setContentView() to inflate and set layout (defined in main.xml)
        setContentView(R.layout.main);
```

```
        . . .
    }

    . . .
}
```

While this is a very simple call, a few things happen under the hood when `setContentView()` is called:

- Android reads the application's resource data (in the APK file, stored either on internal storage or SD card).

- The resource data is parsed and the layout is inflated.

- The inflated layout becomes the top-level view of the activity.

How much time this call will take depends on the complexity of the layout: the bigger the resource data the slower the parsing is, and the more classes to instantiate the slower the layout instantiation.

When you create an Android project in Eclipse, a default layout is generated in main.xml, as shown in Listing 8–2. The TextView's text is defined in strings.xml.

Listing 8–2. *Default Layout*

```xml
<?xml version="1.0" encoding="utf-8"?>
<LinearLayout xmlns:android="http://schemas.android.com/apk/res/android"
    android:layout_width="fill_parent"
    android:layout_height="fill_parent"
    android:orientation="vertical" >

    <TextView
        android:layout_width="fill_parent"
        android:layout_height="wrap_content"
        android:text="@string/hello" />

</LinearLayout>
```

A call to `setContentView()` as shown in Listing 8–1 using this particular layout takes about 17 milliseconds to complete on a Samsung Galaxy Tab 10.1. While this is quite quick, it is also an extremely simple layout that is not really representative of a typical Android application: only two classes will be instantiated (`LinearLayout` and `TextView`) and very few properties are specified in the XML file.

> **NOTE:** Layouts can be created programmatically as well but XML is usually preferred.

After adding multiple widgets to the default layout to reach a total of thirty widgets (including ScrollView, EditText, and ProgressBar), the call to `setContentView()` took more than 163 milliseconds to complete.

As you can see, the time it takes to inflate a layout grows almost linearly with the number of widgets to create. Moreover, the call to `setContentView()` represented almost 99% of the time spent between the beginning of `onCreate()` and the end of `onResume()`.

You can perform your own measurements by simply adding widgets to or removing widgets from the layout. Using the graphical layout view of the XML files in Eclipse makes it very easy. If you already have defined your application's layout, the first thing you should do is to measure how much time it takes to inflate it. Because the layout is typically inflated in your activity's onCreate() method, the time it takes to inflate it will have a direct impact on your activity's start-up time, as well as your application's. It is therefore recommended you try to minimize the time spent inflating layouts.

To achieve this, several techniques are available, most of them based on the same principle: reducing the number of objects to create. You can do this by using different layouts while still achieving the same visual result, by eliminating unnecessary objects, or by deferring the creation of objects.

RelativeLayout

Linear layouts are typically the first layout application developers learn to use. As a matter of fact, this layout is part of the default layout shown in Listing 8–1 and therefore is one of the first ViewGroups developers get familiar with. It is also an easy layout to understand as a linear layout is basically a container for widgets that are aligned either horizontally or vertically.

Most developers who are new to Android start nesting linear layouts to achieve the desired result. Listing 8–3 shows an example of nested linear layouts.

Listing 8–3. *Nested Linear Layout*

```xml
<?xml version="1.0" encoding="utf-8"?>
<LinearLayout xmlns:android="http://schemas.android.com/apk/res/android"
    android:layout_width="fill_parent"
    android:layout_height="fill_parent"
    android:orientation="vertical" >

    <LinearLayout xmlns:android="http://schemas.android.com/apk/res/android"
        android:layout_width="fill_parent"
        android:layout_height="wrap_content"
        android:orientation="horizontal" >
        <TextView
            android:id="@+id/text1"
            android:layout_width="wrap_content" android:layout_height="wrap_content"
            android:text="str1"
android:textAppearance="?android:attr/textAppearanceLarge" />
        <TextView
            android:id="@+id/text2"
            android:layout_width="wrap_content" android:layout_height="wrap_content"
            android:text="str2"
android:textAppearance="?android:attr/textAppearanceLarge" />
    </LinearLayout>

    <LinearLayout xmlns:android="http://schemas.android.com/apk/res/android"
        android:layout_width="fill_parent"
        android:layout_height="wrap_content"
        android:orientation="horizontal" >
        <TextView
```

```
                    android:id="@+id/text3"
                    android:layout_width="wrap_content" android:layout_height="wrap_content"
                    android:text="str3"
        android:textAppearance="?android:attr/textAppearanceLarge" />
            <TextView
                    android:id="@+id/text4"
                    android:layout_width="wrap_content" android:layout_height="wrap_content"
                    android:text="str4"
        android:textAppearance="?android:attr/textAppearanceLarge" />
        </LinearLayout>

        <LinearLayout xmlns:android="http://schemas.android.com/apk/res/android"
            android:layout_width="fill_parent"
            android:layout_height="wrap_content"
            android:orientation="horizontal" >
            <TextView
                    android:id="@+id/text5"
                    android:layout_width="wrap_content" android:layout_height="wrap_content"
                    android:text="str5"
        android:textAppearance="?android:attr/textAppearanceLarge" />
            <TextView
                    android:id="@+id/text6"
                    android:layout_width="wrap_content" android:layout_height="wrap_content"
                    android:text="str6"
        android:textAppearance="?android:attr/textAppearanceLarge" />
        </LinearLayout>

</LinearLayout>
```

This layout's core views are the six text views. The four linear layouts are simply here to help with positioning.

This layout exposes two issues:

- As linear layouts are nested, the layout hierarchy becomes deeper (causing layout and key handling to be slower).

- Out of ten objects, four exist only for positioning.

These two issues are easily solved by replacing all these linear layouts with a single relative layout, as shown in Listing 8–4.

Listing 8–4. *Relative Layout*

```
<?xml version="1.0" encoding="utf-8"?>
<RelativeLayout xmlns:android="http://schemas.android.com/apk/res/android"
    android:layout_width="fill_parent"
    android:layout_height="fill_parent"
    android:orientation="vertical" >

    <TextView
        android:id="@+id/text1"
        android:layout_width="wrap_content" android:layout_height="wrap_content"
        android:layout_alignParentLeft="true"
        android:layout_alignParentTop="true"
        android:text="@string/str1"
android:textAppearance="?android:attr/textAppearanceLarge" />
    <TextView
```

```
        android:id="@+id/text2"
        android:layout_width="wrap_content" android:layout_height="wrap_content"
        android:layout_toRightOf="@id/text1"
        android:layout_alignParentTop="true"
        android:text="@string/str2"
android:textAppearance="?android:attr/textAppearanceLarge" />
    <TextView
        android:id="@+id/text3"
        android:layout_alignParentLeft="true"
        android:layout_below="@id/text1"
        android:layout_width="wrap_content" android:layout_height="wrap_content"
        android:text="@string/str3"
android:textAppearance="?android:attr/textAppearanceLarge" />
    <TextView
        android:id="@+id/text4"
        android:layout_width="wrap_content" android:layout_height="wrap_content"
        android:layout_toRightOf="@id/text3"
        android:layout_below="@id/text2"
        android:text="@string/str4"
android:textAppearance="?android:attr/textAppearanceLarge" />
    <TextView
        android:id="@+id/text5"
        android:layout_alignParentLeft="true"
        android:layout_below="@id/text3"
        android:layout_width="wrap_content" android:layout_height="wrap_content"
        android:text="@string/str5"
android:textAppearance="?android:attr/textAppearanceLarge" />
    <TextView
        android:id="@+id/text6"
        android:layout_width="wrap_content" android:layout_height="wrap_content"
        android:layout_toRightOf="@id/text5"
        android:layout_below="@id/text4"
        android:text="@string/str6"
android:textAppearance="?android:attr/textAppearanceLarge" />

</RelativeLayout>
```

As you can see, all six text views are now within a single relative layout, and therefore only seven objects are created instead of 10. The layout is also not as deep as it used to be: the text views are now one level higher. The key to positioning the widgets is in the layout_*** attributes. Android defines many such attributes that you can use to determine the positioning of the various elements in your layout:

- layout_above
- layout_alignBaseline
- layout_alignBottom
- layout_alignLeft
- layout_alignRight
- layout_alignTop
- layout_alignParentBottom
- layout_alignParentLeft

- layout_alignParentRight
- layout_alignParentTop
- layout_alignWithParentIfMissing
- layout_below
- layout_centerHorizontal
- layout_centerInParent
- layout_centerVertical
- layout_column
- layout_columnSpan
- layout_gravity
- layout_height
- layout_margin
- layout_marginBottom
- layout_marginLeft
- layout_marginRight
- layout_marginTop
- layout_row
- layout_rowSpan
- layout_scale
- layout_span
- layout_toLeftOf
- layout_toRightOf
- layout_weight
- layout_width
- layout_x
- layout_y

NOTE: Some attributes are specific to a certain type of layout. For example, the `layout_column`, `layout_columnSpan`, `layout_row`, and `layout_rowSpan` are to be used with the grid layout.

Relative layouts are especially important in list items as it is quite common for applications to show ten or more such items on the screen at any given time.

Merging Layouts

Another way to reduce the height of the layout hierarchy is to merge layouts with the <merge /> tag. Quite often the top element of your own layout will be a FrameLayout, as shown in Listing 8–5.

Listing 8–5. *Frame Layout*

```xml
<?xml version="1.0" encoding="utf-8"?>
<FrameLayout xmlns:android="http://schemas.android.com/apk/res/android"
    android:layout_width="fill_parent"
    android:layout_height="fill_parent"
    android:id="@+id/my_top_layout" >

    <ImageView
        android:layout_width="fill_parent"
        android:layout_height="fill_parent" />

    <TextView
        android:layout_width="fill_parent"
        android:layout_height="wrap_content"
        android:text="@string/hello" />

</FrameLayout>
```

Because the parent of an activity's content view is also a FrameLayout, you would end up with two FrameLayout objects in the layout:

- Your own FrameLayout

- The parent of the activity's content view, another FrameLayout, which has only one child (your own FrameLayout)

Figure 8–1 shows the layout you would obtain assuming your own FrameLayout had two children: an ImageView and a TextView.

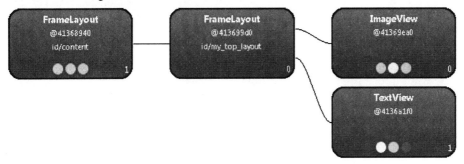

Figure 8–1. *FrameLayout child of another* FrameLayout

This is one FrameLayout too many, and you can reduce the height of the layout by replacing your own FrameLayout with a <merge /> tag. By doing so, Android simply attaches the children of the <merge /> tag to the parent FrameLayout. Listing 8–6 shows the new XML layout.

Listing 8–6. *Merge Tag*

```
<?xml version="1.0" encoding="utf-8"?>
<merge xmlns:android="http://schemas.android.com/apk/res/android">

    <ImageView
        android:layout_width="fill_parent"
        android:layout_height="fill_parent" />

    <TextView
        android:layout_width="fill_parent"
        android:layout_height="wrap_content"
        android:text="@string/hello" />

</merge>
```

As you can see, it is just a matter of replacing the <FrameLayout /> tag with a <merge /> tag. Figure 8–2 shows the resulting layout.

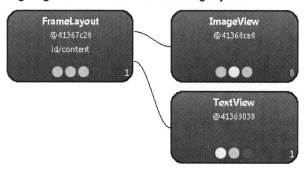

Figure 8–2. *<FrameLayout /> replaced With <merge />*

Reusing Layouts

Similar to the #include directive in C or C++, Android supports the <include /> tag in the XML layouts. Simply put, the <include /> tag includes another XML layout, as shown in Listing 8–7.

The <include /> tag can be used for two purposes:

- ▣ You want to use the same layout multiple times.

- ▣ Your layout has a common part and also parts that depend on the device configuration (for example, screen orientation—landscape or portrait).

Listing 8–7 shows how you can include a layout multiple times while overriding some of the included layout's parameters.

Listing 8–7. *Including Layout Multiple Times*

```
<LinearLayout xmlns:android="http://schemas.android.com/apk/res/android"
    android:layout_width="fill_parent"
    android:layout_height="fill_parent"
    android:orientation="vertical" >

    <include android:id="@+id/myid1" android:layout="@layout/mylayout"
android:layout_margin="9dip" />
    <include android:id="@+id/myid2" android:layout="@layout/mylayout"
android:layout_margin="3dip" />
    <include android:id="@+id/myid3" android:layout="@layout/mylayout" />

</LinearLayout>
```

Listing 8–8 shows how you can include a layout just once, but depending on the device's screen orientation, either layout-land/mylayout.xml or layout-port/mylayout.xml will be included. (It is assumed here there are two versions of mylayout.xml, one in the res/layout-land directory and the other in the res/layout-port directory.)

Listing 8–8. *Including Layout Depending On Screen Orientation*

```
<LinearLayout xmlns:android="http://schemas.android.com/apk/res/android"
    android:layout_width="fill_parent"
    android:layout_height="fill_parent"
    android:orientation="vertical" >

    <include android:id="@+id/myid" android:layout="@layout/mylayout" />

</LinearLayout>
```

When a layout is included, it is possible to override some of the layout's parameters, such as:

- ▨ The root view's id (android:id)
- ▨ The layout parameters (android:layout_*)

> **NOTE:** Overriding the layout's parameters is optional. Only the android:layout attribute is mandatory in the <include /> tag.

As Listing 8–8 demonstrates, the inclusion of the layout is done dynamically when the layout is inflated. Should the inclusion be done at compile time Android would not know which of the two layouts to include (layout-land/mylayout.xml or layout-port/mylayout.xml). This is different from the #include directive in C or C++, which is handled by the preprocessor at compile time.

View Stubs

As we saw in Chapter 1, lazy initialization is a convenient technique to defer instantiations, improve performance, and potentially save memory (when objects never have to be created).

Android defines the ViewStub class for that purpose. A ViewStub is a lightweight invisible view that you can use in your layout to allow you to lazily inflate layout resources when you need them. Listing 8–9, a modified version of Listing 8–8, shows how to use ViewStub in an XML layout.

Listing 8–9. *ViewStub In XML*

```xml
<LinearLayout xmlns:android="http://schemas.android.com/apk/res/android"
    android:layout_width="fill_parent"
    android:layout_height="fill_parent"
    android:orientation="vertical" >

    <ViewStub
        android:id="@+id/mystubid"
        android:inflatedId="@+id/myid"
        android:layout="@layout/mylayout" />

</LinearLayout>
```

When the LineaLayout is inflated, it will contain only one child, a ViewStub. The layout the ViewStub is referring to, @layout/mylayout, could be a very complicated layout, requiring significant time to be inflated, but it is not inflated yet. To inflate the layout defined in mylayout.xml, you have two options in your code, as shown in Listing 8–10 and Listing 8–11.

Listing 8–10. *Inflating Layout In Code*

```java
ViewStub stub = (ViewStub) findViewById(R.id.mystubid);
View inflatedView = stub.inflate(); // inflatedView will be the layout defined in
mylayout.xml
```

Listing 8–11. *Inflating Layout In Code Using* setVisibility()

```java
View view = findViewById(R.id.mystubid);
view.setVisibility(View.VISIBLE); // view stub replaced with inflated layout
view = findViewById(R.id.myid); // we need to get the newly inflated view now
```

While the first way of inflating the layout (in Listing 8–10) seems more convenient, some may argue it has a slight problem: the code is aware of the fact that the view is a stub and explicitly needs to inflate the layout. In most cases, this won't be an issue though, and it will be the recommended way of inflating a layout when your application uses ViewStub in its layout.

The second way of inflating the layout, shown in Listing 8–11, is more generic as it does not refer to the ViewStub class. However, the code as shown above is still aware of the fact that it uses a ViewStub since it uses two distinct ids: R.id.mystubid and R.id.myid. To be fully generic, the layout should be defined as shown in Listing 8–12, and inflating the layout should be done as shown in Listing 8–13. Listing 8–12 is identical to Listing 8–9 except for the fact that only one id is created, R.id.myid, instead of two. Similarly, Listing 8–13 is identical to Listing 8–11 except for R.id.mystubid being replaced with R.id.myid.

Listing 8–12. *ViewStub In XML Without Overriding ID*

```
<LinearLayout xmlns:android="http://schemas.android.com/apk/res/android"
    android:layout_width="fill_parent"
    android:layout_height="fill_parent"
    android:orientation="vertical" >

    <ViewStub
        android:id="@+id/myid"
        android:layout="@layout/mylayout" />

</LinearLayout>
```

Listing 8–13. *Inflating Layout In Code Using setVisibility()*

```
View view = findViewById(R.id.myid);
view.setVisibility(View.VISIBLE); // view stub replaced with inflated layout
view = findViewById(R.id.myid); // we need to get the newly inflated view now
```

As a matter of fact, Listing 8–13 would be valid whether or not a ViewStub is used in the layout. If it is important for your code to be generic and work fine regardless of the use of ViewStub in the layout, then this approach is preferred. However, the two calls to findViewById() would affect performance negatively. To partially fix this problem, since a ViewStub will be removed from its parent when setVisibility(View.VISIBLE) is called, you could first check whether the view still has a parent before calling findViewById() the second time. While this is not optimal as a second call to findViewById() would still be needed when you used a ViewStub in your layout, it would guarantee that findViewById() is only called once when you did not use a ViewStub. The modified code is shown in Listing 8–14.

Listing 8–14. *Calling findViewById() Once When Possible*

```
View view = findViewById(R.id.myid);
view.setVisibility(View.VISIBLE); // view stub replaced with inflated layout (if
stub is used in layout)
if (view.getParent() == null) {
    // a stub was used so we need to find the newly inflated view that replaced it
    view = findViewById(R.id.myid);
} else {
    // nothing to do, the view we found the first time is what we want
}
```

What is shown in Listing 8–13 and Listing 8–14 is uncommon, and you usually won't have to follow this approach. Typically, it will be acceptable for your code to know that ViewStubs are used in the layouts and therefore the simple way of inflating stubs shown in Listing 8–10 will be sufficient.

Layout Tools

To assist you in creating the best layouts, the Android SDK provides two easy-to-use tools: hierarchyviewer and layoutopt. You can find these tools, among others, in the SDK tools directory.

Hierarchy Viewer

The Android SDK comes with a very useful tool to view and analyze your application's layout: hierarchyviewer. As a matter of fact, Figure 8–1 and Figure 8–2 were generated using that tool. In addition to showing you the detailed layout of your application, this tool also measures how much time it takes to measure, lay out, and draw each widget, and identifies which widgets took longer to measure, lay out, and draw.

You can use hierarchyviewer as a standalone tool or directly in Eclipse with the "Hierarchy View" perspective.

layoutopt

The Android SDK comes with another tool that can help you with your layouts: layoutopt. This tool analyzes your layout files and can recommend changes in order to make the layout more efficient.

For example, using layoutopt on the layout from Listing 8–5 results in the following output:

```
The root-level <FrameLayout/> can be replaced with <merge/>
```

As it turns out, this is exactly what Listing 8–6 did. Running layoutopt in Listing 8–6 did not result in any recommendation.

> **TIP:** Use the latest version of the layoutopt tool to make sure you get the best results.

Make sure all issues reported by layoutopt are taken care of before you release your application. Unoptimized layouts can slow down your application, and it is usually quite easy to remedy such layouts.

OpenGL ES

Three-dimensional rendering is becoming a more and more important feature of today's Android devices and applications. While becoming an expert in 3D rendering would take quite some time, the following section introduces some simple techniques that are easy to implement as well as some basic concepts you need to be aware of in order to start working with 3D rendering. If you want to learn more about OpenGL ES for Android, you can refer to "Pro OpenGL ES for Android" by Mike Smithwick and Mayank Verma.

Most recent Android devices support both OpenGL ES 1.1 and OpenGL ES 2.0 while older devices would support only OpenGL ES 1.1. As of December 2011, about 90% of the devices connecting to Android Market support OpenGL ES 2.0.

While OpenGL ES is a standard from the Khronos Group, several implementations exist. The most common GPUs supporting OpenGL ES in Android devices are:

- ARM Mali (example: Mali 400-MP4)

- Imagination Technologies PowerVR (example: PowerVR SGX543)

- Nvidia GeForce (Nvidia Tegra)

- Qualcomm Adreno (acquired from AMD, formerly ATI Imageon, and integrated into Qualcomm Snapdragon)

Extensions

The OpenGL standard supports extensions, allowing new features to be incorporated in certain GPUs. For example, the following extensions are supported by the Samsung Galaxy Tab 10.1 (based on Nvidia Tegra 2):

- GL_NV_platform_binary

- GL_OES_rgb8_rgba8

- GL_OES_EGL_sync

- GL_OES_fbo_render_mipmap

- GL_NV_depth_nonlinear

- GL_NV_draw_path

- GL_NV_texture_npot_2D_mipmap

- GL_OES_EGL_image

- GL_OES_EGL_image_external

- GL_OES_vertex_half_float

- GL_NV_framebuffer_vertex_attrib_array

- GL_NV_coverage_sample

- GL_OES_mapbuffer

- GL_ARB_draw_buffers

- GL_EXT_Cg_shaders

- GL_EXT_packed_float

- GL_OES_texture_half_float

- GL_OES_texture_float

- GL_EXT_texture_array

- GL_OES_compressed_ETC1_RGB8_texture

- GL_EXT_texture_compression_latc
- GL_EXT_texture_compression_dxt1
- GL_EXT_texture_compression_s3tc
- GL_EXT_texture_filter_anisotropic
- GL_NV_get_text_image
- GL_NV_read_buffer
- GL_NV_shader_framebuffer_fetch
- GL_NV_fbo_color_attachements
- GL_EXT_bgra
- GL_EXT_texture_format_BGRA8888
- GL_EXT_unpack_subimage
- GL_NV_texture_compression_st3c_update

Listing 8–15 shows how to retrieve the list of the extensions a device supports. Since OpenGL ES 2.0 is currently not supported by the Android emulator, make sure you run that code on an actual device.

Listing 8–15. *OpenGL ES Extensions*

```
// list of extensions returned as a single string (parse it to find a specific
extension)

String extensions = GLES20.glGetString(GLES20.GL_EXTENSIONS);

Log.d(TAG, "Extensions: " + extensions);
```

You will need an OpenGL context to be able to successfully execute the code in Listing 8–15 and retrieve the list of extensions. For example, you can execute the code in your GLSurfaceView.Renderer's onSurfaceChanged() method. If you run that code and no OpenGL is available, then you will see a "call to OpenGL ES API with no current context" message in LogCat.

As you can see, the extensions above can be separated into multiple groups:

- GL_OES_*
- GL_ARB_*
- GL_EXT_*
- GL_NV_*

The GL_OES_* extensions are extensions that have been approved by the Khronos OpenGL ES Working Group. Even though these extensions are not required by OpenGL ES, they are widely available.

The GL_ARB_* extensions have been approved by the OpenGL Architecture Review Board. The GL_EXT_* extensions have been agreed upon by multiple vendors, whereas the GL_NV_* extensions are specific to Nvidia. By looking at what extensions are supported, you can usually tell which company provides a device's GPU:

- ARM extensions use the GL_ARM prefix.

- Imagination Technologies extensions use the GL_IMG prefix.

- Nvidia extensions use the GL_NV prefix.

- Qualcomm extensions use the GL_QUALCOMM, GL_AMD and GL_ATI prefixes.

> **NOTE:** Visit http://www.khronos.org/registry/gles and http://www.opengl.org/registry for more information.

Because not all devices support the same extensions (hello, fragmentation), you have to be extremely careful when optimizing for a specific device, as something that works on one device may not work on another. Typical examples include using Non-Power-Of-Two (NPOT) textures or a texture compression format that is supported on the device you test your application on but not on other devices. If you plan on supported non-Android devices, also check which extensions these devices support. For example, current Apple iPhone/iPod/iPad devices are all Imagination Technologies PowerVR-based (which may or may not share the same extensions) but future models may not be PowerVR-based.

Texture Compression

Textures will define what your OpenGL ES applications will look like. While it is easy to use uncompressed textures, such textures can quickly bloat your application. For example, an uncompressed 256x256 RGBA8888 texture could use 256 kilobytes of memory.

Uncompressed textures impact performance negatively as they are not as cacheable as compressed texture (because of their size), and they require more memory access (affecting also power consumption). Applications that use uncompressed textures are also bigger and therefore require more time to be downloaded and installed. Besides, the amount of memory on Android devices is typically limited, so your applications should use as little memory as possible.

In the list above, the following extensions show which texture compression formats are supported by the Samsung Galaxy Tab 10.1:

- GL_OES_compressed_ETC1_RGB8_texture

- GL_EXT_texture_compression_latc

- GL_EXT_texture_compression_dxt1

- GL_EXT_texture_compression_s3tc

The ETC1 compression format was created by Ericsson (ETC stands for Ericsson Texture Compression) and is supported by most Android devices (and by all Android devices that support OpenGL ES 2.0). It is therefore the safest choice to target as many devices as possible. This compression format uses 4 bits per pixel instead of 24 (ETC1 does not support alpha) and therefore achieves a 6x compression ratio: including the 16-byte header, a 256-by-256 ETC1 texture would use 32,784 bytes.

Multiple tools exist to create ETC1 textures. The Android SDK includes etc1tool, a command-line tool to encode PNG images to compressed ETC1 images. For example, the following line shows how to compress lassen.png (183 kilobytes) and generate the difference between the original image and the compressed one:

```
etc1tool lassen.png --encode --showDifference lassen_diff.png
```

The output file, if not specified, is generated based on the name of the input file. In this particular case, the output file will be lassen.pkm (33 kilobytes). Figure 8–3 shows the difference between the compressed image and the original.

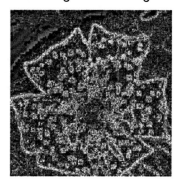

Figure 8–3. *Original image (left) and difference with compressed image (right)*

> **NOTE:** etc1tool can also be used to decode an ETC1 image into a PNG image. For more information about etc1tool, refer to
> http://d.android.com/guide/developing/tools/etc1tool.html.

Unfortunately, the Android SDK's etc1tool does not provide many options. For those who want to be able to fine tune the compression and visual quality, another tool is recommended: etcpack. The etcpack tool can be downloaded from the Ericsson website (http://devtools.ericsson.com/etc) and allows for more options:

- Compression speed (slower speed = higher quality)
- Error metric (perceptual or non-perceptual)
- Orientation

You should always use the best quality possible before releasing your application when ETC1 textures are generated offline (that is, not on the Android device itself). Since the human eye is more sensitive to green than red or blue, you should also select "perceptual" as the error metric. (The algorithm will make green be closer to its original value at the expense of red and blue, decreasing the peak signal-to-noise ratio.)

While the difference may not be obvious, there is no reason to release an application that uses lower-quality textures as a higher-quality ETC1 texture will be the same size as a lower-quality one. Even though generating higher-quality textures takes more time and therefore many developers choose to work with lower-quality textures during development, you should always remember to switch to high-quality textures before releasing your application.

Alternatively, you can use the ARM Mali GPU Compression Tool, available for free at http://www.malideveloper.com/developer-resources/tools. This tool offers options similar to etcpack but with a graphical interface (a command-line version is also provided). Figure 8–4 shows the ARM Mali GPU Compression Tool in action with the same input file as above.

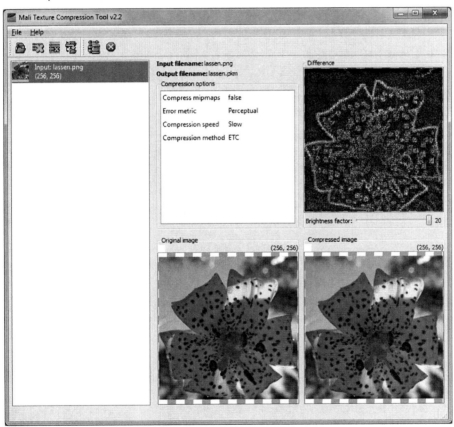

Figure 8–4. *ARM Mali GPU compression tool*

Figure 8–5 shows the difference in quality between a higher-quality (slow) compression and a lower-quality (fast) compression. Once again, the differences are not obvious.

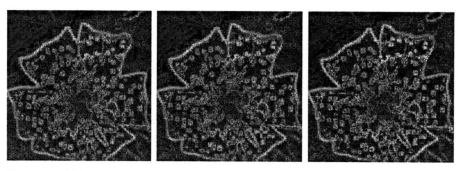

Figure 8–5. *Higher quality (left), medium (middle), and lower-quality (right)*

As you can see on the ARM Mali developer website, many other tools are available. You can find many authoring and debugging tools on the ARM, Imagination Technologies, Nvidia, and Qualcomm websites:

- http://www.malideveloper.com/developer-resources/tools

- http://www.imgtec.com/powervr/insider/sdkdownloads

- http://developer.nvidia.com/tegra-android-development-pack

- http://developer.qualcomm.com/develop/mobile-technologies/graphics-optimization-adreno

For example, Imagination Technologies also provides a tool to create compressed textures, PVRTexTool, and the Nvidia website offers a complete SDK (including Android SDK, NDK, Eclipse, and sample code).

> **NOTE:** You may have to register to gain access to the various tools and documents on these websites.

Starting in Android 2.2 (API level 8), the following classes are defined to help you work with ETC1 textures:

- android.opengl.ETC1

- android.opengl.ETC1Util

- android.opengl.ETC1Util.ETC1Texture

Your application can compress images into ETC1 textures dynamically with the ETC1.encodeImage() and ETC1Util.compressTexture() methods. This is useful when ETC1 textures cannot be generated offline, for example when the textures are based on pictures stored on the device (perhaps a picture of one of the user's contacts).

> **TIP:** Even though ETC1 does not support transparency (there is no alpha component in the compressed texture), you can use another single-channel texture that contains only the transparency information and combine the two textures in a shader.

Other Texture Compression Formats

While ETC1 is the most common texture compression format, other formats exist and are supported by some devices. Among these are:

- PowerVR Texture Compression (PVRTC)
- ATI Texture Compression (ATC or ATITC)
- S3 Texture Compression (S3TC), with DXT1 to DXT5 variants

You should experiment with various compression formats depending on which devices you target. Because a particular GPU may be optimized for its own compression format (for example, PowerVR GPU optimized for PVRTC compression format), you may achieve better results with a proprietary compression format than with the more standard ETC1 compression format.

> **NOTE:** You can also use Apple's iOS texturetool to generate PVRTC textures.

Manifest

Your OpenGL application's manifest should specify two things:

- Which OpenGL version it requires the device to support
- Which texture compression formats the application supports

Listing 8–16 shows how to specify the device should support OpenGL ES 2.0 and shows the application supports only two texture compression formats: ETC1 and PVRTC.

Listing 8–16. *Manifest and OpenGL*

```
<?xml version="1.0" encoding="utf-8"?>
<manifest xmlns:android="http://schemas.android.com/apk/res/android"
    package="com.apress.proandroid.opengl"
    android:versionCode="1" android:versionName="1.0" >

    <uses-sdk android:minSdkVersion="8" />

    <uses-feature android:glEsVersion="0x00020000" />

    <supports-gl-texture android:name="GL_OES_compressed_ETC1_RGB8_texture" />
    <supports-gl-texture android:name="GL_IMG_texture_compression_pvrtc" />
```

...

```
</manifest>
```

> **NOTE:** The OpenGL ES version is a 16.16 number, so 0x0002000 is for OpenGL ES 2.0.

Android Market will use this information to filter applications when a device connects to Market. For example, a device that supports only OpenGL ES 1.1 will not see applications that use OpenGL ES 2.0. Similarly, a device that supports only ETC1 texture compression will not see applications that support only PVRTC and ATC textures.

If your application does not specify any texture compression format in its manifest, then Android Market will not apply any filtering based on compression format (and therefore will assume your application supports all compression formats). This could lead to users installing your application only to find out that the application does not work, potentially leading to bad reviews.

Mipmaps

Often, objects in a 3D scene appear in the background and do not use that much space on the screen. For example, using a 256x256 texture on an object that is only 10x10 pixels on the screen is a waste of resources (memory, bandwidth). Mipmaps solve this by providing multiple levels of detail for a texture, as shown in Figure 8–6.

Fig 8–6. *Mipmaps from 256x256 to 1x1*

While a mipmap set uses about 33% more memory than its lone original image, it may improve not only performance but also visual quality.

As you can see in Figure 8–6, each image is a version of the original image but at a different level of detail. Obviously, it is quite hard to see a flower in the 1x1 version of the texture.

The ARM Mali GPU Texture Compression Tool can generate mipmaps for you. Instead of generating only a single .pkm file, the tool will generate all levels of details all the way to 1x1 and will create a single .pkm file for each. Your application will then have to load these different levels one by one, for example by calling `ETC1Util.loadTexture()` or `GLES20.glTexImage2D()`.

Because not all devices are equal, they may not all require the same levels of detail. For example, a Google TV device with a resolution of 1920x1080 (HD resolution) would typically require a higher level of detail than a Samsung Nexus S with a resolution of 800x480 (WVGA). Consequently, while a 256x256 texture may be needed for a Google TV device, the Nexus S may never have any use for such texture and would be ok using a 128x128 texture.

> **NOTE:** Do not simply rely on the resolution of a device to determine what your application should do. For example, Sony Google TV televisions (1920x1080 resolution) use a PowerVR SGX535 at 400MHz, which is not as powerful as the PowerVR SGX540 at 384MHz found in the newer Samsung Galaxy Nexus (1280x720 resolution).

How the textures will be rendered also depends on what texture parameters are set with one of the `glTexParameter()` methods (for example, `glTexParameteri()`). For example, you can set the minifying function by calling `glTexParameteri(GL_TEXTURE_2D, GL_TEXTURE_MIN_FILTER, param)` with `param` being one of the following values:

- GL_NEAREST
- GL_LINEAR
- GL_NEAREST_MIPMAP_NEAREST
- GL_NEAREST_MIPMAP_LINEAR
- GL_LINEAR_MIPMAP_NEAREST
- GL_LINEAR_MIPMAP_LINEAR

While GL_NEAREST is generally faster than GL_LINEAR, and GL_LINEAR is faster than the other four, better visual quality will be achieved with slower functions. What parameters your application will choose may depend on the user's preferences (if you provide a way for the user to configure the quality of rendering), however many users won't have the patience to try various settings to find a combination that works well on their devices. As a consequence, your application should do its best to determine the OpenGL configuration it should use.

Many things can be configured in OpenGL and some default values favor visual quality over performance, so you should become familiar with what your application can configure. For example, as far as textures are concerned, the documentation on `http://www.khronos.org/opengles/sdk/docs/man/` will show you all the different parameters you can set.

Multiple APKs

Because you may want to support multiple texture compression formats (optimizing as much as possible for each device) and because mipmaps take more space, your application may go over the size limit defined by Android Market (currently 50 megabytes).

If that happens, you have basically three options:

- Reduce the size of your application, for example by supporting only ETC1 texture compression.

- Download textures from a remote server after the application is installed.

- Generate multiple APKs, each with its own set of textures.

Android Market lets you publish different APKs for your application, each targeting a different configuration. For example, you could have one APK using only ETC1 textures and a second one using only PVRTC textures—that is, an APK optimized for PowerVR-based Android devices. These APKs will share the same Android Market listing, and Android Market will take care of selecting the right APK for each device. Users won't have to worry about downloading and installing the right APK as the selection is automatic and transparent.

> **NOTE:** Not all Android application stores support this feature, so if you plan on distributing your application in multiple stores, try to use a single APK for all devices whenever possible.

Of course, textures may not be the sole reason why you would need or want to release multiple APKs. For example, you may want to release a smaller APK for older devices and a larger APK with more features for newer devices. While shipping multiple APKs is possible, it makes your maintenance and release process more complicated and therefore it is recommended you try to ship a single APK whenever possible.

Shaders

OpenGL ES 2.0 supports the OpenGL ES Shading Language, replacing the fixed function transformation and fragment pipeline of OpenGL ES 1.x. Based on C, the language allows you to have more control over the OpenGL pipeline by writing your own vertex and fragment shaders.

Like any C program, shaders can go from very simple to extremely complex. While there is no single rule you have to follow, you should try to reduce complexity as much as possible in your shaders as it can have a significant impact on performance.

Scene Complexity

Obviously, a complex scene will take longer to render than a simple one. An easy way to increase the frame rate therefore is to simplify the scenes to render while maintaining an acceptable visual quality. For example, as you have already seen with textures, objects that are further away can be less detailed and can be made of fewer triangles. Simpler objects will use less memory and bandwidth.

Culling

Even though GPUs are good at geometry and can determine what has to be rendered, your application should do its best to eliminate objects that are outside of the viewing frustum so it does not send draw commands for objects that will simply be discarded because they are not visible.

There are numerous methods to cull objects or even triangles and while these methods are outside the scope of this book, a lower-than-expected frame rate may be caused by poor culling. For example, it is pretty easy to quickly eliminate objects that are behind the camera.

> **NOTE:** More often than not you want to enable back face culling so that back facing triangles in objects are not rendered.

Render Mode

By default, the OpenGL renderer keeps rendering the scene, regardless of what might have changed. In some cases, the scene may not change between frames, and you may want to explicitly tell the renderer to only render the scene when you request it. You can achieve this by changing the GLSurfaceView's render mode.

You can set a GLSurfaceView's render mode by calling setRenderMode() with one of the following two values:

- RENDERMODE_CONTINUOUSLY
- RENDERMODE_WHEN_DIRTY

When the render mode is set to RENDERMODE_WHEN_DIRTY, the renderer will render the scene when the surface is created, or when GLSurfaceView.requestRender() is called.

Power Consumption

One of the great qualities of modern GPUs is that they can fall asleep or at least slow down very quickly during periods of inactivity. For example, the GPU can shut down (partially or fully) between two frames if it has nothing to do for a while, reducing power consumption and therefore increasing battery life.

Once you have achieved an acceptable frame rate for your application, you may still want to optimize further if only to reduce power consumption. The faster a frame is being rendered, the sooner the GPU can idle and the longer the battery life (and the longer a user can use your application). For some applications, one of the great ways to increase battery life with OpenGL is to render frames only when the scene changed (as described above with the RENDERMODE_WHEN_DIRTY render mode).

Summary

The latest Android devices are very powerful pieces of hardware and are capable of great graphics, both 2D and 3D. While some optimizations may become less important than just a couple of years ago, new challenges present themselves with the higher and higher resolutions the devices support, the almost ubiquitous support for OpenGL ES 2.0, and the increasingly higher expectations from users. This chapter only scratched the surface of OpenGL ES and only introduced some techniques that are easy to implement and yet can give tremendous results. Luckily for you, there exist many resources to learn about OpenGL, whether you are looking for beginner or advanced material. Also remember to refer to the documentation offered by the GPU vendors (ARM, Imagination Technologies, Nvidia, Qualcomm) as they explain ways to optimize rendering for their own GPU.

Chapter 9

RenderScript

Introduced in Honeycomb (API level 11), RenderScript is a new framework targeted at high-performance 3D rendering and compute operations. While RenderScript was already used back in Android 2.1 (Éclair), Honeycomb is the first Android version where RenderScript is made publicly available.

After a brief overview of RenderScript, you will learn how to create a simple script and how to use it from your Java application. Then you will learn how to perform rendering operations from your script and how to access your script's data from Java. We will review one of the sample applications provided in the Android SDK, HelloCompute, and compare two implementations of the same application, one based on Honeycomb APIs and the other based on Ice Cream Sandwich (Android 4.0) APIs. To conclude this chapter, we will review the RenderScript header files for both Honeycomb and Ice Cream Sandwich, and the functions you can use in your scripts.

> **NOTE:** This chapter is not meant to be a complete guide to 3D rendering. For example, one should acquire knowledge of the OpenGL Shading Language (GLSL) as well in order to use advanced features of RenderScript. Whole books are dedicated to OpenGL and GLSL, and mastering 3D rendering can take years of practice.

Overview

There aren't that many applications currently using RenderScript. Since a picture is worth a thousand words, let's see examples of where RenderScript is used. Perhaps the most popular example is the YouTube application and its carousel view, as shown in Figure 9–1. For clarity, the screenshot was taken when the videos were not loaded yet, and you can see what each rectangle looks like (each rectangle would then contain a video thumbnail). Another example, Balls, is available as sample code in the Android SDK and uses sensors' information and physic to compute the position of the balls on the screen, as shown in Figure 9–2.

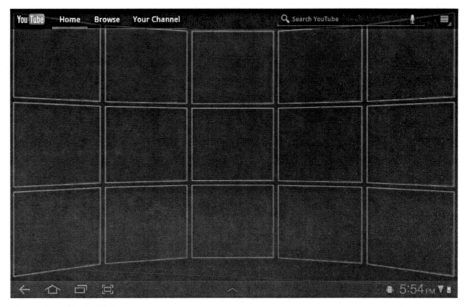

Figure 9–1. *YouTube Carousel view*

Figure 9–2. *Balls sample application*

> **NOTE:** To create a project from sample code (for example, Balls), create a new Android project in Eclipse and select "Create project from existing sample," or simply create a new Android Sample project (option available with newer versions of the Eclipse ADT plugin). RenderScript samples are available only when you select 3.0 or above as the target. You can download a carousel example from `http://code.google.com/p/android-ui-utils/downloads/list`.

RenderScript uses C99 as its language but is not meant to completely replace your Java application. Instead, your application will use RenderScript for certain parts and Java for others. When you use RenderScript, your scripts will be compiled to Low-Level Virtual Machine (LLVM) bitcode on the host machine (for example, your Windows PC on which you installed Eclipse), and the LLVM bitcode will then be compiled to native code on the Android device itself. In that respect, it is similar to your Java code being compiled to Dalvik bytecode on the host, which can be compiled to native code on the device by the Dalvik Just-In-Time compiler.

The native code is then cached on your device, so subsequent executions of the script will be faster as the script will already be compiled to native code. As compilation of the bitcode to native code occurs on the device, the resulting native code can be optimized for the device, or even hardware module (for example, GPU), and you as a developer won't have to worry about the various architectures and features. This is a major difference with the NDK, where, for example, your code has to check whether NEON is available, and should simplify your workflow significantly.

> **NOTE:** For more information about LLVM, visit `http://llvm.org`. You can download and install various LLVM tools from there as well. LLVM is not an Android-specific technology. As a matter of fact, it is used by Apple's Xcode 4.

Before we talk in more detail about what you can do in RenderScript, we are going to walk through how to create a basic RenderScript script in a project. Since the emulator does not support all the features needed by RenderScript you will need an actual Android device to use RenderScript. You will often find that a RenderScript script is simply referred to as a RenderScript.

Hello World

As always when introduced to a new framework, your first instinct should be to say "hello" to the world from a RenderScript script. To create a script, simply create a new file in your Android project and call it helloworld.rs. Listing 9–1 shows how we can create a simple function that will output the "Hello, World" string using a simple RenderScript debugging function.

Listing 9–1. *"Hello, World" Script*

```
#pragma version(1)
#pragma rs java_package_name(com.apress.proandroid.ch9)

void hello_world() {
    rsDebug("Hello, World", 0); // 0 is because we cannot send only a string to the
debug output...
}
```

The first line declares which version of RenderScript your script uses. The second line declares the package name of the Java reflection of this script. As you build your Android project, many things will happen under the hood, and the build tools will create the following three files:

- ScriptC_helloworld.java (in gen/ directory)

- helloworld.d (in gen/ directory)

- helloworld.bc (in res/raw/ directory)

Listing 9–2 shows the content of the auto-generated `ScriptC_helloworld.java` file. You can find that file in your project's gen directory, which is the same directory R.java is generated. This file is part of the reflected layer of your script and contains the definition of the class that will allow you to invoke functions from your script and communicate with your script in general. In that same directory you will also find helloworld.d, which simply lists the dependencies for the helloworld.bc file (that is, helloworld.bc would have to be generated again if any of the listed dependencies in helloworld.d is modified).

Listing 9–2. `ScriptC_helloworld.java`

```
/*
 * Copyright (C) 2011 The Android Open Source Project
 *
 * Licensed under the Apache License, Version 2.0 (the "License");
 * you may not use this file except in compliance with the License.
 * You may obtain a copy of the License at
 *
 *      http://www.apache.org/licenses/LICENSE-2.0
 *
 * Unless required by applicable law or agreed to in writing, software
 * distributed under the License is distributed on an "AS IS" BASIS,
 * WITHOUT WARRANTIES OR CONDITIONS OF ANY KIND, either express or implied.
 * See the License for the specific language governing permissions and
 * limitations under the License.
 */

/*
 * This file is auto-generated. DO NOT MODIFY!
 * The source RenderScript file: E:\ws\Chapter
9\src\com\apress\proandroid\ch9\helloworld.rs
 */
package com.apress.proandroid.ch9;

import android.renderscript.*;
import android.content.res.Resources;
```

```
/**
 * @hide
 */
public class ScriptC_helloworld extends ScriptC {
    // Constructor
    public  ScriptC_helloworld(RenderScript rs, Resources resources, int id) {
        super(rs, resources, id);
    }

    private final static int mExportFuncIdx_hello_world = 0;
    public void invoke_hello_world() {
        invoke(mExportFuncIdx_hello_world);
    }

}
```

Three things stand out in this auto-generated file:

- The package name is the one defined in the script with #pragma

- The public constructor

- The invoke_hello_world function

Parts of this auto-generated file, even though they are important, are not relevant to you. For example, the private mExportFuncIdx_hello_world constant in Listing 9–2 refers to the index of a function in the script, but its actual value is of no importance to you or your application.

To use the script, you will have to create an instance of ScriptC_helloworld in your Java code, which will then allow you to call the script's hello_world function via the reflected invoke_hello_world method, as shown in Listing 9–3.

Listing 9–3. *Calling RenderScript Function*

```
public class Chapter9Activity extends Activity {
    /** Called when the activity is first created. */
    @Override
    public void onCreate(Bundle savedInstanceState) {
        super.onCreate(savedInstanceState);
        setContentView(R.layout.main);

        HelloWorldRenderScript();
    }

    private void HelloWorldRenderScript() {
        RenderScript rs = RenderScript.create(this); // needs a Context as parameter

        // script created using the helloworld bitcode in res/raw/helloworld.bc
        ScriptC_helloworld helloworldScript = new ScriptC_helloworld(rs, getResources(),
R.raw.helloworld);

        // now we can call the script's hello_world function using the reflected method
        helloworldScript.invoke_hello_world();
    }
}
```

Executing this code will result in "Hello, World 0 0x0" being displayed in logcat with the tag "RenderScript".

> **NOTE:** Use DDMS perspective in Eclipse to observe that RenderScript-related threads are now running in the application (with the name RSMessageThread). You can also see the following output in logcat: "RS Launching thread(s), reported CPU count 2" (if your device has 2 cores). As you learn about RenderScript, observe the outputs generated with the tag "RenderScript".

While the helloworld.bc file is critical as it contains the script bitcode, its actual content is not of great value to you. All you should care about is the fact that the LLVM bitcode is the platform-independent representation of your script. That being said, it is possible to disassemble this file and convert it to human-readable LLVM assembly language using the LLVM disassembler llvm-dis (available as part of the LLVM suite). Listing 9–4 shows the LLVM assembly language version of helloworld.bc.

Listing 9–4. *LLVM Assembly Language (helloworld.bc)*

```
; ModuleID = '/home/herve/helloworld.bc'
target datalayout = "e-p:32:32:32-i1:8:8-i8:8:8-i16:16:16-i32:32:32-i64:64:64-f32:32:32-
f64:64:64-v64:64:64-v128:128:128-a0:0:64-n32"
target triple = "armv7-none-linux-gnueabi"

@.str = private constant [13 x i8] c"Hello, World\00"

define void @hello_world() nounwind {
  tail call void @_Z7rsDebugPKci(i8* getelementptr inbounds ([13 x i8]* @.str, i32 0,
i32 0), i32 0) nounwind
  ret void
}

declare void @_Z7rsDebugPKci(i8*, i32)

!#pragma = !{!0, !1}
!#rs_export_func = !{!2}

!0 = metadata !{metadata !"version", metadata !"1"}
!1 = metadata !{metadata !"java_package_name", metadata !"com.apress.proandroid.ch9"}
!2 = metadata !{metadata !"hello_world"}
```

This example did not perform any rendering using RenderScript. In fact, the activity's layout was still defined using XML and the activity content was still set from a layout resource which was inflated when setContentView() was called. Now that you know how to create a basic script, it is time to see how rendering can be performed with RenderScript.

Hello Rendering

Rendering with RenderScript is a little bit more complicated than simply invoking a script function, and requires a little more work before you can see anything on the screen. You will need to:

- Create a script that does the rendering.
- Create a RenderScriptGL context object.
- Create a class that extends RSSurfaceView.
- Set your RSSurfaceView as the content view for your activity.

Creating a Rendering Script

Our first rendering script will be extremely simple as it will only change the background color to some random color. The script is shown in Listing 9–5 and is in a file called hellorendering.rs. The names of the RenderScript files are important as they define the resource name (in that case R.raw.hellorendering, which is simply defined as an integer in R.java).

Listing 9–5. *Changing Background Color*

```
#pragma version(1)
#pragma rs java_package_name(com.apress.proandroid.ch9)

#include "rs_graphics.rsh"

// invoked automatically when the script is created
void init() {
    // do whatever you need to do here...
}

int root() {
    float red = rsRand(1.0f);
    float green = rsRand(1.0f);
    float blue = rsRand(1.0f);

    // clear the background color with random color
    rsgClearColor(red, green, blue, 1.0f); // alpha is 1.0f, i.e. opaque

    // 50 frames per second = 20 milliseconds per frame
    return 20;
}
```

The first two lines of the files are the same as in Listing 9–1. The following line is to include the rs_graphics.rsh header file, where rsgClearColor() is defined. Header files are automatically included except for rs_graphics.rsh, so you will have to explicitly include that file when you use graphics RenderScript functions such as rsgClearColor() or rsgBindFont().

The init() function here is for informational purpose only as its implementation is empty. The init() function is optional and, if present, will be called automatically when the script is created. This allows you to perform any initialization before other routines are executed. A script that does no rendering, like the one shown in Listing 9–1, could also have an init() function.

The root() function is where the rendering actually happens. The implementation here is trivial as all it does is clear the background with a random color. What is interesting though is the return value of the function as it specifies how often rendering will occur. In this particular case we return 20, which means the frame should be updated every 20 milliseconds (that is, frame rate of 50 frames per second).

> **NOTE:** `init()` and `root()` are reserved functions and do not result in `invoke_init()` and `invoke_root()` methods being created in the reflected layer (ScriptC_hellorendering.java in this case).

Creating a RenderScriptGL Context

Now that the rendering script is complete, you will need a RenderScriptGL context object. Here the RenderScriptGL context object is created when the RSSurfaceView's surfaceChanged() method is called. The HelloRenderingView implementation is shown in Listing 9–6.

Listing 9–6. *HelloRenderingView.java*

```java
public class HelloRenderingView extends RSSurfaceView {

    public HelloRenderingView(Context context) {
        super(context);
    }

    private RenderScriptGL mRS;
    private HelloRenderingRS mRender; // helper class

    public void surfaceChanged(SurfaceHolder holder, int format, int w, int h) {
        super.surfaceChanged(holder, format, w, h);
        if (mRS == null) {
            RenderScriptGL.SurfaceConfig sc = new RenderScriptGL.SurfaceConfig();
            mRS = createRenderScriptGL(sc);
            mRender = new HelloRenderingRS();
            mRender.init(mRS, getResources());
        }
        mRS.setSurface(holder, w, h);
    }

    @Override
    protected void onDetachedFromWindow() {
        if(mRS != null) {
            mRS = null;
            destroyRenderScriptGL();
        }
    }
}
```

As you can see in Listing 9–6, a `HelloRenderingRS` helper class is used as well.

Extending RSSurfaceView

The implementation of this class is shown in Listing 9–7.

Listing 9–7. *HelloRenderingRS.java*

```java
public class HelloRenderingRS {

    public HelloRenderingRS() {
    }

    private Resources mRes;
    private RenderScriptGL mRS;
    private ScriptC_hellorendering mScript;

    public void init(RenderScriptGL rs, Resources res) {
        mRS = rs;
        mRes = res;

        mScript = new ScriptC_hellorendering(mRS, mRes, R.raw.hellorendering);

        mRS.bindRootScript(mScript);
    }
}
```

In this class, we create the actual ScriptC_hellorendering script and bind it to the RenderScriptGL object. Without the call to bindRootScript(), nothing would actually get rendered as the script's root() function would not be called. If you find yourself staring at a black screen when you were expecting some rendering to happen, first check you did not forget to call bindRootScript().

Setting the Content View

Now that all these files exist, you can create an instance of HelloRenderingView and set the activity's content to this instance, as shown in Listing 9–8.

Listing 9–8. *Activity*

```java
public class Chapter9Activity extends Activity {
    static final String TAG = "Chapter9Activity";

    private HelloRenderingView mHelloRenderingView;

    /** Called when the activity is first created. */
    @Override
    public void onCreate(Bundle savedInstanceState) {
        super.onCreate(savedInstanceState);
        //setContentView(R.layout.main); // we don't use the XML layout anymore here so
we comment it out

        HelloWorldRenderScript();

        mHelloRenderingView = new HelloRenderingView(this);
        setContentView(mHelloRenderingView);
```

```
    }

    @Override
    protected void onPause() {
        super.onPause();
        mHelloRenderingView.pause(); // to pause the rendering thread
    }

    @Override
    protected void onResume() {
        super.onResume();
        mHelloRenderingView.resume(); // to resume the rendering thread
    }

    private void HelloWorldRenderScript() {
        // see Listing 9-3 for implementation
    }
}
```

While most of this file should be trivial to you now, there is one thing in this file worth noting: the RSSurfaceView must be told when the activity is paused and resumed. Without the calls to RSSurfaceView.pause() and RSSurfaceView.resume(), the rendering thread would not be aware of the activity's state and would carry on rendering things even when the activity is not necessarily visible.

In Android 4.0 two new important features are added:

- Your application can use an allocation as an off-screen buffer by setting the Allocation.USAGE_GRAPHICS_RENDER_TARGET flag when creating the allocation object.

- You can use an RSTextureView in your layout (together with other views). While an RSSurfaceView creates a separate window, an RSTextureView does not.

Adding Variables to Script

Let's modify Listing 9–5 a little bit to learn more about the reflected layer. So far, we only saw how the hello_world routine from the script was reflected in Listing 9–2. Here we are going to add more variables in the script, which we will call hellorendering2.rs, as shown in Listing 9–9.

Listing 9–9. *Changing Background Color (Second Version)*

```
#pragma version(1)
#pragma rs java_package_name(com.apress.proandroid.ch9)

#include "rs_graphics.rsh"

// we removed init() as it was empty anyway

float red = 0.0f; // initialized to 1.0f

float green; // purposely not initialized
```

```
static float blue; // purposely not initialized, static

const float alpha = 1.0f; // constant

int root() {
    // clear the background color
    blue = rsRand(1.0f);
    rsgClearColor(red, green, blue, alpha);

    // 50 frames per second = 20 milliseconds per frame
    return 20;
}
```

As you can see, the four variables—red, green, blue, and alpha—are all defined
differently. While this does not necessarily make sense for the actual script, it allows us
to see how the reflected layer is created. Listing 9–10 shows the
ScriptC_hellorendering2.java class.

Listing 9–10. *ScriptC_hellorendering2.java*

```
/*
 * Copyright (C) 2011 The Android Open Source Project
 *
 * Licensed under the Apache License, Version 2.0 (the "License");
 * you may not use this file except in compliance with the License.
 * You may obtain a copy of the License at
 *
 *      http://www.apache.org/licenses/LICENSE-2.0
 *
 * Unless required by applicable law or agreed to in writing, software
 * distributed under the License is distributed on an "AS IS" BASIS,
 * WITHOUT WARRANTIES OR CONDITIONS OF ANY KIND, either express or implied.
 * See the License for the specific language governing permissions and
 * limitations under the License.
 */

/*
 * This file is auto-generated. DO NOT MODIFY!
 * The source RenderScript file: E:\ws\Chapter
9\src\com\apress\proandroid\ch9\hellorendering2.rs
 */
package com.apress.proandroid.ch9;

import android.renderscript.*;
import android.content.res.Resources;

/**
 * @hide
 */
public class ScriptC_hellorendering2 extends ScriptC {
    // Constructor
    public  ScriptC_hellorendering2(RenderScript rs, Resources resources, int id) {
        super(rs, resources, id);
        mExportVar_red = 0f;
        mExportVar_alpha = 1f;
    }
```

```java
        private final static int mExportVarIdx_red = 0;
        private float mExportVar_red;
        public void set_red(float v) {
            mExportVar_red = v;
            setVar(mExportVarIdx_red, v);
        }

        public float get_red() {
            return mExportVar_red;
        }

        private final static int mExportVarIdx_green = 1;
        private float mExportVar_green;
        public void set_green(float v) {
            mExportVar_green = v;
            setVar(mExportVarIdx_green, v);
        }

        public float get_green() {
            return mExportVar_green;
        }

        private final static int mExportVarIdx_alpha = 2;
        private float mExportVar_alpha;
        public float get_alpha() {
            return mExportVar_alpha;
        }
}
```

The global red variable was defined in the script and initialized to zero. Consequently, the reflected layer defines a private mExportVar_red floating-point member, initialized to zero in the constructor, as well as two methods to set and get the red value: set_red() and get_red().

The global green variable in the script was very similar to the red one, except for the fact that it was not initialized. The reflected layer therefore also defines a private mExportVar_green floating-point member as well as two methods, set_green() and get_green(). However, the mExportVar_green member is not initialized in the constructor.

The blue variable was defined as static, which means it is not exported outside the script. As a consequence, the reflected layer does not define any member or method related to the script's blue component.

Finally, the alpha component was defined as a constant, and therefore the reflected layer contains the initialization of the mExportVar_alpha member in the constructor and only defines one method, get_alpha(), to access the value of the member. Since the alpha component is constant, there is indeed no need to define any set_alpha() method in Java.

> **NOTE:** Global pointers defined in the script would result in a bind_pointer_name() method in the reflected layer instead of a set_pointer_name() method.

As you can see, a get() method in the reflected layer returns the last value set in Java. For example, get_green() simply returns mExportVar_green, which can only be modified by a call to set_green(). This basically means that if the script modifies the value of the global green variable, the change won't propagate to the Java layer. This is a very important detail to be aware of.

We will now review one of the simple examples provided by Android as sample code to learn more about one of the most important RenderScript functions.

HelloCompute

The Android HelloCompute sample application simply converts a color picture to black and white. Listing 9–11 shows the script implementation (build target is Honeycomb).

Listing 9–11. *RenderScript mono.rs*

```
/*
 * Copyright (C) 2011 The Android Open Source Project
 *
 * Licensed under the Apache License, Version 2.0 (the "License");
 * you may not use this file except in compliance with the License.
 * You may obtain a copy of the License at
 *
 *      http://www.apache.org/licenses/LICENSE-2.0
 *
 * Unless required by applicable law or agreed to in writing, software
 * distributed under the License is distributed on an "AS IS" BASIS,
 * WITHOUT WARRANTIES OR CONDITIONS OF ANY KIND, either express or implied.
 * See the License for the specific language governing permissions and
 * limitations under the License.
 */

#pragma version(1)
#pragma rs java_package_name(com.android.example.hellocompute)

rs_allocation gIn;
rs_allocation gOut;
rs_script gScript;

const static float3 gMonoMult = {0.299f, 0.587f, 0.114f};

void root(const uchar4 *v_in, uchar4 *v_out, const void *usrData, uint32_t x, uint32_t
y) {
    float4 f4 = rsUnpackColor8888(*v_in);

    float3 mono = dot(f4.rgb, gMonoMult);

    *v_out = rsPackColorTo8888(mono);
}

void filter() {
    rsForEach(gScript, gIn, gOut, 0); // first: script; second: input allocation; third:
output allocation
}
```

The root() function converts a single pixel to black and white. It does so in four steps:

1. The ARGB value (*v_in) is converted to a floating-point vector.

2. root() performs the dot product of f4.rgb and gMonoMult, which returns a single floating-point value (the luminance).

3. All three entries in the mono vector are given the same value (the result of the dot product, that is, the luminance).

4. The mono vector is converted to an ARGB value that is copied into *v_out.

> **NOTE:** The gMonoMult values are defined by the NTSC standard.

In order for the script to convert a whole picture to black and white, it has to be told to execute the root() function on each pixel. This is what the filter() function is doing by calling the rsForEach() function. The rsForEach() function executes the script (first parameter) for each pair of elements in the input and output allocations (second and third parameters). The fourth parameter, usrData, is set to zero here and is ignored by the root() function.

Allocations

As rsForEach() uses allocations as parameters, allocations have to be created in Java and must then be passed down to the script. This is what createScript() in HelloCompute.java does among other things, as shown in Listing 9–12.

Listing 9–12. *Allocations*

```
private RenderScript mRS;
private Allocation mInAllocation; // input allocation
private Allocation mOutAllocation; // output allocation
private ScriptC_mono mScript;

...

private void createScript() {
    mRS = RenderScript.create(this);

    mInAllocation = Allocation.createFromBitmap(mRS, mBitmapIn,
                                Allocation.MipmapControl.MIPMAP_NONE,
                                Allocation.USAGE_SCRIPT);

    mOutAllocation = Allocation.createTyped(mRS, mInAllocation.getType());

    mScript = new ScriptC_mono(mRS, getResources(), R.raw.mono);
```

```
        mScript.set_gIn(mInAllocation);
        mScript.set_gOut(mOutAllocation);
        mScript.set_gScript(mScript);

        mScript.invoke_filter();

        mOutAllocation.copyTo(mBitmapOutRS);
    }
```

In this example, the input memory allocation is created from a bitmap, and the allocation will be used by the script. Other possible uses include texture source (USAGE_GRAPHICS_TEXTURE) and graphics mesh (USAGE_GRAPHICS_VERTEX). You can review the various methods defined in the Allocation class to create allocations. Allocations can be one dimensional (for example, array), two-dimensional (for example, bitmap), or three-dimensional.

rsForEach

The rsForEach function exists in three different flavors:

- rsForEach(rs_script script, rs_allocation input, rs_allocation output) (only in Android 4.0 and above)

- rsForEach(rs_script script, rs_allocation input, rs_allocation output, const void * usrData)

- rsForEach(rs_script script, rs_allocation input, rs_allocation output, const void * usrData, const rs_script_call_t*)

As we saw in Listing 9–11, the first parameter is a script. It will define which root() function to execute. The second and third parameters specify the input and output allocations. The fourth parameter, if present, is some private user data that can be used by the script. Android will not use this value and it can be set to zero or any other value when not used by the root() function. The fifth parameter, when present, will specify how the root() function will be executed. Listing 9–13 shows the definitions of the rs_script_call_t structure.

Listing 9–13. *rs_script_call_t*

```
enum rs_for_each_strategy {
    RS_FOR_EACH_STRATEGY_SERIAL,
    RS_FOR_EACH_STRATEGY_DONT_CARE,
    RS_FOR_EACH_STRATEGY_DST_LINEAR,
    RS_FOR_EACH_STRATEGY_TILE_SMALL,
    RS_FOR_EACH_STRATEGY_TILE_MEDIUM,
    RS_FOR_EACH_STRATEGY_TILE_LARGE
};

typedef struct rs_script_call {
    enum rs_for_each_strategy strategy;
    uint32_t xStart;
```

```
        uint32_t xEnd;
        uint32_t yStart;
        uint32_t yEnd;
        uint32_t zStart;
        uint32_t zEnd;
        uint32_t arrayStart;
        uint32_t arrayEnd;
} rs_script_call_t;
```

You can configure the strategy as well as the start and end parameters (for all dimensions of the allocations). The strategy is only a hint and there is no guarantee implementations will obey the order.

For convenience, Android 4.0 (Ice Cream Sandwich) defines the Script.forEach() method. While you should not be calling this method in your code directly, it is being used in the reflected code. Thanks to this new method, the mono.rs script can be simplified, and Listing 9–14 shows the implementation of the script when the build target is set to Android 4.0.

Listing 9–14. *RenderScript mono.rs (Android 4.0 Version)*

```
/*
 * Copyright (C) 2011 The Android Open Source Project
 *
 * Licensed under the Apache License, Version 2.0 (the "License");
 * you may not use this file except in compliance with the License.
 * You may obtain a copy of the License at
 *
 *      http://www.apache.org/licenses/LICENSE-2.0
 *
 * Unless required by applicable law or agreed to in writing, software
 * distributed under the License is distributed on an "AS IS" BASIS,
 * WITHOUT WARRANTIES OR CONDITIONS OF ANY KIND, either express or implied.
 * See the License for the specific language governing permissions and
 * limitations under the License.
 */

#pragma version(1)
#pragma rs java_package_name(com.example.android.rs.hellocompute)

const static float3 gMonoMult = {0.299f, 0.587f, 0.114f};

void root(const uchar4 *v_in, uchar4 *v_out) {
    float4 f4 = rsUnpackColor8888(*v_in);

    float3 mono = dot(f4.rgb, gMonoMult);
    *v_out = rsPackColorTo8888(mono);
}
```

As you can see, the filter() function has been removed and so were the gIn, gOut, and gScript variables. To understand why it was possible to remove this function in the Android 4.0 sample application, one has to look at the reflected layer that is generated when the project is built. Listing 9–15 shows the new reflected layer.

Listing 9–15. *ScriptC_mono.java (Android 4.0 Version)*

```java
/*
 * Copyright (C) 2011 The Android Open Source Project
 *
 * Licensed under the Apache License, Version 2.0 (the "License");
 * you may not use this file except in compliance with the License.
 * You may obtain a copy of the License at
 *
 *      http://www.apache.org/licenses/LICENSE-2.0
 *
 * Unless required by applicable law or agreed to in writing, software
 * distributed under the License is distributed on an "AS IS" BASIS,
 * WITHOUT WARRANTIES OR CONDITIONS OF ANY KIND, either express or implied.
 * See the License for the specific language governing permissions and
 * limitations under the License.
 */

/*
 * This file is auto-generated. DO NOT MODIFY!
 * The source Renderscript file:
 E:\ws\HelloCompute\src\com\example\android\rs\hellocompute\mono.rs
 */
package com.example.android.rs.hellocompute;

import android.renderscript.*;
import android.content.res.Resources;

/**
 * @hide
 */
public class ScriptC_mono extends ScriptC {
    // Constructor
    public  ScriptC_mono(RenderScript rs, Resources resources, int id) {
        super(rs, resources, id);
        __U8_4 = Element.U8_4(rs);
    }

    private Element __U8_4;
    private final static int mExportForEachIdx_root = 0;
    public void forEach_root(Allocation ain, Allocation aout) {
        // check ain
        if (!ain.getType().getElement().isCompatible(__U8_4)) {
            throw new RSRuntimeException("Type mismatch with U8_4!");
        }
        // check aout
        if (!aout.getType().getElement().isCompatible(__U8_4)) {
            throw new RSRuntimeException("Type mismatch with U8_4!");
        }
        // Verify dimensions
        Type tIn = ain.getType();
        Type tOut = aout.getType();
        if ((tIn.getCount() != tOut.getCount()) ||
            (tIn.getX() != tOut.getX()) ||
            (tIn.getY() != tOut.getY()) ||
            (tIn.getZ() != tOut.getZ()) ||
            (tIn.hasFaces() != tOut.hasFaces()) ||
            (tIn.hasMipmaps() != tOut.hasMipmaps())) {
```

```
            throw new RSRuntimeException("Dimension mismatch between input and output
parameters!");
        }
        forEach(mExportForEachIdx_root, ain, aout, null);
    }
}
```

Obviously the invoke_filter() method does not appear in the reflected layer as
filter() is not defined in the script anymore. Because the gIn, gOut, and gScript
variables were removed, all the set/get methods in the reflected layer are also gone. The
key method now is forEach_root(), which is called in createScript() in
HelloCompute.java, as shown in Listing 9–16 (the Honeycomb version is shown in
Listing 9–12).

Listing 9–16. *createScript() Method (Android 4.0 Version)*

```
    private void createScript() {
        mRS = RenderScript.create(this);

        mInAllocation = Allocation.createFromBitmap(mRS, mBitmapIn,
                                        Allocation.MipmapControl.MIPMAP_NONE,
                                        Allocation.USAGE_SCRIPT);

        mOutAllocation = Allocation.createTyped(mRS, mInAllocation.getType());

        mScript = new ScriptC_mono(mRS, getResources(), R.raw.mono);

        mScript.forEach_root(mInAllocation, mOutAllocation);

        mOutAllocation.copyTo(mBitmapOut);
    }
```

> **NOTE:** Allocations have to be compatible (for example, same sizes in all dimensions).

As you can see, createScript() now simply calls the forEach_root() method from the
reflected layer. Because the Script.forEach() method does not exist in Honeycomb,
you may want to avoid using that method and instead use the original Honeycomb way
of doing things. Although it is more complicated, it also allows your application to be
compatible with Android 3.x devices.

Performance

Since RenderScript is targeted at high-performance 3D rendering and compute
operations, it is important to compare the performance of a script to its Java counterpart
to give you an idea of how much gain you can achieve with RenderScript. For this
purpose, a simple Java implementation of the black-and-white filter is provided in
Listing 9–17.

Listing 9–17. *Java Filter*

```
    // mBitmapIn is the input bitmap, mBitmapOut is the output bitmap

    int w = mBitmapIn.getWidth();
    int h = mBitmapIn.getHeight();
    int size = w * h;
    int[] pixels = new int[size];

    mBitmapIn.getPixels(pixels, 0, w, 0, 0, w, h); // we get all the pixels (as 32-bit
integer values)

    for (int i = 0; i < size; i++) {
        int c = pixels[i]; // 0xAARRGGBB

        // we extract red, green and blue components (each one in [0, 255] range)
        int r = (c >> 16) & 0xFF;
        int g = (c >> 8)  & 0xFF;
        int b =  c        & 0xFF;

        // approximation of the formula using integer arithmetic
        r *= 76;
        g *= 151;
        b *= 29;
        int y = (r + g + b) >> 8; // luminance

        pixels[i] = y | (y << 8) | (y << 16) | ( c & 0xFF000000);
    }

    mBitmapOut.setPixels(pixels, 0, w, 0, 0, w, h); // we set the output bitmap's pixels
```

While the RenderScript version of the filter took about 115 milliseconds to complete on a Galaxy Tab 10.1 (using the bitmap resource provided in the sample application as input), the Java version took only 48 milliseconds! The no-JIT version (android:vmSafeMode="true" in the application's manifest) took about 130 milliseconds to complete.The results may sound surprising but one has to consider the overhead of creating the script, allocations, and floating-point operations. A more complicated script may perform better than its Java counterpart, and may benefit in the future from more powerful processing units. For example, in the future a script could run on the GPU instead of the CPU, possibly taking advantage of better support for parallel execution. Not all scripts will be slower, but this example shows that using RenderScript may not always make your code faster.

Native RenderScript APIs

Your RenderScript code has access to a limited set of APIs as it cannot simply call APIs from the NDK or C library. The RenderScript APIs are defined in six header files, located in the SDK's platform/android-xx/renderscript/include (where xx is the API level, for example, 13):

- rs_types.rsh
- rs_core.rsh

- rs_cl.rsh

- rs_math.rsh

- rs_graphics.rsh

- rs_time.rsh

In Ice Cream Sandwich, the RenderScript APIs are defined in 12 header files. In addition to the six header files above, the following six files were added:

- rs_allocation.rsh

- rs_atomic.rsh

- rs_debug.rsh

- rs_matrix.rsh

- rs_object.rsh

- rs_quaternion.rsh

Again, as online documentation for RenderScript is currently quite scant, it is recommended you review these files. One of the big differences between Honeycomb and Ice Cream Sandwich is the addition of comments in these header files. You should therefore refer to the Android 4.0 RenderScript header files whenever possible since you will find more information in those than in the Honeycomb header files.

rs_types.rsh

- This header file defines the basic types used in RenderScript (in addition to the C99 standard types `char`, `short`, `int`, `long`, and `float`):

- int8_t

- int16_t

- int32_t

- int64_t

- uint8_t

- uint16_t

- uint32_t

- uint64_t

- uchar (defined as uint8_t)

- ushort (defined as uint16_t)

- uint (defined as uint32_t)

- ulong (defined as uint64_t)

In addition to these basic types, this file defines vector types:

- float2
- float3
- float4
- double2 (Android 4.0 and above)
- double3 (Android 4.0 and above)
- double4 (Android 4.0 and above)
- char2
- char3
- char4
- uchar2
- uchar3
- uchar4
- short2
- short3
- short4
- ushort2
- ushort3
- ushort4
- int2
- int3
- int4
- uint2
- uint3
- uint4

Since a 3D framework would not be complete without matrices, several matrix types are also defined:

- rs_matrix2x2 (square matrix of order 2)
- rs_matrix3x3 (square matrix of order 3)
- rs_matrix4x4 (square matrix of order 4)

> **NOTE:** While vector types are defined for both floating-point and integer vectors (for example, `float2`, `ushort3`, and `int4`), matrix types use float only.

Honeycomb MR1 (API level 12) introduced the quaternion type `rs_quaternion` (defined as `float4`). Additional APIs were also introduced to manipulate this new type.

As you can see, the number of types is relatively high, however each of these types can be seen as a scalar, a vector, or a matrix.

The following types are also defined in `rs_types.rsh` and are opaque handles to their Java counterparts:

- rs_element
- rs_type
- rs_allocation
- rs_sampler
- rs_script
- rs_mesh
- rs_program_fragment
- rs_program_vertex
- rs_program_raster
- rs_program_store
- rs_font

All these types are also exposed in the Java layer in the `android.renderscript` package:

- Byte2
- Byte3
- Byte4
- Double2 (Android 4.0 and above)
- Double3 (Android 4.0 and above)
- Double4 (Android 4.0 and above)
- Float2
- Float3
- Float4
- Int2
- Int3

- Int4
- Long2
- Long3
- Long4
- Matrix2f
- Matrix3f
- Matrix4f
- Short2
- Short3
- Short4
- Element
- Type
- Allocation
- Sampler
- Script
- Mesh
- ProgramFragment
- ProgramVertex
- ProgramRaster
- ProgramStore
- Font

rs_core.rsh

This header file defines the following functions in Honeycomb:

- rsDebug
- rsPackColorTo8888
- rsUnpackColor8888
- rsMatrixSet
- rsMatrixGet
- rsMatrixLoadIdentity
- rsMatrixLoad

- rsMatrixLoadRotate
- rsMatrixLoadScale
- rsMatrixLoadTranslate
- rsMatrixLoadMultiply
- rsMatrixMultiply
- rsMatrixRotate
- rsMatrixScale
- rsMatrixTranslate
- rsMatrixLoadOrtho
- rsMatrixLoadFrustum
- rsMatrixLoadPerspective
- rsMatrixInverse
- rsMatrixInverseTranspose
- rsMatrixTranspose
- rsClamp

The matrix functions were moved to a dedicated header file in Android 4.0: `rs_matrix.rsh`.

As the quaternion type was introduced in Honeycomb MR1 (Android 3.1), new functions were also added to `rs_core.rsh`:

- rsQuaternionSet
- rsQuaternionMultiply
- rsQuaternionAdd
- rsQuaternionLoadRotateUnit
- rsQuaternionLoadRotate
- rsQuaternionConjugate
- rsQuaternionDot
- rsQuaternionNormalize
- rsQuaternionSlerp
- rsQuaternionGetMatrixUnit

This header file went through a metamorphosis in Android 4.0. As a matter of fact, the Honeycomb version of this file was a little bit all over the place, containing matrix, quaternion, debugging, and some math functions. The file was dramatically reorganized in Android 4.0 to define only the following functions:

- rsSendToClient
- rsSendToClientBlocking
- rsForEach

The matrix, quaternion, and debugging functions were moved to their new respective files (rs_matrix.rsh, rs_quaternion.rsh, and rs_debug.rsh) while the math functions were naturally moved to rs_math.rsh. Since header files are automatically included, the fact that functions were moved from one header file to another should not affect your script.

rs_cl.rsh

This header file is actually somewhat hard to read as it uses many macros to define functions. It contains the main "compute" APIs, and if you played hooky instead of attending math classes, you are in for a shock.

This header file defines the following math functions:

- acos   arc cosine
- acosh   inverse hyperbolic cosine
- acospi   acos(x) / pi
- asin   arc sine
- asinh   inverse hyperbolic sine
- asinpi   asin(x) / pi
- atan   arc tangent
- atan2   arc tangent with 2 parameters
- atanh   hyperbolic arc tangent
- atanpi   atan(x) / pi
- atan2pi   atan2(x,y) / pi
- cbrt   cubic root
- ceil   round up value
- copysign   x with its sign changed to sign of y
- cos   cosine
- cosh   hyperbolic cosine
- cospi   cos(pi * x)
- erf   error function encountered in integrating the normal distribution
- erfc   complimentary error function

- exp — e^x
- exp2 — 2^x
- exp10 — 10^x
- expm1 — $e^x - 1.0$
- fabs — absolute value of floating-point value
- fdim — positive difference between x and y
- floor — largest integer less than or equal to x
- fma — (x * y) + z, rounded
- fmax — maximum of 2 floating-point values
- fmin — minimum of 2 floating-point values
- fmod — modulus
- fract — fractional value in x (floor(x) also returned)
- frexp — extract mantissa and exponent
- hypot — square root of $x^2 + y^2$
- ilogb — exponent as integer value
- ldexp — $x * 2^y$
- lgamma — natural logarithm of the absolute value of the gamma
- log — natural logarithm (base e)
- log10 — common logarithm (base 10)
- log2 — logarithm base 2
- log1p — natural logarithm of 1+x
- logb — exponent of x, which is the integral part of $\log_r|x|$
- mad — approximation of (x * y) + z (when speed is preferred over accuracy)
- modf — decompose floating-point number into integral and fractional parts
- nextafter — next representable floating-point value following x in the direction of y
- pow — x^y
- pown — x^y (y is integer)
- powr — x^y (x greater than or equal to zero)
- remainder — remainder

- remquo   remainder and quotient
- rint   round to nearest integer (in floating-point format)
- rootn $x^{1/y}$
- round   nearest integer value (in floating-point format)
- sqrt   square root
- rsqrt   reciprocal of square root (i.e. 1.0 / sqrt(x))
- sin   sine
- sincos   sine and cosine
- sinh   hyperbolic sine
- sinpi   sin(pi * x)
- tan   tangent
- tanh   hyperbolic tangent
- tanpi   tan(pi * x)
- tgamma   gamma function
- trunc   truncate floating-point value

It also defines these few integer functions:

- abs   absolute value
- clz   number of leading 0-bits
- min   minimum of two integers
- max   maximum of two integers

Some other common functions are also defined:

- clamp   clamp *amount* to range given by *low* and *high*
- degrees   convert radians to degrees
- mix   *start* + (*stop* − *start*)*amount* (linear blend)
- radians   convert degrees to radians
- step   0.0 if *v* is less than *edge*, else 1.0
- smoothstep   0.0 if v ≤ edge0, 1.0 if v ≥ edge1, else smooth Hermite interpolation
- sign   sign (-1.0, -0.0, +0.0 or 1.0)

Last but not least, this header file defines some geometric functions:

- cross   cross product

- ■ dot   dot product
- ■ length   vector length
- ■ distance   distance between 2 points
- ■ normalize   normalize vector (length will be 1.0)

If you are familiar with OpenCL, you should recognize these APIs. As a matter of fact, the Honeycomb rs_cl.rsh header file itself refers to the OpenCL documentation as it contains comments referring to sections 6.11.2, 6.11.3, 6.11.4, and 6.11.5, which are the sections in the OpenCL 1.1 specifications covering the math, integer, common, and geometric functions respectively. Listing 9–18 shows these comments from rs_cl.rsh. You can also refer to the OpenCL documentation for more information, which is freely available on the Khronos website (www.khronos.org/opencl).

Listing 9–18. *Comments Referring To OpenCL In* rs_cl.rsh

```
#ifndef __RS_CL_RSH__
#define __RS_CL_RSH__

...

// Float ops, 6.11.2

...
extern float __attribute__((overloadable)) trunc(float);
FN_FUNC_FN(trunc)

// Int ops (partial), 6.11.3

...
IN_FUNC_IN_IN_BODY(max, (v1 > v2 ? v1 : v2))
FN_FUNC_FN_F(max)

// 6.11.4

_RS_RUNTIME float __attribute__((overloadable)) clamp(float amount, float low, float
high);
...

// 6.11.5
_RS_RUNTIME float3 __attribute__((overloadable)) cross(float3 lhs, float3 rhs);

...

#endif
```

This header file also defines some conversion functions such as convert_int3, which converts a vector of three elements to a vector of three integers.

rs_math.rsh

This header file defines the following functions in Honeycomb:

- rsSetObject
- rsClearObject
- rsIsObject
- rsGetAllocation
- rsAllocationGetDimX
- rsAllocationGetDimY
- rsAllocationGetDimZ
- rsAllocationGetDimLOD
- rsAllocationGetDimFaces
- rsGetElementAt
- rsRand
- rsFrac
- rsSendToClient
- rsSendToClientBlocking
- rsForEach

As we saw earlier, `rsForEach()` is one of the most important functions.

The `rsSendToClient()` and `rsSendToClientBlocking()` functions (moved to `rs_core.rsh` in Android 4.0) are worth mentioning as they allow a script to send data to the Java layer. For the Java layer to be able to receive data, your application will have to register a message handler, as shown in Listing 9–19.

Listing 9–19. *Message Handler*

```
RenderScript rs = RenderScript.create(this); // needs a Context as parameter

rs.setMessageHandler(new RenderScript.RSMessageHandler() {

    @Override
    public void run() {
        super.run();
        Log.d(TAG, String.valueOf(this.mID) + " " + mData + ", length:" + mLength);
    }
});
```

The handler's `mID`, `mData`, and `mLength` fields will contain the information passed by the script. If your script sends data to the Java layer but no handler is registered, an exception will be thrown.

In Android 4.0, the `rs_math.rsh` was also modified to focus exclusively on mathematical functions:

- rsRand
- rsFrac
- rsClamp
- rsExtractFrustumPlanes (new in Android 4.0)
- rsIsSphereInFrustum (new in Android 4.0)
- rsPackColorTo8888
- rsUnpackColor8888

The allocation functions were moved to a new file, `rs_allocation.rsh`, which, in addition to the functions introduced in Honeycomb, defines the following two new functions:

- rsAllocationCopy1DRange
- rsAllocationCopy2DRange

The object functions were also moved to a new header file: `rs_object.rsh`.

rs_graphics.rsh

This header files defines the following functions:

- rsgBindProgramFragment
- rsgBindProgramStore
- rsgBindProgramVertex
- rsgBindProgramRaster
- rsgBindSampler
- rsgBindTexture
- rsgProgramVertexLoadProjectionMatrix
- rsgProgramVertexLoadModelMatrix
- rsgProgramVertexLoadTextureMatrix
- rsgProgramVertexGetProjectionMatrix
- rsgProgramFragmentConstantColor
- rsgGetWidth
- rsgGetHeight
- rsgAllocationsSyncAll (new overloaded function added in Android 4.0)
- rsgDrawRect

- rsgDrawQuad
- rsgDrawQuadTexCoords
- rsgDrawSpriteScreenspace
- rsgDrawMesh
- rsgClearColor
- rsgClearDepth
- rsgDrawText
- rsgBindFont
- rsgFontColor
- rsgMeasureText
- rsgMeshComputeBoundingBox

In Android 4.0 the following functions were added to `rs_graphics.rsh`:

- rsgBindColorTarget
- rsgClearColorTarget
- rsgBindDepthTarget
- rsgClearDepthTarget
- rsgClearAllRenderTargets
- rsgFinish

Since the focus of this chapter is not on making you an expert in 3D rendering, we won't review these functions in detail. If you are already familiar with OpenGL, then you should easily be able to use these functions. If you are not, then it is recommended you first get familiar with 3D terms like fragment, vertex, and mesh before you dive into RenderScript.

rs_time.rsh

This file defines the following:

- rsTime
- rsLocalTime
- rsUptimeMillis
- rsUptimeNanos
- rsGetDt

Of particular interest is the rsGetDt() function, which returns the number of seconds (as a floating-point value) since it was last called. Listing 9–20 shows how this would typically be used in a script.

Listing 9–20. *Calling* rsGetDt()

```
#pragma version(1)
#pragma rs java_package_name(com.yourpackagehere)

typedef struct __attribute__((packed, aligned(4))) MyObject {
    float x;
    float other_property;
} MyObject_t;
MyObject_t *object; // Java layer would have to call bind_object

int root() {
    float dt = rsGetDt();
    float dx = dt * 10.f; // 10 pixels per second

    object->x += dx; // new x position of object

    // do something else here, for example to draw the object

    return 20;
}
```

> **NOTE:** While the root() function returns 20 (that is, 20 milliseconds between frames, or 50 frames per second), the frame rate is not guaranteed. This is why your code should use rsGetDt() instead of assuming the duration between two frames is the value root() returns.

rs_atomic.rsh

New in Android 4.0, this file defines functions that were not defined in Honeycomb:

- rsAtomicInc
- rsAtomicDec
- rsAtomicAdd
- rsAtomicSub
- rsAtomicAnd
- rsAtomicOr
- rsAtomicXor
- rsAtomicMin
- rsAtomicMax
- rsAtomicCas

As their names indicate, these functions perform various operations atomically.

RenderScript vs. NDK

Both RenderScript and NDK are here to improve the performance of applications. While they share a common goal, you should think carefully about using one versus the other. Each has its own advantages and drawbacks, and not thinking things through could result in you being stuck during development or finding out the hard way that something is extremely difficult to implement.

The advantages of RenderScript can be summarized as follows:

- Platform-independent (ARM, MIPS, Intel, for example)

- Easy parallel execution

- Can use CPU, GPU, or other processing units

On the other hand, RenderScript does have some drawbacks:

- Android-only (scripts cannot be used with other platforms like iOS)

- Learning curve

- Limited number of APIs

Actual RenderScript performance results are hard to obtain as they will heavily depend on the Android version and the hardware device. Some scripts may run much faster than their Java or NDK counterpart while others may not. Because of legacy code or because it simply makes sense in your application, you can actually use both RenderScript and the NDK in the same application.

Summary

While it still appears to be a somewhat immature technology in Honeycomb, RenderScript is already improving in Android 4.0 and is going to take advantage of more hardware features in the future. Even though ARM is clearly the dominant architecture in Android portable devices nowadays and using the NDK can therefore be justified, the fact that RenderScript is platform-independent can be a huge benefit as it can ultimately reduce your maintenance cost significantly. All in all, RenderScript shows some promises and is likely to be an important part of your applications in the future should you need to reach performance levels not attainable with Java alone.

Index

B, C

▓N, O

▓P, Q

▓R

CPSIA information can be obtained at www.ICGtesting.com
Printed in the USA
LVOW130219280112

265993LV00006B/1/P